CRACKING THE SHOW

Also by Thomas Boswell

The Heart of the Order
Game Day
Strokes of Genius
How Life Imitates the World Series
Why Time Begins on Opening Day

THOMAS BOSWELL

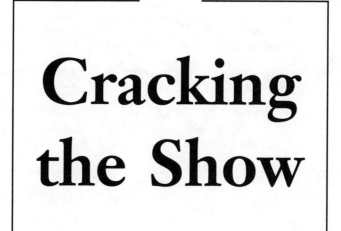

Cracking the Show

DOUBLEDAY

New York London Toronto Sydney Auckland

PUBLISHED BY DOUBLEDAY
a division of Bantam Doubleday Dell Publishing Group, Inc.
1540 Broadway, New York, New York 10036

DOUBLEDAY and the portrayal of an anchor with a dolphin
are trademarks of Doubleday, a division of
Bantam Doubleday Dell Publishing Group, Inc.

Articles appearing herein have previously appeared in *The Washington Post*, *The
Washington Post Magazine*, *Playboy*, and *Inside Sports*.

Library of Congress Cataloging-in-Publication Data

Boswell, Thomas, 1947–
Cracking the show/Thomas Boswell.—1st ed.
p. cm.
1. Baseball—United States. 2. Newspapers—Sections, columns,
etc.—Sports. I. Title.
GV863.A1B65 1994
796.357'0973—dc20 93-42585
CIP

ISBN 0-385-47286-2
Printed in the United States of America
April 1994
First Edition

1 3 5 7 9 10 8 6 4 2

Contents

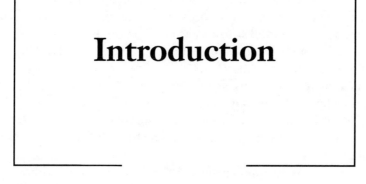

Introduction

W. B. YEATS once tried to imagine the ideal reader for his poetry. He settled on a "wise and simple" fisherman, casting his fly in a stream at dawn.

In the upper deck of a ballpark an usher once said to me, "You're Boswell, right? You write a great shithouse book. I got 'em all."

"Thanks . . . I guess."

"I keep one in my bathroom and read it a few pages at a time," he said.

"Just don't tear out the pages when you're finished."

Though he wore an orange cap, not gray Connemara cloth, I'm fond of my usher. If you asked me why you might want to read this book, I'd say because it comes highly recommended—all the way from the upper deck.

If you love baseball—that's to say, if you think a ballpark usher has it pretty good—then you'd probably enjoy sitting next to me for a few innings. We'd do what all fans do: spend an hour figuring some new angle on the game.

Maybe we'd put Pete Rose on the couch, like a school buddy gone off track. Or wonder whether the Streak represents the best or worst part of Cal Ripken. Perhaps we'd debate why more hitters don't swing at the 0–0 pitch. Or redigest a 15–14 World Series game. Maybe we'd pick each other's brains about some young star like Juan Gonzalez or Frank Thomas who's only half in focus.

We'd be "cracking the show."

For years, bush leaguers have said they wanted to "crack the show" —meaning make the majors, once and for all. However, cracking the show—the participle, not the infinitive—is a continual, leisurely process, the work of a lifetime's worth of summer nights and rain delays. It's not a destination. Baseball is, as much as anything, a lifelong conversation among friends. The game is our excuse to talk. This book continues our lengthening chat.

One tone of voice is largely missing from this collection, although it occasionally finds its way into my daily newspaper writing. The Prophet of Doom is on vacation. After twenty years of covering baseball, I have no sense that the sport has any basic difficulties that matter in the long view.

Yes, money is corrupting the sport. But money has also been corrupting American business, politics, religion, and entertainment right along. Baseball is just playing catch-up. None of Elizabeth Taylor's marriages or goofy diets or tragicomic depressions or ten-pound diamond rings has ever kept a single person away from one of her movies. A presidential candidate without skeletons in his closet is considered too bloodless for the job. In our culture, getting corrupted has always been half the fun. Or at least watching somebody else get corrupted. Every reporter hates vice—in print. Yet we rub our hands whenever we see her sashaying down the road in her skimpy gown of headlines.

Most criticism of baseball begins and ends with the observation that money brings out the worst in people. This is news? Those who deal most intimately with baseball's money issues are, unfortunately, people who have spent their lives being interested primarily in . . . money. You wouldn't like them much. They barely like themselves. The game's recent de facto commissioner, Bud Selig, and union boss, Don Fehr, are about the best of the lot—two dutiful dweebs with decent values. Neither has exercised or exposed his skin to direct sunlight in years. Now, after decades of arguing-for-a-living, they're like two aging punched-out tomato cans who'd rather go have a beer together than finish the fifteenth round.

In the relentlessly boring spitting contest between baseball labor and baseball management, the sole constructive purpose of daily journalism is to administer evenhanded beatings to all parties on a regular basis. They expect it. They know they deserve it. Still, if we step back, we sense that it's all foolishness that will pass. Within wide limits, a sport has little reason to fear controversy or public wailing about large sums of money. Golf is so civilized it has lower TV ratings than bowling. The only thing a major sport needs to fear is boredom. If a game stops being fun to watch, then the whole structure starts to crumble. It's the product, stupid.

If, ten years from now, a baseball game still lasts three hours, rather than two and a half, then my elementary-school-age son may not grow up in a culture of baseball fans. However, even this does not worry me greatly. The forces of corruption are dependable, if nothing else. Money talks. And the smart money says if baseball wants good TV ratings, everybody better get the lead out of their rear ends. Hustle will become cool again and the problem will disappear.

Some of us—cut out my tongue—would stay if the games were even longer.

One night last summer, I could not get myself to leave Camden Yards, despite a three-hour rain delay. The game was not important. My work was done. Midnight passed. But the emptier the park became, the more beautiful it seemed. When would there ever be another game played in this yard before an old-fashioned—that is to say, small—crowd?

Like the SkyDome, Camden Yards has sold out almost every ticket in its existence. Soon baseball will have more new/old parks in Cleveland, Texas, and elsewhere built on the Camden Yards model. And they, too, will probably stay full to the brim for decades, just as Dodger Stadium did for more than twenty-five years. The only trend of the '90s that will infuse much of baseball's twenty-first century will probably be Camden Yards' architecture. Part of the price of such popularity, however, is that you never get to feel at home. You're always a visitor with a particular seat in a packed house and no room to roam.

Eventually, about five thousand of us were left in the stands—everybody sitting in exactly the seat he'd always coveted but probably couldn't get. My choice was an angled section in the rightfield corner that looks like the old Baker Bowl. The whole place felt like the Grand Canyon with lights. We were at the bottom of a deep-green cavern with more than forty thousand empty seats stacked above us. The whole scene looked like every Washington Senators home game of the 1960s—a private party, a private joke, for an extremely odd but gentle group of people.

Finally, the rain stopped. Several Orioles gathered in front of us to do their stretching. Cal Ripken, Jr., the ultimate baseball stoic, the player so maniacally diligent that Orioles fans call him the Prisoner of the Streak, jogged up behind them. He planned his attack perfectly. With one giant leap-frog hop into the largest puddle, he drenched every dry pair of pants in the bunch. Maybe he hadn't laughed that hard in public in years.

That scene is probably what this book is about. Most reporters love initiative. Perhaps my gift is for inertia. It's sad but true that I'll wait years to see Cal Ripken jump into a puddle in the middle of the night. Such stories might not appeal to a wise and simple fly fisherman. But they'd please an upper deck usher. Or anyone who would ignore a three-hour rain delay just to see what a majestic park looks like when it is almost empty and the night clouds break, giving us a new moon on wet grass.

This book is for everybody who stays until the last out, not really knowing why. Or even wishes that they could.

CRACKING THE SHOW

Greed Strikes Out

AS I STEPPED into All-Pro Sports Cards, carrying a sack so heavy that I leaned as I walked, I felt like one of those old prospectors who staggers into a western saloon to show the boys the nuggets he's found in the hills. They all have the same thought: Has the crazy coot found fool's gold? Or is it the real thing? And, if so, how can we jump his claim?

"I've only touched these cards once in thirty years," I said as I laid 3,000 pieces of cardboard on the counter at the strip-mall shop in Edgewater, Maryland. "A long time ago, I took them to a friend who's a collector. He said they were worth $200. I found them again today. Are they worth anything?"

The next few minutes are still a blur in my memory. Within seconds, a crowd had gathered. Phone calls were made. Grown men, summoned from who knows where by who knows whom, began surrounding me, looking over my shoulder, handling my cards. They talked amazing nonsense.

"Look, mint Mantles. God, there must be a dozen Mickeys. Mays, Koufax, Maris. He's got hundreds of stars," said one.

The store owners, without consulting me, began inserting my cards into screw-down Lucite cases or individual plastic holders. They put each card into its protective sheath with the exaggerated care one might expect of a surgeon.

"Topps 1958, No. 150," said one man, inspecting a card. "Excellent-plus."

Another, running his finger down a column of figures in a magazine, said, "325 to 500 and going up."

"The guy's whole '59, '60, and '61 sets are full of mints. Looks like they've never been touched. What kind of kid were you, anyway?" a middle-aged man said, turning to me. "Didn't you *play* with 'em? Where've you been keeping these? In a vault?"

"Take the rubber bands off that pack of '57s," snapped another fellow sternly. "Don't ever do that again."

As I helped unpack, I was told not to touch the corners of my cards. A bit later I was informed, with an indulgent firmness, that I probably shouldn't touch them at all.

Children in the store were nudged to the back by adults. Business stopped. Sorry, kids, no sale for now.

"Football cards too! Here's a '59 Unitas. Looks like it just came out of the pack. . . . Ever see Doak Walker in a '55 Bowman? . . . I didn't know there were '62 Giffords with black borders this perfect."

I was excited. But I had no frame of reference. That $200 estimate felt real outdated, and mentally, I had already added a zero. But I was still acting cool, even letting my four-year-old son continue to rummage through the cards.

Vince Chick, co-owner of the store, got out a cotton swab and gently washed the bubble gum residue off Carl Yastrzemski's face. "There," he said turning to me proudly. "It's worth $100 more now."

I told my kid to get his hands off my cards.

"Mister, you better get yourself an insurance policy," said an onlooker. "Or an armed guard."

"Daddy, I need to go potty," said a voice.

"Not now, Russell," I said.

"Daddy, I *really* need to go potty."

We went potty in the back as unknown hands scooped up my cards (or Russ's freshman year tuition in 2005, whichever way you chose to think of them).

When I got back, Chick was muttering to himself.

"What did you say?" I asked.

"Must be fifty here," he repeated.

"Fifty what?"

"Fifty thousand dollars."

I got a very cold feeling all over my body, like a general anesthetic, as the local experts began an impromptu pool, with $42,000 the low guess. Then I phoned my wife. "Come get Russ at the card store right away," I said.

"What's the rush?" she said.

"While I'm taking him potty, a lot of men are deciding whether to slip $500 Mickey Mantles into their pockets."

"Be right there," she said.

No good deed goes unpunished, it's said. This time I think that's wrong. But I'm not sure yet. When the good deed leads to big-money paranoia, a reawakened obsession-compulsion, and a return to childhood in middle age—not to mention spouse neglect and an urge toward tax evasion—the moral score sheet can get complicated. Finding that bag of old cards has become one of the most defining, but also upsetting, events I've experienced in years.

I was just trying to help a friend. He wanted to buy a box of cards for his friend's infant son—a gift that would combine fun for the kid someday with a little yuppie investment potential. Buy 'em now for $50, open 'em in five years for $500? After we found a card store, I asked casually, "What are old '50s cards worth now?"

"A beat-up Mantle—at least $180."

I went directly to my truck and drove in a straight line to my childhood home on Capitol Hill. "Hi, Dad," I said, and headed up to my old bedroom.

The first thing I noticed was . . . the bureau was gone! The one that had held about 100 pounds of '50s Senators junk (excuse me, rare memorabilia). In there, I probably could have found a calcified chaw of tobacco that could be carbon-dated back to Rocky Bridges. And someone, somewhere, would have bought every old magazine, program, yearbook, and ticket stub in that war chest. As far as I can tell, the only thing my mother *ever* threw away was *that* bureau.

But my cards were in a brown paper bag in the bedroom closet, right where I left them years before with orders never to touch them under threat of excommunication. Not because they might be valuable, just because *they were my baseball cards.*

As is the case with millions of kids—or millions of boys, at least—sports cards were the first material possession that I bought with my own earned money and then took care of with an adult level of concern. Looking at them three decades later, I saw that the cards I acquired from age seven to thirteen improved in condition like a line on a graph—from worn-to-the-bone to handled-with-care to treated-like-fine-china. It was like reading a diary I never kept.

For many, baseball cards are the last toy as well as the first possession. You fall in love with them as a child, then leave them behind at puberty. They link the blue-water, lazy-day joy of childhood summers with the pride of blossoming maturity.

Building a card collection was a six-month commitment. To get the whole year's "set," you had to start in the spring and not miss a "series"—a fresh group of about 150 cards that came out every few weeks—until school began again.

I still remember how appalled I was the first time I met a boy whose parents had bought him the entire Topps Co. set as a one-lump present. I did not consider that he owned *any cards at all* because he had neither worked for them nor collected them.

The poor guy didn't know the delight of opening a pack and getting a missing superstar card. "My God, I really got Ted Williams!" Or of trading doubles to fill a set. "Oh, Lord, how many Herb Plews must I spare for one miserable Mantle with a bent corner?"

He didn't know about finding an ideal cigar box to keep his cards perfect so he could trade one-for-one. Above all, he didn't share the agony of spending his own money, then screaming, "All doubles again!"

I hated the Topps Co. then (and now) for the way it stole my nickels with its debased marketing strategy of printing more bums than stars just to keep you buying more product. May Upper Deck, Score, and the rest continue to drive Topps out of the empire it once monopolized. Serves 'em right. I still have *four* Wynn Hawkins cards ('61—No. 34), and at least six others must have been thrown away.

No, my parents would have known better than to throw away a single card. Which is why I made two trips to my old home on that day of discovery. The first was sensible and quick. The second, after the $50,000 appraisal, was a scene out of *The Treasure of the Sierra Madre* with me as Fred C. Dobbs.

"Where are the rest of them?" was the thought that drove me crazy. Where were the '59 and '60 duplicate cards? There had to be hundreds of them. What if I opened a drawer or shoebox and found *thousands* more cards? Why not? I'd completely forgotten I ever bought a football card, yet I'd found hundreds. Why did I have '55, '57, '59, and '62? Where were all the other years, replete with $450 Jim Brown rookie cards and gem-quality Johnny U.'s?

My father is lucky that, before I left on that hot evening, I did not tear down his brick walls. Because, in our old row house, there were baseball cards everywhere. On the second manic visit, I found Mantle as a bookmark in a detective novel. I found Fleer cards of Hank Greenberg and Charlie Gehringer in the attic under a pile of tiny rubber toy soldiers. Hank Aaron, batting lefty due to a reversed photo negative, was under a stack of Nats bleacher stubs. The card had been carried in my wallet for so many years (imagine, a left-handed Aaron!) that Hank's face was worn away as well as all of his $240 "book" value. To my horror, Willie Mays's four rounded corners had been clipped with scissors in 1957 for a neater look—at a 1991 cost of about $50 a snip.

One '57 Roy Sievers was entirely encased in Scotch tape, presumably so that, had I been hit by a truck at age nine, I could have been buried with it.

In sum, every card on which I had showered my love was rendered worthless by the affection. Every card I'd never cared about or touched was priceless.

The other way to look at it is that the cards I wore out with kindness were mostly old Senators, who now sell for $1 to $3, while the mighty Yanks, whom I hated, now sell for ten to one hundred times that much. My Yank cards are perfect. Revenge!

Some of my discoveries were embarrassing. For instance, I unearthed an extremely incriminating '56 Dick Donovan—what we elementary school criminals called a "doubleheader." To make one, you glued two identical cards back-to-back so it always came up heads when you were playing flip. And you won the whole pile.

Unless, of course, the other guy flipped heads too. If he won the pile later and discovered your doubleheader, the solution was simple: You rolled around on the asphalt playground until one of you died or the teacher came.

I prefer to assume that the discovery of only one double—okay, okay, two, but none after '56—is proof of normal acculturation. Of course, I might have shredded the others as a teenager to cover my trail. My memory fails on this point, your honor.

By the time I finished my attic-to-cellar excavations, I was so sweaty and filthy I looked as if I'd climbed out of a mine shaft. But the sense of relief—that there couldn't possibly be much more to find—was enormous. I could move on. I could take the next step. I could make myself and my family miserable as I turned into the Greedy Card Miser from Hell.

For weeks I spent every spare minute studying the ultra-sick world of card commerce. I'd stay up until all hours, oblivious of time, so I could evaluate, collate, and maximize my stash. I found excuses to arrange those 3,000 cards by year, by card number, by stars, and by teams. I had the entire '60 set (572 cards), but decided I could net more by breaking it up into stars, commons, old Nats, and old Orioles. I'd become a car thief cannibalizing parts.

My son looked perplexed. Wasn't *he* supposed to be the child? My wife wasn't confused. She was mad.

I couldn't help it. Nobody was going to jump *my* claim, steal *my* childhood, swindle me out of cards I'd earned with chores and hoarded allowance. This was real nickel-a-pack money, not the stuff you earn in inflated gobs and waste as an adult.

A man doesn't know what the word *value* means until he tries to put a price on his slightly dinged '58 Harmon Killebrew. The more I handled my cards and played with them—yes, *played*, though I always had some other name for it—the more I enjoyed them. However, the more I tried to figure out what they were worth and take steps to sell them, the more depressed I got.

The sums involved started to seem disproportionately large, as though a zero had been added to the value of each card. Being told your childhood purchase is worth $100 makes you feel as though it were worth $1,000. Is it possible that the child in you hears the price and translates it into a number with the same emotional impact that $100 would have had on a ten-year-old in 1958?

It still takes my breath away that my '56 Sandy Koufax, in basic beat-up kid condition, is worth $120. What happens to people who find '52 Mantles, which sell for $20,000? Heck, it takes my breath away that a Gil Hodges, so long as the card isn't torn in half, is $16.50. Where does that 50 cents come from, anyway? And what about the notation in the margin of the Beckett *Baseball Card Monthly* saying the card has gone down 9 percent in value this year? Is the late Mr. Hodges in a slump? Does he know it? Can he do something about it? Doesn't seem fair.

Inevitably, the estimated value of my cards went down. And when it did, my disappointment was much worse than it should have been.

Within thirty-six hours (spent largely in the company of Vince

Chick, a pocket calculator, and the Beckett price-and-condition guide), I realized the $50,000 guess was a gold-fever fantasy. No matter how I fiddled and gave myself the benefit of the doubt, the truth looked more like $25,000.

And that's retail. Most card dealers will give you only about 50 cents on the dollar for the "common" cards (hello, Elmer Valo) that languish in their inventories and perhaps 67 percent for Hall of Famers. In a blink, I had gone from $50,000 to $15,000. And that's before taxes.

Don't say anything about "taxes" around card people. They blanch. No one in America, it seems, has ever paid taxes on a card sale. We're talking all cash. "That notebook where you keep a record of your cards?" one dealer told me. "Well, if you ever decide to sell, just use it to start a fire some February night."

This may be the dirty little secret that explains why the card "hobby" now involves as many as ten million people and has become an investment fad among the three-piece-suit set. It's not just that cards went up faster than the stock market in the '80s, it's that nobody's declaring squat.

I understand why. First, simple greed. Second, the perfect rationalization: The idea of paying adult taxes on a childhood purchase insults something deep inside.

The more the estimated value of my cards shrank, the more I obsessed about maxing out what I had. At least that's what I thought my compulsion was about at first. Few things in my life have kept me up so late so many times.

In those first days, I was still awake at 3 A.M.—evaluating the exact condition of each card, guessing its value, then putting it in a binder, a plastic box, or single holder, depending on the guess.

You think this is easy? Here's Beckett's, the bible of card mavens: "An Excellent-Mint (EX-MT) card is one with micro defects, but no minor defects. Two or three of the following would lower the grade of a card from mint to excellent-mint. Layering at some of the corners (fuzzy corners). A very small amount of the original gloss lost. Minor wear on the edges. Slightly off-center borders. Slight off-whiteness of the borders. An EX-MT card is valued at 65-to-80 percent of Near Mint."

Aaaagggghhhh!

All Beckett's definitions of other conditions are the same: exact on the surface, yet, in reality, totally vague and infuriating. Is it "two" or is it "three" micro defects that lowers the grade? When is a card corner "layered" or fuzzy and when is it "rounded"? How much loss of gloss is a "small" amount? How slight is "slightly"?

With a particularly valuable card, like my precious more-than-fuzzy, less-than-rounded, semi-glossy, slightly edged, almost centered (yet extremely attractive, I must say) 1958 Mantle, these vague terms mean hundreds of dollars. One expert, an aesthetic-collector type, told me the card was worth $400. Another, the technical-investor type, said $150. A third, the practical kind, threw up his hands, said the question was impossible, and told me I should auction it.

In reality, cards are worth what you can get for them. It's pure horse-trading and gamesmanship. That makes you even crazier as you try to figure how much you should try to get for 3,000 cards when nobody on earth really knows how much any single card is worth.

My mania abates about 1 A.M. now. Still, the cards won't let up. It's been weeks. My wife says, "When does it end?" I say, "I don't know. It's partly money. It's partly fun. Mostly I just can't stop."

The kicker is I've never been like this before. I don't collect anything. I'm not neat. My lack of sensible care for money is a lifelong bleak joke.

At All-Pro Cards, they must chuckle at me. I'm in there every other day on some lame excuse. I've got some junky '57s on consignment and I worry about their fate. I hope they sell. I hope they don't. When an offer was made for 100 mundane cards, I studied every one to make sure that I wouldn't feel some huge loss.

In one card, the sky behind Jim Brosnan's head is so blue it must be Wrigley Field in the fall. He looks young, but the promise of *The Long Season* and *Pennant Race* is in his face. A man with 1½ real books in him—how can you sell him? I took the card out of the deal.

I took Tom Cheney's rookie card out too. A career 19–29 pitcher, he now sells propane for trailers in Cordele, Georgia. But the year before his elbow blew, he struck out 21 men in a 16-inning game. That and Walter Johnson's 110 shutouts are the only serious records still held by old Senators.

When John McCarthy, All-Pro's other owner, sees me, he says, "Sell 'em quick. Everybody who finds their old cards is just like you. It drives 'em crazy to sell to a dealer for half what they're worth. So they go to weekend card shows, trying to sell to collectors for a decent price. Damned if they don't end up hooked on collecting themselves. This hobby is worse than shooting up."

"Remember the guy who bought $100 to $150 worth of cards every day? I thought he was rich," says Vince Chick. "One day his wife came in here in tears. The phone and electric had been shut off. They were about to be evicted. He'd spent everything on cards."

So far, I've been to three card shows, several card stores, gone through my collection card by card with two experts, read a book by someone named "Mr. Mint," and planned a trip to America's biggest card show. My son has 100 cards in a binder and another 100 for us to play flip with.

As we speak, I've developed a preposterous scheme for making a 50-to-1 profit by cornering the market on two future Hall of Famers whose cards are now selling for pennies. All I have to do is (1) scour America to buy a few thousand of their cards, (2) hope neither of them gets hurt, (3) pray that the whole card market doesn't collapse, and (4) wait until the next century to earn back the first cent.

The sign on All-Pro's door should be "Abandon Hope, All Ye Who Enter Here."

My house of cards began collapsing at the House of Cards. Everyone told me to go there. Everyone said Bill Huggins, the owner of the store and a relative of the old Yankee manager Miller Huggins, was smart and fair about antique cards. He'd tell me what I was holding and maybe buy them too.

This time, nobody encircled me. Nobody told me to get an insurance policy or a bodyguard. This time, somebody just told me the truth.

"Sorry to hurt your feelings," said Huggins, watching my face fall. "These are nice cards. But they're not that nice. You *played* with them. Everything is, basically, a level lower than you thought. The '56s and '57s are good. The '58s very good. The '59s excellent and the '60s excellent-mint. Only the '61s and '62s are near mint—or 100 percent of book value."

How much difference could that make?

"They're worth about $15,000 retail," he said. "I'll give you $10,000."

All I thought was, "Before taxes."

I must've looked like my dog died. Maybe it was because, the day before, my wife had informed me that solving our most recent home disaster (a defunct heating-and-cooling system) would require writing a check for $7,000 to Mr. Frosty. I hate cosmic irony.

At any rate, Huggins sensed a sad man on his doorstep and began to console me. "In 1976, when all of this was starting and we'd just opened, people would drive up all weekend, open the trunks of their cars, and thank me for paying them $50 apiece to take big boxes of their old cards. One lady misunderstood and was ready to pay *me* $50 to take all the cards that her kids had saved over the years.

"At least you're getting something for yours," he said. "This is probably the top of the market. It's crazy. I can't imagine it going much higher. But I've said that before. There are a lot of rich guys in Potomac, Maryland. They say, 'Give me that Mantle, this Mays and the Clemente over there.' In five minutes, they peel off $1,300 and leave."

You can tell the whole thing hits him wrong. "The condition freaks may kill the hobby," he says. "All they're interested in is the investment, not the cards. They come in with magnifying glasses to examine every corner. So we have to be the same way when we buy."

Almost everybody I've met in the card subculture seems to have similar ambivalent feelings, as though they're part of something intoxicating yet subtly debilitating. The fact is, the days when baseball cards were just baseball cards are gone.

Sports memorabilia have appreciated faster than any other collectible on earth in the last decade. Forget diamonds, stamps, and stocks. If you wanted to buy something and watch it make money while sitting in a box, you bought baseball cards, especially old ones. The vintage card business is now up to $500 million a year, with new cards doing roughly twice that. The National Sports Collectors convention drew 70,000 in July 1991. These puppies'll buy anything. A ticket stub, like mine from the '69 All-Star Game in RFK? An easy $30. (That old bureau must be *somewhere*.) One 1910 Honus Wagner card was auctioned at Sotheby's for $451,000.

As a result, there are now about fifteen different brands of baseball cards, one of which costs $5 for a pack of twelve. The ritzy cards, all fancier than White House invitations, are so excessively ornate—embossed, bas-reliefed, or individually hologrammed (no kidding)—that they make an Abrams coffee-table art book look inexpensive. But these wretched-excess cards also make any '56 Topps look classy by contrast.

No marketing excess is too comical. One brand offers scouting reports on the back of each player's card—including how he hits against low fastballs or inside curves. No credible scout would pretend such exact knowledge existed. If it did, the "book" would change every time a player altered his stance. Oh, never mind. Another brand has Nolan Ryan posing in a tuxedo.

Stand in a card shop and watch the kids sometime. They don't open a pack to see if they got their favorite player, let alone to chew the bubble gum. (Gum disappeared long ago in all but cheap brands because it defaced and devalued the cards.) Beckett's in hand, they look to see the value of the players they just bought.

It's stock market speculation for munchkins. The "hot brand" is the one that's out first with a torrid rookie whose card price will go up. One Stadium Club card of White Sox slugger Frank Thomas is worth $12 already. Or thirty times what it cost. Our children now buy last year's cards, looking for a jackpot. Hey, get a $1.19 pack of those '89 Upper Decks and you might hit for a $50 Ken Griffey Jr. rookie card or a $70 Dale Murphy (photo reversed).

My low point came when I sat down with a respected dealer who found barely visible flaws in all but *three* of my 3,000 cards. "Keep these," he said. "They're 'blazers' "—meaning totally perfect and beyond criticism.

"But that's the ugliest picture Mantle ever took," I said.

"That card is worth double-book and it will never stop going up," he said.

I asked this fellow why a certain dealer was selling cards for twice what he claimed his retail price would be. "That guy's the biggest crook," erupted my new friend, who's renowned for inventing a legitimate but still secret method for taking creases out of cards. "A few years ago, mail-order dealers started shaving old cards to create perfect corners. They were selling short cards and some of them got arrested. This guy has a new gimmick. He wets the cards, puts them under a hydraulic press to make them bigger, then shaves them back to normal size with perfect new corners.

"But I can tell the fakes," he said. "They feel just a little thin."

And I was starting to feel more than a little sick.

The rehumanization of my card collection started slowly. In the days following the session with the dealer, I found myself asking friends if they had any favorite old players, then giving them an Ernie Banks or half a dozen New York Giants.

Their disproportionate gratitude was embarrassing, but instructive. They loved the cards the way baseball cards were meant to be loved.

"You'll never know what this means to me," gushed the Banks fan. "My mom threw all mine away."

"I'm going to put these in Lucite holders and make rec-room coasters out of them," said the recipient of Windy McCall and Dusty Rhodes.

But what really started to heal me was that, card by card, I found myself regaining misplaced parts of my childhood—parts I needed more than I knew.

I remembered how I used to be at Kendall's Market, one hundred yards from our house, as soon as it opened at 7 A.M., for my morning pack. In the afternoon, I'd walk across the park to another store for my evening pack. On weekends, I'd trek ten blocks to Tommy T.'s.

By buying from different stores out of different shipments, I was convinced I'd cut down on doubles and make my funds go further. I even saved card money for visits to my grandparents so I could beat those nefarious Topps bastards. The card distribution pattern was different in Selbyville, Delaware. Every year I'd march into Hastings Pharmacy like a blackjack card counter into a Las Vegas casino. I knew I was going to beat the house. And I always did.

What patience my parents must have had. My mother actually kept track of which cards I wanted badly or needed to finish a series and would ask if I had gotten them yet. In a family where waste was abhorred and Depression tales were periodically invoked, I never heard the words "That's *enough* baseball cards."

The first summer I went away to camp, my parents faithfully bought cards for me while I was gone. That's why, to this day, there is no six-week gap in the middle of my '60 set.

Finding the cards—and the old cigar box I'd kept them in, which turned up inside my camp trunk—helped me open some doors into the past. I started to realize that I had never gone through my parents' house—closets, attic, basement, every corner—since my mother died. She was everywhere, and I hadn't wanted to see her in each detail. But to complete the card search, I had to. And some balloon of tension popped.

Like most families, we had arguments and painful, imperfect reconciliations. Don't bother listening for melodramatic theme music here: I'm talking about the usual family stuff that bores everybody else but rips you apart at the time. People gain distance on their childhood and their parents as they grow. But independence has a cost.

I'd never understood the degree to which my memories of growing up had been diminished in sweetness, in intensity, by all those necessary adult understandings and demythologizings. I hadn't realized that very little from my youth still felt as innocently rich as it had back then.

Until the baseball cards came back.

Through them, I reconnected with some of my unalloyed pleasure as a kid—as well as the sincerity of my parents' flawed love. Just being around the cards, "playing" with them, made me feel secure, cared for, and appreciated. So, obviously, that's how the seven-to-thirteen-year-old who owned the cards must have felt about the home they were part of.

A touchstone like that is hard to find. And difficult, perhaps even stupid, to give up. Maybe that's why, one autumn day with the World Series approaching, I realized that I was glad my cards were *not* worth $50,000. If they were, I'd *have* to sell them, like a stock that's peaked, because I can't help thinking the card market must be headed for the trendoid dumpster.

Still, I couldn't decide whether to hold 'em for sentiment or fold 'em for a heating system that works.

Then one day I was watching my son—who gets Ken Griffey Jr. or Juan Gonzalez every time he opens a pack—merrily abuse his cards, just like I'd taught him, as he prepared to trounce me again at flip.

"Show me some of your good players," he said. "Show me Willie Mays."

So I did. He even wanted to hear about Pete Runnels and Camilo Pascual.

"Daddy, are you going to sell all your baseball cards?" he asked.

"No," I decided. "I'm going to save all the good ones for you."

Rose and Thorns

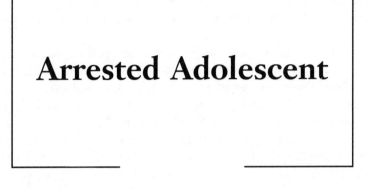

Arrested Adolescent

March 24, 1989—Whoever dreamed that Pete Rose, who's given us such childish pleasure, would now give us such deeply adult pain?

For thirty years, America has cheered Rose for remaining a child. He was selfish but charming. Vain but joyous. Shallow but shrewd. Crude but funny. Greedy for all the candy but generous once he got it. Prone to the vices but honest about it. Oblivious to society's conventions but also mythically large. Given no gift, save his obsession for baseball, he made himself a hero.

His world bought the package. So why would such a common man ever change?

Now, precisely because he obeyed our wishes (and his own) by staying a child in almost every way, Rose's life may soon be a public and private shambles.

Failed husband. Apparently worse father. Apparently out of control gambler. That's probably the best public verdict that Rose can hope a few days hence. Far worse is possible. Is Rose bankrupt? Will he be banned for a year from baseball for betting on his sport? Or, worst of all, will he be banned for life for betting on his own team?

The priest defrocked, the lawyer disbarred, the captain court-martialed, the doctor stripped of his license faces no greater pain or shame than Rose does now. Life without baseball would be purgatory for him, if not hell itself.

Whatever the commissioner's probe reveals, one familiar truism has been borne out again: What goes around comes around. Even for Rose.

He devoted his life to baseball and it rewarded him with wealth, adulation, and sports immortality. He was paid in gold for every drop of sweat.

For the best in himself, he got full compensation. But at a great price. The worst we can say is that Rose and Ty Cobb are starting to look more alike. Rose apparently cheated on a good wife, neglected two children, and hurt his family more than he ever hurt Ray Fosse.

Those, however, were not Rose's only adolescent flaws. In every idle hour and deep into the night, as though allowing nothing else into his mind, he watched games of all kinds. The devil sent him cable. It helped keep his mind as free of ideas as the day he signed at Macon.

At the least, Rose is a damaged man. His managing career is in grave jeopardy even if the commissioner lets him stay in his job. For a manager, maturity is the equivalent of hustle to a player. Rose's players, like Billy Martin's in a different way, know he doesn't have a handle on adult behavior. Dave Parker isn't alone among former Reds when he says he has "no respect" for Rose.

As a player, Rose's escapades and foibles made him one of the boys, even in his mid-forties; bizarre as it sounds, they may have helped him be a roughhouse clubhouse leader. Now, those same traits are baggage.

Despite everything we already know, despite everything we soon may learn, Rose deserves our empathy, though maybe not too much sympathy. To grasp how Rose got where he is, we have to sense his weird relationship with fame.

Like many, he got famous fast—Rookie of the Year at twenty-two. Rose and glory always seemed to be racing full speed to lock arms around each other. Once they embraced, the passion only grew. Instead of loosening their hold on each other as Rose aged, they grabbed tighter.

Free agency late in his career brought Rose his first millions (and let him graduate to the $100 window). Batting .325 at forty made him beloved. His staggering pursuit of Ty Cobb, instead of being seen as ornery and even pathetic as he bounced to three different teams in his last five mediocre years, was magnified as doggedly heroic.

After thirty-five, most players are forced to face their athletic mortality. (Many become nicer people. "He learned to say hello when it was time to say goodbye" is the cliché.) Instead, over a heady decade, Rose went from star to superstar to world figure to all-time hit king.

The common sense and modesty that most people have beaten into them in their twenties, and even ballplayers gain in their thirties, Rose was able to postpone indefinitely—perhaps forever. At forty-eight, he still has not officially retired and sometimes threatens to pinch-hit again. At ages when players traditionally have gained humility, Rose was learning pride. Even as a manager, with his team on the verge of a pennant, he could see his legend rising.

In sports, as in politics, we hear the most exceptionally successful and driven people described as "larger than life." But what happens when you become larger than life? The ego needed to be great and the judgment required to be wise aren't often found in the same package.

We celebrate heroes when they accomplish tasks that demand that they go beyond normal human limits. Then we're shocked when they act as though normal human limits do not apply to their private conduct.

What must someone like Rose tell himself as he tries to do things the whole world says are impossible? Surely, in his own mind, he must build the case for his own specialness: "I can, because I'm different." Won't those same words—the hallmark of hubris—tempt a person into mischief on a hundred other occasions?

Within a few days, perhaps a few hours, we may hear stories about Rose that will curl our hair. And we may watch him suffer punishments that sadden our hearts, no matter how much we try to harden them. We may be tempted to ask: How could a man so blessed by fortune lose touch with common sense to such a degree?

If compassion moves us a little, we might also ask: How could he not?

Last Standing O

CINCINNATI, April 4, 1989—Regardless of whatever dark nights lie ahead for him, Pete Rose had a thunderous minute in the sun Monday. Regardless of whatever guilt he may, or may not, have to bear in a nation's eyes someday, Rose was presumed innocent Monday afternoon by both the court of hometown opinion and by a jury of his peers.

On Opening Day, baseball's symbolic afternoon of rebirth, Cincinnati fans poured their love upon him, and even the Los Angeles Dodgers, his archrival foes, were moved to oratory to defend him.

An hour before the first pitch of a new season, Rose was asked how he thought the Riverfront Stadium crowd would respond when he was introduced. After all, he's been persecuted by innuendo coast to coast for weeks, even though no one has prosecuted him for anything as yet.

"How would I know?" said Rose.

"You've lived here all your life," came the response.

"Not yet," said Rose, quietly, slyly, cutting a look out of the corner of his eye to see if his meaning was taken.

It's going to take a lot to run Rose out of this town. "Now, the manager of the Cincinnati Reds," intoned the public address announcer as Rose ran from the dugout.

What followed was like a sonic boom. The sellout crowd of 55,385 bellowed for a full minute as Rose took his place at home plate, his feet in the same batter's box where he stood four years ago to break Ty Cobb's hit record. Not a boo in the house.

"I got goose bumps. Anybody'd be moved by that. I could stand here all day and describe what the fans of Cincinnati have meant to me. They treated me like a king," said Rose after his team's 6–4 win over the world champion Dodgers. "I feel like I'm playin' again. Everybody is pulling for me."

Rose may, or may not, have done plenty wrong. The office of the baseball commissioner has taken a hard look at his life. There are reports that federal authorities are also looking—at his extensive gambling, his possible serious debts, his questionable friends, his duplicate sales of personal memorabilia, and his reporting of taxable cash income.

To the rest of the world, charges will have to be proved beyond a reasonable doubt before Rose can be punished. Here in Cincinnati, where one of the biggest streets is named Pete Rose Way, such sins may have to be proved beyond a shadow of a doubt.

T-shirts in a downtown store window read: "Take The Heat Off Pete." Rose jerseys also were for sale as well as duplicates of the front page of the September 12, 1985, edition of the *Cincinnati Enquirer* (for $15). Bedsheet signs ran the range from "Free Pete" to "You Bet We Back Pete." However, a security guard tore down one long upper-deck sign that said, "We're Bettin' On Pete."

Cincinnati has long been known as perhaps the most ferociously loyal, and defiantly provincial, town in baseball. To this crowd, dressed in a sea of red, the Reds are demigods. Their foes are merely foils.

No one in Cincinnati could have defended Rose more vehemently than Dodgers star Kirk Gibson. "I don't think this [investigation] has been handled right," Gibson said. "There's going to be a scar beside his name now whether he's guilty or not. I don't think that's fair. For all he's done [for baseball], he has to prove his innocence for how many weeks now?

"We forgive people over and over in this game. When people do drugs, they go to rehab. They're forgiven. Why should they put this on him? Anybody who booed him today, if there were any, should be ashamed."

Then Gibson took the most radical pro-Rose position possible: "If he were guilty of some wrongdoing, that wouldn't change my opinion of Pete Rose as a man. I make mistakes. I wouldn't crucify him. . . . He's a Hall of Famer. I don't care what he's done."

On this day, which baseball dedicates to forgetfulness of past transgressions, Dodgers manager Tommy Lasorda was in Rose's corner.

But he was worried. "I just pray that Pete has never bet on a baseball game and that his reputation will never be tarnished."

Even Lasorda could not free his mind of reports that Rose has gambled himself into problems that could get him suspended from baseball for a year, or for life. "Seventy-five percent of the people think this guy's guilty," said Lasorda. "I don't understand why Pete hasn't come out and said, 'I never bet on baseball. I never bet on baseball in my life.' "

Perhaps the core cause of sympathy for Rose, aside from the lack of hard public evidence, is the growing sense that baseball has slipped into a double standard. For being addicted to drugs, you get twenty-eight days. For being addicted to gambling, you can get life. Yet both, medically, can be viewed as diseases. Also, the danger to baseball posed by both problems is the same: the ultimate fixing of a game.

Much has come out already that will permanently darken our perception of Rose. Still, the worst that can be said of him is that he has been as poor a husband and father as Robert Frost and as bad a gambler as Fyodor Dostoyevsky. Yet no one rejects Frost's poetry or ignores *Crime and Punishment* because gambling impoverished its author. Few can perfect both their life and their work.

Rose has said, "I feel like a piece of raw meat." Yet he claims his ordeal is tolerable. "It's not hard. I'm waiting for the same thing you are," he said Monday. "I'm very confident. . . . That's one thing about being in America. You always get your chance."

Another American principle of jurisprudence, however, may be getting short shrift. The feeling grows that, for Rose, justice delayed is justice denied.

The Empty Wall

COOPERSTOWN, New York, May 23, 1989—As you step into the Hall of Fame Museum, the first thing you see is a portrait of Babe Ruth, the symbol of everything joyous, full-blooded, and mythic in baseball's first century. The fat man with the moon face who ate and drank to excess, drove his roadster like a maniac, punched a couple of cops, and signed a ton of autographs for sick kids is captured exactly as he should be—swinging lustily for the farthest fence.

Just a step behind the Babe, more prominently displayed than any other mural—ahead of Hank Aaron, Jackie Robinson, Sandy Koufax, Joe DiMaggio, or Ted Williams—stands a huge black-and-white tribute to Pete Rose, the symbol of everything that's most jubilant, childlike, and greedy in baseball's young second century. The squat man with the square jaw, who hustled and punched his way through the sport for twenty-five years, is captured exactly as he should be—barreling out of the batter's box at the age of forty-five, heading hell-bent for first base, looking for infielders to scatter like candlepins.

Rose's poster in this room of great achievements has only one thing printed on it—"4,192." No more is needed, any more than the big placards for Lou Gehrig ("2,130"), Rickey Henderson ("130"), Roger Clemens ("20"), DiMaggio ("56"), or Williams (".406") need explanation to the visitors here.

The museum itself is a single towering room full of marble, natural light, and bronze plaques. The first carved head you meet is that of the man Rose chased and caught—Ty Cobb. His face is grim, as befits a sociopath who was hated and feared by his peers. Diagonally across from Cobb, in the farthest corner of the Hall, a small patch of wall is still empty. Two alcoves, each with room for twenty more plaques, are bare. This summer, Carl Yastrzemski and Johnny Bench, Rose's old teammate, will start that new gallery.

The one where Rose should hang.

Everyone who comes here wonders and worries and argues as they march past the plaques and peek ahead at the empty wall where Rose may, or may not, have a place. Many note that, next to Rose's wall, is a large bronze inscription dedicating the Hall. It's signed by Kenesaw Landis, the commissioner who banned eight Chicago White Sox for life, including the great Joe Jackson.

Seventy years ago, fans echoed the child who begged Shoeless Joe to "Say it ain't so, Joe." Now, Charlie Hustle says it ain't so; says he never bet on baseball or his Reds; says he'll clear his name at a hearing next month.

Opinion is divided among the pilgrims here. Emotion isn't. They are on Rose's side. Hoping against hope. Hoping against a 225-page investigative report. Hoping against seven more volumes of documentation against him. Yet many seem resigned that Rose and baseball soon will be divorced, perhaps forever. At least, many of them say, if Rose is to be out of baseball and, perhaps, in hot water with the IRS, then at least let him keep the place he earned here.

"They ought to have a petition right here for people to sign to help Pete get in the Hall," said Pat Carlozzi of Burrville, Rhode Island. "It's a shame they don't ask the fans to vote or call one of those 900 numbers. Then Rose would get in for sure. . . . You think a guy like that could throw a game? 'I'm not going to run to first base today, guys.' That's tantamount to foolishness."

If the worst public allegation against Rose is true—that he bet on the Reds—what would Carlozzi say to the other young Carlozzis traipsing through the Hall with him? "You tell your children just what you'd tell them if they have an uncle who's an alcoholic. You can't stop liking someone or giving him his due just 'cause he's human and has problems."

Tom Zambarano of North Providence, Rhode Island, expressed succinctly what many fans said: "All it says on the plaques is what you did, not what kind of father you were or what kind of man you were. We should be able to make that distinction. They're not heroes, just

larger than life people. They're not here because they were
saints. . . .

"This is a guy who gave everything he had to the game. Now, they
may take his future away from him. They can't take the past away
from him, too."

"I've never been a Rose fan, but I think he belongs in here on his
baseball abilities. If I owned a team, I'd want nine Roses," said Jim
McNulty of Portland, Oregon. "In many respects, Pete is already
here. He's in, really. His records are all over the place."

McNulty's wife, Dorene, disagreed. She saw the Hall as a symbolic
place, a shrine. "You hate to see baseball tainted. None of them are
angels. But the sport is the best, so you want to see it kept as clean as
possible."

Those who felt both sides of the argument were, of course, most
pained. "It's a tough call. Betting on your own team is hard to forgive.
But if you look beyond the field, there're a lot of skeletons in the
closets [of Hall of Famers]," said Greg Ryan of Colonia, New Jersey.

"It's especially a shame, because gambling is an illness, like alcohol.
I'm a lawyer, so I deal with people on both sides of the law. I can
really understand how Rose is getting into these problems. And once
you start dealing with the people he's dealing with, you're vulnerable
to getting in even deeper.

"I'm glad I don't have to make the decision."

That job will fall to the baseball writers. Their instructions for
voting are carved at the entrance to the Hall. "Voting shall be based
upon the player's record, playing ability, integrity, sportsmanship,
character, contribution to the team[s] on which he played and not on
what he may have done otherwise in baseball."

Before coming here, I thought I'd never vote for Rose if it were
proven that he bet on the Reds. That's just too close to betting against
your own team. And that's only a whisker away from fixing a game.
And fixers have no business whatsoever here.

Now, I've changed my mind, thanks to the simple logic of fans. If
Rose has broken the law, then let the IRS or courts handle that. If
Rose has bet on baseball or the Reds, let Commissioner A. Bartlett
Giamatti administer the game's simple and longstanding rules, even
though they're harsh.

If Rose deserves punishment, we can assume he'll get it. However,
as long as he hasn't fixed a game or bet against his team—and no one
has suggested either—Pete Rose deserves to be in the Hall of Fame.

Denial

August 25, 1989—In keeping with the central theme of his tragedy, Pete Rose was banned from baseball for life yesterday. And he is the only one who doesn't know it yet.

Rose's almost infinite capacity for self-delusion completed a full and sad circle as a watching nation saw the horrible power of psychological denial.

Clear as a bell, Commissioner A. Bartlett Giamatti told the world: "The banishment for life of Pete Rose from baseball is the sad end of a sorry episode. . . . One of the game's greatest players has engaged in a variety of acts which have stained the game and he must now live with the consequences of those acts. . . . There is absolutely no deal for reinstatement. That is exactly what we did not agree to in terms of fixed number of years."

As if that weren't enough, Giamatti said point-blank that he personally believed Rose had bet on his own team, the Cincinnati Reds.

In the face of this sword through his heart, Rose stood before the cameras, looked the reality of his past and his future squarely in the face—and didn't see a thing.

Where the rest of the world saw incredible disgrace, he saw exoneration, simply because he had refused to confess to any wrongdoing. Like a movie mobster saying, "They couldn't pin nothin' on me," Rose took great pride in pointing out that his agreement with the commissioner did not force him to confess any specific wrongdoing.

Where others saw indefinite banishment, Rose saw the technical glimmer of reinstatement in a year if Giamatti will reconsider his case.

"I've been in baseball three decades and to think I'm going to be out of baseball for a very short period of time hurts," said Rose. "My life is baseball. I hope to get back in as soon as I possibly can. I'm never looking forward to a birthday like I'm looking forward to my new daughter's birthday. Because two days after that I can apply for reinstatement."

Most incredible, Rose said, once more without a shred of evidence to back it up: "I never bet on baseball. . . . I only regret that I won't have the opportunity to tell my side of the story."

Who knows, perhaps the trauma of the last six months has been so awful that Rose has truly convinced himself that he never bet on a baseball game, much less the games of his Reds.

The betting slips in his handwriting, the calls to bookies made from his telephone, the court testimony by his criminal buddies, even his fingerprints found on the betting paraphernalia—maybe he has wished them all out of existence.

Like countless alcoholics, drug addicts, and habitual gamblers before him, Rose continues to swear: "I have no problem. I don't need help."

Rose hasn't gone low enough yet. But, if the history of addicts and their denials repeats itself, he probably will. That's what's saddest of all.

Still hanging over Rose's neck is an investigation into several varieties of possible tax evasion. Rose could end up in prison. Would that snap him back into focus? Can anything?

Regarding any gambling rehabilitation for Rose, Giamatti said: "We have not required it. It seems to be entirely in Mr. Rose's hands."

In other words, heaven help him.

Giamatti may have fumbled the Rose Case from day one until the whole mess became a maze of legal mumbo jumbo. At times, the new commissioner, a victim of on-the-job training, had so much egg on his face you could barely see his beard. However, in the end, Giamatti protected the integrity of baseball admirably by slipping a curveball past Rose for a called third strike.

The commissioner had a trump card: He understood Rose's problem and Rose did not. So he could turn Rose's inverted worldview back against him. The former Yale president understood that only one thing was dearer to Rose than his life in baseball—and that was maintaining his grip on his castle of illusions. So a trade was made. Baseball got rid of both Rose and his dangerous lawsuits, which could have eroded the power of the office of commissioner. And Rose got to save face, at least in his own eyes, with one last brassy news conference. Rose could crow that there had been no final hearing, no formal guilty verdict.

No commissioner in his right mind ever will reinstate Rose—especially if he stays in so obvious a state of denial. Let this swaggering, unrepentant loose cannon back into the game? He'd be a ticking bomb. In addition, no team would touch Rose now if it could. Just as no team touches Billy Martin. You can ruin your reputation so badly that you blackball yourself.

Baseball has had blacker days than August 24, 1989. But perhaps none more full to the brim with sorrow. If Rose is not a modern approximation of a tragic figure in Greek drama, then who would be?

All his adult life he has thought, and been encouraged to think, that he was outside the normal rules of human behavior and above punishment. In his private life, in his friendships, in his habits, he went to the edge, then stepped over, trusting his luck because—well, because he was the Great Pete Rose. He still appears to believe that his 4,256 hits will save him.

Balanced against this one great flaw stand all Rose's gifts and charms. His hard work and his humor are real. His common touch with little people and his generosity are not fake. The praise he received for thirty years was not a fraud, although it may have helped lure him down his path.

Now, the worst seems to have happened. No, not banishment from baseball. Or the possibility, which seems so trivial, that he won't be voted into the Hall of Fame. What looms before us now is the uglier possibility that Rose simply does not know what has happened to him or his life.

Rose always liked to say, "I was raised, but I never did grow up." For his sake, let's hope he starts soon. Because, at the moment, Pete Rose seems to have regressed past childhood, all the way to a world of fantasy.

Revisionist's Delight

April 21, 1990—When time has boiled away the inessentials, how will Pete Rose be remembered? Might the following citation appear in an encyclopedia in 2090?

> Pete Rose was one of the most colorful and generous of baseball's great players. A single-minded, simple man, he loved the game exuberantly and did more to help the popularity of the national pastime than anyone since Babe Ruth. In the end, however, he was banned from the sport for life because it was believed that he had bet on his own team to win its games. Then, he was sent to prison for neglecting to pay taxes on his fees for signing thousands of autographs. Ironically, in a time when many corporations paid no taxes at all, Rose paid a dozen times more to the IRS than he evaded.

> Rose is now generally considered to be the most tragically wronged and misunderstood athlete in the history of his sport. Few Americans have ever given so much to so many, yet been penalized so grievously for so little. Rose, who accepted punishment stoically, said all he ever wanted was to be in the Hall of Fame. This too he was denied. Rose was a good-hearted though badly flawed man who was crushed by the relentless application of the letter of the law.

Many other things have been written about Pete Rose in the last year, most of them far harsher and more judgmental than this. Some of them have appeared in this column. The feeling here is still firm that Rose should have been banned from baseball and that he should stay banned for a long time. Perhaps forever. The idea of reinstatement after one year should be dismissed in a split second. Rose should also pay every cent of back income tax that the IRS can prove he owes. With interest and penalties, like everybody else.

Yet Rose also belongs in the Hall of Fame. And not in jail.

This guy has suffered enough.

Perspective is especially difficult in these Rose matters. Because of his swagger and self-assurance, and his habit of hanging out with disreputable characters, Rose evokes memories of movie felons. On the other hand, Rose's open, blunt manner, his wit, and (on the nonlegal issues) his candor make it hard to believe that lifetime banishments and prison sentences are the proper fate for such a man. In ten or twenty years, will Rose's sins seem much grayer and his virtues much brighter than they do now?

History refuses to stand still. It keeps getting rewritten and reframed in new contexts. When we look at the politicians who have been rehabilitated in the public mind, can we doubt that enterprising fact jugglers will someday make a cottage industry of reinventing Rose as Victim? And will they, to some degree, be correct?

Many will be shocked that Rose underreported his income by about $355,000 between 1984 and 1987. But some inside baseball will be surprised that it wasn't considerably more. Rose got $10,000 and more for a single autograph session.

If U.S. District Judge S. Arthur Spiegel sends Rose to jail, as he has already sentenced Rose's friend Tommy Gioiosa to five years, Rose will have been imprisoned for neglecting to report about three percent of his income. How does that compare to the national average?

Perhaps the most fascinating aspect of the Rose case is the way it shimmers and shifts according to the light. One day you wake up and your sympathies are with Pete—the free-living common man with common vices who suddenly finds himself surrounded by lawyers, IRS agents, intellectuals, commissioners, and other perfect moralists. The next day you reread the Dowd report and think that Rose's arrogance was grotesquely out of control and that he's getting just what he deserved. If you're going to make somebody an example, what a good place to start—with a guy who thought he was above everybody and everything.

Although it will bring scant relief to Rose, the drama over Should Pete Go to Jail will only magnify the dimensions of this whole sad saga. Rose is quickly moving out of baseball history and into American history. So far he's been the subject of sportswriting. Now it's just a matter of time before literature gets perpetrated on him.

Great fame and historic feats, coupled with a Gordian knot of moral ambiguity, plus a hint of untold secrets, make a potboiler plot that can stand the test of time. Long after Rose is dead, his relative guilt or innocence and the true nature of his character will be debated. Anybody who has simple feelings or a simple answer when the name "Pete Rose" is mentioned probably hasn't been thinking enough.

The other day I opened a book of photo portraits of baseball players. There was Rose, his huge hungry face leaping out of the page like the bogeyman in a horror movie. I had to hold the book at arm's length to get the face far enough away so it didn't seem scary. Then, in a moment, I remembered fifteen years in which all my memories of Rose were of his laughter, his gentleness with little people, his patience with fools, and, always, that great commonsense, smart-aleck humor.

I could almost hear Pete say: "Hey, I finally hit a big one at the track today. Ten more and I'll be even. Yeah, sure, I told the IRS all about it. Got any idea how much money I've paid those guys over the years? They ought to name a bridge after me."

Shoeless Joe Jackson refused to rat on his Black Sox buddies seventy years ago. And they're still writing books and making movies with him as a central character. If Rose has the misfortune to go to jail, even if it's only for a fraction of the maximum six-year term that he might face, the story of Charlie Hustle will make "Say it ain't so, Joe" seem like small potatoes in the gallery of American pop-culture pathos.

Let's hope Pete gets off light if only so we don't have to keep hearing from him and about him for the rest of our lives. And feel lousy inside every time.

White-Collar
Lynching

February 5, 1991—The righteous lynching, with the townsfolk taking justice into their own hands, is an American tradition as old as the frontier and as fresh as Pete Rose's banishment from the Hall of Fame ballot yesterday.

Rose was strung up by the most distinguished men in the game—including past and present league presidents and a former commissioner. Fair play was ignored. But vengeance was served. In a vigilante act, both passionate in motive and arrogant in execution, the friends of the late commissioner, Bart Giamatti, and current commissioner, Fay Vincent, lashed out at Rose in the fiercest and most final way they could manage. In effect, they probably barred Rose from the Hall of Fame for life. No doubt, they feel they've acted for the ends of justice and the good of the game, though their means may have stunk.

The 12–0 vote by the Hall of Fame board to "exclude players on the permanently ineligible list from the ballot" was a personal act of revenge by the sport's hierarchy against Rose—a man whom the game's establishment reviles for the pain and embarrassment he brought them. For the record, there is only one living human on the permanently ineligible list: Rose.

Heretofore, every member of the Hall of Fame has been elected by the Baseball Writers Association of America or the Old-Timers Committee. Some great players, like Shoeless Joe Jackson, have been left out of the Hall because of the "morals" clause in the voting instructions. The Rose issue, however, was seen as too vital to entrust to anyone outside the sport's inner sanctum. So, with Rose eligible for the ballot this December, due process and precedent were ignored so the game's most powerful men could do what they pleased.

In an attempt to rationalize what was probably an emotion-driven decision, Hall of Fame President Ed Stack said: "The directors felt that it would be incongruous to have a person who has been declared ineligible by baseball to be eligible for baseball's highest honor. . . . If such individual is reinstated by baseball, then such individual would be a candidate for election."

Why would such leaders of the sport as Bobby Brown, Lee Mac-Phail, Bowie Kuhn, Bill White, and Chub Feeney stoop to such bare-knuckles tactics? Nobody knows or, at least, can prove what they suspect. But many in baseball think they know what this is really about.

It's about Fay Vincent—Bart Giamatti's best friend—shaking hands with Pete Rose on the back porch of the Hall of Fame at his induction ceremony. A lot of people in baseball—good people—just don't have the stomach to allow this Vincent-Rose moment to occur. If they have to abuse their power, tarnish their reputations, and embarrass themselves to prevent it, they'll do it. And they did it yesterday.

Everyone knows that Giamatti, who died at age fifty-one, ate too much, smoked too much, worked too hard, and worried too much.

But if you were one of the dozen men who voted in New York yesterday—if you knew Giamatti, the former Yale president who brought prestige, affection, and competence to the sport—how would you have felt about the raw, undeniable fact that he died one week after barring Rose for life? In the crunch, would you stick to proper procedure or would you stick it to Rose?

Within the baseball establishment, Rose is held in contempt on three levels. First, according to the Dowd report, for betting on baseball, including his own team's games. Second, for dragging the sport through the mud after he was caught red-handed, rather than throwing himself on the mercy of the court. And third, for refusing—to this day—to admit that he bet on baseball. To these men, Rose is as unrepentant and destructive as he ever was.

To many on the Hall board, such as former Expos president John McHale, Brewers owner Bud Selig, and Tigers chairman John Campbell, Giamatti and Vincent are a modern Damon and Pythias. They are heroic figures—one the stout, earthy, charismatic intellectual; the other, the brilliant businessman and gentle compromiser. To the members of the board, Giamatti's death and Vincent's pain over it—not to mention the suffering of Giamatti's family—are everyday facts.

On top of all that, the Hall of Fame board had every reason to suspect that, eventually, the baseball writers might have voted Rose into the Hall. The writers never had a better friend, a better source, a richer continuing story—right to the ugly end—than Rose. Journalists see lots of human foibles. For some reason, they tend to be quick to judge but also prone to forgive.

It's easy to see why baseball's wise men orchestrated this charade in recent weeks—pretending that Operation Get Pete was never on their agenda. The Hall even went to the dissembling length of stacking a "study committee" against Rose, then inviting two members of the BBWAA to join that committee to lend it credibility. The two writers, Jack Lang and Phil Pepe, reported back that the committee meeting on Rose was totally cordial and totally a sham.

Some still hold out hope for a bizarre "happy" ending to this saga. In fact, the wording of Stack's statement implies it. Let's say that the game's old guard breaks Rose's resistance with this Hall blackball and, in time, gets a bet-on-baseball confession out of him. Then, maybe, someday, Vincent or another commissioner might take him off the permanently ineligible list. Theoretically, Rose could then be voted into the Hall of Fame—the sinner chastened, the prodigal son returned home at last.

Maybe. But don't bet on it. When the words "Rose" and "Hall of Fame" are mentioned in the same sentence, many of the most powerful men in the sport have the same gut-level response: not in my lifetime.

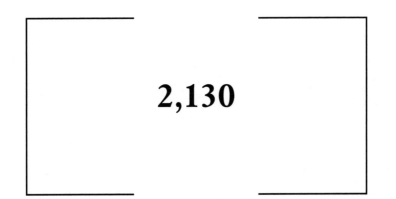

2,130

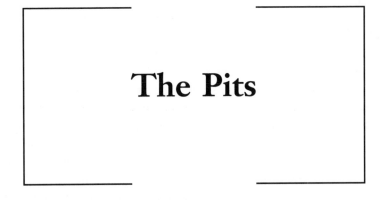

The Pits

June 29, 1990—Earlier this month, Cal Ripken Jr. reached rock bottom. That's what it usually takes to convince a successful man to make drastic changes.

At the moment he was passing Everett Scott's mark of 1,307 consecutive games, second all-time, Ripken also was hearing boos at Memorial Stadium.

As he was building a streak of errorless games at shortstop—which has reached 70, three short of the AL record—Ripken was being savaged on talk shows for being selfish.

You see, Ripken's batting average had plunged to .209. And in baseball your average and the public's estimation of your character usually go hand in hand. Ripken's failure to hit his weight became symbolic of a four-and-a-half-season span. Since 1985, the six-time All-Star starter had proved, beyond any statistical doubt, that he no longer bore much resemblance to the hitter who'd masticated AL pitching in his first four seasons.

In those early years, Ripken averaged .293 with 27 homers, 69 extra-base hits, 108 runs scored, and 98 RBI a year. In the four seasons since, he has averaged .264 with 24 homers, 55 extra-base hits, 91 runs scored, and 88 RBI.

Holy atrophy.

Everybody had a solution. Take a rest to avoid those slumps from exhaustion the past two Septembers. Break the streak, forget about

Lou Gehrig's mark of 2,130 games and take the "pressure" off. Move to third base—a physically easier and less mentally demanding position. Bat lower in the order where there's less responsibility.

Only one suggestion seemed verboten.

Maybe Cal should start taking batting instruction from somebody besides the third-base coach, his dad.

Over the past two weeks, strange doings have been afoot. The Ripken rumor mill has been buzzing because, suddenly, Ripken's appearance at home plate has become radically different. He stopped wrapping the bat around his neck like a contortionist. He stopped waggling the bat as the pitcher delivered. Ripken even stopped standing so deep in the box, with an extremely closed stance.

Finally, Ripken began looking a bit like a modern hitter—one influenced by the Charlie Lau–Walt Hriniak school of hitting. Weight back. Commit late. Hit to all fields. Don't uppercut. Line drives, not fly balls. Hit off a firm left side that extends, rather than collapses, at the moment of impact.

A funny thing happened: Ripken got hot immediately. One line drive or smoking grounder after another. Plus a couple of seeing-eye bonuses. In his last fourteen games, Ripken has been one of the hotter batters in baseball—23 for 56 (.411). His average has risen from .209 to .250. Last week, Ripken had a new kind of streak—four straight three-hit games, a first for him.

Ripken merely may be in a nice streak that's gotten him back to his modest level of the past four years. But Ripken doesn't think so. He thinks Frank Robinson (1966 Triple Crown winner, 586 career home runs) has turned him around.

Yes, Frank.

The secret's out.

"It's ludicrous for people to say that I've never had any other teacher but my father," said Ripken yesterday, knowing that, basically, that is what most people in baseball believe. "We're all in this together. I'm just taking advantage of expertise. What I'm doing is something we all agreed with. Maybe Frank said it differently than my father would have, so I heard it."

Gee, does that ever happen with fathers and sons?

"Anyway, it dawned on me."

Ripken asked Robinson, "Am I lunging at the ball?"

"No," said Robinson, chuckling, "you're sprinting at it. Looks like you're trying to run to the mound to get the ball out of the pitcher's hand."

"From trying to succeed too much, I got into the habit of starting too soon. And that's a hard habit to break," Ripken said. "Everything I'm doing is to try to wait longer. Not be jumpy.

"When you lunge, you pop up and nothing good can happen. When you wait, you can hit the ball hard to right. You're still in hitting position. . . . I was getting myself in a position where I'd expended my energy and I had nothing left to hit the ball with.

"I can't be my own eyes. You need somebody to watch you."

And perhaps not with family eyes. Where a father might see minor problems, an outsider might see the need for a major overhaul.

"He's giving himself a chance to be the hitter he can be," said Robinson.

If Ripken ever straightens out his mechanics—and he's been an eccentric-looking hitter for years—then other controversies around him would subside.

Already, Ripken Sr. is happy to take shots at his son's critics. "If he was so tired at 1,307, how'd he get so rested at 1,314?" growled the old coach.

Ripken Jr. lives in a world of stats. He has made two errors in his last 127 games. Nobody's ever played shortstop more flawlessly. Instead of outgrowing the position with age, Ripken seems to be growing into it.

Or is it just his glove?

Ripken says, "If you must know, it's the glove."

Late last July in Minnesota, Kirby Puckett hit two topspin smashes that jumped out of Ripken's glove for errors. "So I switched to my BP [batting practice] glove. It's bigger, looser. More like a third baseman's glove or an outfielder's," he said. "I've never had a glove that broke in just like that one. It's the same series as the others, but it's just different. In-between hops don't bounce out of it. Balls to the backhand side, where I used to get a lot of errors, don't spin out. But it's still flat enough in the pocket to turn the double play.

"Just a good glove."

Two months from now, if Ripken is still headed for .250 with 20 homers, the boobirds will be yelling: "Hey, dude, have a mental margarita. Kick back. Take a whole day off."

But maybe, just maybe, a summer of hitting lessons from Robinson will smooth the wrinkles forming in Ripken's forehead as his thirtieth birthday approaches in August.

The least controversial player in baseball really shouldn't be surrounded by such constant controversy. Add 50 points to this guy's batting average and, suddenly, his insidious character flaws will disappear.

The Groove

TORONTO, July 9, 1991—Years from now, when ballplayers talk about the 1991 All-Star Game, their most vivid memory may be of what Cal Ripken did the day before the classic.

What Michael Jordan and Larry Bird have done for slam-dunk and three-point contests, Ripken did yesterday for the long ball. Forget the old "Home Run Derby" from 1950s TV. This was new legend.

In 22 swings, the Orioles shortstop hit an astonishing 12 home runs, including several that may have been longer than any he's hit in Memorial Stadium.

"Unbelievable," said Kirby Puckett. "Unbelievable," said Carlton Fisk. "Unbelievable," said Ripken himself.

No, not unbelievable.

However, to a game that can't afford to lose one more iota of its innocence, Ripken gave an indelibly sweet moment—one worthy of a man who hasn't missed a game in more than nine years.

"I didn't know what I was doing but I didn't want it to stop," said Ripken. "I felt like a little boy."

That's sure not how Ripken felt an hour earlier. Then, he was honestly worried. Was he going to risk wasting a year of work—as well as a rediscovery of himself as a hitter—for the sake of this one gimmicky slugging contest?

"I hate these things. Nothing messes you up faster. Especially me. It puts me right back in all the bad habits I've worked so hard to break," he said. "When we go to Rochester [to play AAA farmhands],

I won't be in them. When the guys have long ball contests before games in BP, I try to stay out of 'em.

"But I've agreed to be in this one. So I'll try to hit home runs. If I hit liners up the middle, it'd look bad."

A year ago at the All-Star break, Ripken was so humiliated by his .208 average that he dismantled his swing, stance, and strategy. Now, one July later, Ripken is leading the league in hitting (.348), total bases (190), and hits (111). He's hit 18 home runs and he's on a pace for 36 for the season and 110 RBI.

Finally, this year, the more he's looked out for No. 1, the better it's been for everybody. Of course, Ted Williams could have told him that.

"All right," said Ripken, finally, "I'm going to stick with what I've been doing all year. Everybody says you hit homers when you aren't trying. So let's see. Maybe I'll hit one by accident."

In last year's All-Star contest in Wrigley Field, the four-man AL team hit one homer. Yesterday, National Leaguers Howard Johnson and Chris Sabo each swung ten times without one. Other sluggers, such as Joe Carter of the Blue Jays and George Bell of the Cubs, hit a couple.

Ripken, however, was a bit different. After taking two pitches from Toronto coach Hector Torres, he began his turn with a line drive to center. Except that the ball didn't want to come down until it smacked above a billboard 430 feet away.

After a liner to left, Ripken almost decapitated a vendor in the second deck in left center, about 440 feet away. Almost before that landed, his next blow reached the third deck, 450 feet away.

Ripken's next blow looked like a high liner over shortstop. But it kept working until it cleared the wall. An instant later, No. 5 hit the foul pole at third-deck level.

By now, the AL dugout was a madhouse of high fives, comic bows, and awestruck laughter. Oops, there it goes again—another 420-foot second-decker. On the eighth pitch, Ripken hit his seventh ball out of the park.

Finally, a warning-track fly and a popup gave Ripken his second and third outs. He headed to the dugout. Ten swings.

No way. The crowd wanted more. In what may have been an impromptu change of rules, the PA announcer sent Ripken back to the plate for a full ten outs.

First swing: another liner into the stands. Then, after a rope through the box, two more 410-to-420-foot home runs. The crowd may not have known exactly how special this was, but every player did. "I've never done anything remotely like that," said Fisk, who has 360 career homers. "[In 22 seasons] I've only seen one player have a BP like that—Fred Lynn the year he hit 39 homers."

By this time—10 homers in 14 swings—Ripken was worrying again. "I was getting arm-weary," he said. "I just wanted to make a couple of outs." Ripken even started shaking his arm as if he'd hurt his funny bone. "Maybe I did that subconsciously because I was embarrassed I was hitting so many."

After two line-outs and a popup, Ripken decided he'd try to give the crowd a parting shot. "I decided," he said, "to dig down deep."

On the next swing, Ripken hit probably the longest ball of his life— a fourth-deck shot to left that came within a yard of joining Jose Canseco's 1989 playoff blast as the only fifth-deck homer in SkyDome lore. Distance? At least 475 feet. It was hard to tell. Because Ripken's next swing threatened to send the ball farther. But a brave fan in the third deck stopped it.

On his last two swings, Ripken merely knocked a ball off the leftfield wall, then finished with a second-deck drive that hooked foul by a few feet.

Twelve home runs. On 22 swings.

"The Cal Ripken Hour," intoned the PA man. "What an exhibition!"

"Cal messed it up for everybody else," said Puckett. "Nobody wanted to go up and hit after that."

In all, seven other players in the contest took 85 swings and hit 15 home runs. The final score was NL 7, AL 8, Ripken 12.

For a long time afterward, Ripken could not get the grin off his face. Still, the face of the wary pro peered out from behind the dancing eyes of the little boy. It has cost Ripken years, and probably half of his hair, to get to .348. So, he worries.

"I kept trying not to overswing. But it was hard," he said when, once again, he was almost alone. "I hope this doesn't mess me up too bad."

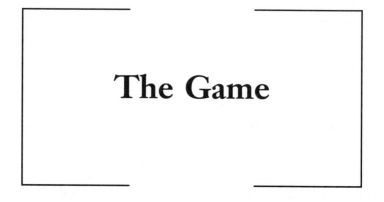

The Game

TORONTO, July 10, 1991—Sometimes, it's your season. Baseball seems to romance you, not claw at your peace of mind. It was like that, fifty years ago, for Ted Williams and Joe DiMaggio. And it may prove to be that way this season for Cal Ripken, whose three-run home run earned him the Most Valuable Player award in the All-Star Game.

Williams and DiMaggio were introduced before Tuesday night's renewal. Or DiMaggio and Williams, depending on how you feel about it.

Since '41, when Williams batted .406 and DiMaggio hit in 56 straight games, baseball has often seemed intent on eradicating its traditional sense of clean, simple style. If it weren't for garish taste, would baseball have any taste at all?

Ripken, who has played in 1,491 consecutive regular-season games, and to round it off to 1,500, nine straight All-Star Games, is one of the few modern players whose defiantly old-fashioned standards and stoic, self-effacing demeanor are of a piece with the days of Williams and DiMaggio.

Generally speaking, ancestor worship is no virtue. But, in the case of the national pastime, the old ways—when a Roger Maris had to be pushed out of the dugout to tip his cap after his 61st homer—may have been better.

This evening, Benito Santiago, who has already changed his number to 09 to draw more attention to himself, wore a cross as an earring. (Ruben Sierra settled for a simple 21 in diamonds.) Many players

wore more wristbands than they have wrists, despite the fact that the
night was almost too cool to sweat.

The baseball commissioner drove around during warm-ups in a
Rolls-Royce golf cart. The ten-man SkyDome grounds crew arrived
to sweep the bases in a white stretch limo as long as a team bus; two
American League outfielders immediately dashed over and jumped in
to check it out.

A marching band worthy of the Chain Saw–Weed Whacker Bowl
cluttered the field before the game. A centerfield magic message
board, bigger than a football field, dominated every minute of the
evening, pandering to inane interviews with players in wraparound
sunglasses.

Ripken, by contrast, was his usual restrained self. Earlier in the day,
a poll of major leaguers (in *USA Today*) had voted him the best player
in the sport. Before the game, he had lots of nice homey quotes. Of
the bat with which he hit a dozen home runs in Monday's home run
contest, Ripken said, "I'm not letting this bat out of my sight." Asked
if he would like to hit a homer in the All-Star Game itself, Ripken
gave the obligatory answer, circa 1941: "I like line-drive singles to
center better. That's what I'll try to do."

So, in his first at-bat, with his first swing, Ripken lined a single to
center.

His next time up, with two men on base, he hit a slightly higher line
drive—thanks largely to former Orioles teammate Dennis Martinez,
who hung a 2–1 slider. This one landed 416 feet away in the black,
empty centerfield seats.

"I wish I could say I was trying to hit a home run," said Ripken.
"But I wasn't."

That's typical. Ripken is the kind of player who, asked about all his
homers on Monday, said he thought the balls were probably juiced up
and what had really impressed him wasn't his performance but two
blasts by Cecil Fielder that landed in somebody's lobster bisque in the
Sightline Restaurant in the third deck in centerfield. The Sightline is,
of course, above the Windows Restaurant. Neither of which is to be
confused with the Hard Rock Café or the world's largest McDonald's,
which are also part of this modest pleasure dome.

Normally, the TV broadcast of the All-Star Game makes an excellent night light for your plants. That's because, normally, nobody hits
the ball. Especially in the clutch with men on base. The average score
of the last seven "Classics" had been 3.3 to 1.1. That's about half of

the action, and scoring, of an average game. This game might have fallen into the same drab category, except for Ripken's three-run blow that equaled all the rest of the scoring in this 4–2 AL victory.

Before this game, Commissioner Fay Vincent told the story of what he called a "fantasy day" in his life—one in which he got to sit with DiMaggio and Williams for three hours and listen to them discuss hitting. Vincent also got to fly from Washington on Air Force One and chat with President Bush. But it was the time with Williams and DiMaggio that was special for him because of the mystique the two legends still carry about them.

Few players these days seem to understand the concept of playing out a legendary life. A wealthy, flashy one, yes. A hedonistic one, perhaps. But one that will grow in stature, that will stand above trends in pop taste and fashions in jewelry and wrist wear? Not many.

Playing 1,491 games in a row is unbelievably hard. Stringing 95 games at shortstop without an error is almost inconceivable. Rebuilding your entire offensive game when you're thirty years old and already headed to the Hall of Fame is above and beyond the call of duty.

Every season is, in some sense, Ripken's season. However, this All-Star break, from its home run contest on Monday, won by Ripken, to its in-the-game home run contest on Tuesday, also won by Ripken, may be as seminal and defining for the Orioles shortstop as 1941 was for Joe and Ted.

"Great players do great things at great times," said AL manager Tony LaRussa. "For Cal to do this, it's a perfect match."

After all, the '41 All-Star Game was won on a three-run homer by Williams.

The Quest

February 1992—Baseball, more than any of our games, is about the long haul. Measured on the calendar of centuries, our pastime is still a baby. Yet the sport loves to pretend that it has always been around and always will be. The conceit took root long ago: Baseball ignores wars and depressions, technological change and revolutions in mores. The game just keeps on keeping on, never better than itself, but never worse, divisible only by itself and sublimely indifferent to judgments from those who don't value it.

What arrogance. And how calming. Baseball's illusion of permanence, in a century of inexorably accelerating change, is a teddy bear for adults to lay at the foot of their beds.

A sport with such an image is a curse to all the Chicken Littles of our media age who can't wait to discover some new piece of sky falling. That's why Howard Cosell hated baseball. It ignored him. It knew he would be gone soon. The sky is always falling. Play ball.

Now, here we go again. Another spring arrives, and, once again, voices clamor for us to pay attention to everything that supposedly threatens baseball. Potential Japanese owners and obscene player salaries compete for headlines with the cold prospect that baseball's first billion-dollar network TV contract may also be its last. Money, always the symbol of temporal concerns, shoulders its way to center stage. Don't watch the game, watch the dollars, we're told. Get mad, feel resentment, hop on a soapbox. Be sure to find a way to prevent the game from making you happy.

Of course, what we should be paying attention to is Cal Ripken at play.

Like Hank Aaron, Pete Rose, and Nolan Ryan before him, Cal Ripken Jr. has become our quintessential player for the long haul. In that sense, he is baseball—a shard of eternity dropped into daily life.

Even Ripken's sliver of the world can't escape the prophets of gloom. As almost anyone in baseball will tell you, this season is sure to be a disappointment for the Orioles shortstop. After a player has had the best season of a deluxe career, after he has been the Most Valuable Player of the American League and the All-Star Game too, there is nowhere to go but down.

This is especially true when a man who will be thirty-two in August has already performed in 1,573 straight games—or about twice as many as it takes to wear out an ordinary human body. Great streakers tend to go downhill fast once their string of games ends. You can look it up.

The rest of Ripken's career, it's thought, should be a graceful glide down to Cooperstown. His stats will pile up, but the days when he evoked wonder will fade into memory. Three errors in a season? Preposterous. A shortstop leading the major leagues in total bases? Once a generation. For Cal, a few more solid years, then erosion.

That's what you hear. Earl Weaver, where are you now when we need you to spit into the wind and growl, "Horse bleep."

Maybe it's Cal's premature bald spot or the weather-beaten look his skin already bears. Of course, anyone's hair would fall out if he wore a baseball cap twenty-five hours a day for twenty-five years. And anyone would get a grizzled sea captain look from squinting into the setting sun during thousands of batting practices.

Whether it's his irredeemably bad haircuts or his old-salt squint or the middle-aged sober-sidedness that Ripken has always shown in public, somehow, somewhere along the way, the amazing misperception has arisen that baseball's best all-around player is nearing the end of the line.

Enjoy Cal while you still can, the smart money mutters. He'll move to third base soon. He's lost a step and survives on smarts.

Yes, the one player in baseball who should never have to hear himself belittled is watching quietly as—once again—few give him the benefit of the doubt.

His consolation, and ours, is that if he will simply hew to his own stubborn, unflappable, self-driven core, he will have the last laugh once again. And a long sweet one too.

This time, the cynical scuttlebutt is wrong. Don't ask if Ripken can break Lou Gehrig's record of 2,130 consecutive games played. That's thinking small. Ask if he can play 2,500 in a row. The bet here is he can. (More on this anon.)

Gehrig's record will go the way of Ty Cobb's 4,191 hits and Babe Ruth's 714 homers—not just broken but smashed.

Please, don't doubt. Trust the force. Once, 130 steals was a fantasy. Just a few years ago, no one ever dreamed a man could pitch seven no-hitters or strike out 5,000 men. (Or will that be 6,000?)

And never fear: If bad luck keeps Ripken from reaching 2,130, he'll do other things just as "impossible." A streak can be derailed. But a whole career? One on Ripken's scale? Not likely.

By the turn of the century, Rip will hold the same place in baseball that Nolan does now, and that Hank and Pete (before he squandered it) achieved before that. He'll be the consensus symbol of what is best and most lasting in his sport and our national pastime.

Just watch.

But no one is watching. We're too busy pointing fingers at the falling sky. "Baseball is sick," we wail. "Greed will ruin the game."

No surprises here. If baseball couldn't begin each season in the grip of some Godzilla malaise, there'd be no Opening Day. The commissioner would have to call it off until everybody had wrung his hands sufficiently for play to begin.

If it's not a midseason strike, it's a preseason lockout. If it's not a cocaine epidemic, then it's bankruptcy. If the next TV contract isn't a harbinger of doom, then the Japanese are trying to buy into our monopoly.

This year, it's the Indecency Issue. It's indecent, during a recession, for ballplayers to make a million dollars a man while the people in the stands, or watching on TV, can't pay the mortgage.

Of course it's indecent. Welcome to capitalism, the best little economic whorehouse on earth. The rich squeeze the rest of us until our screaming gets loud enough to make them step back from the trough for a couple of years. What is the deficit except ten years of checks written by the rich on the bank accounts of everybody else?

But why blame baseball? It's only a mirror. Owners are just '80s kinds of business folks, always buying on margin, betting on the come and putting off the reckoning. Some are floundering in the '90s, but who isn't? (It's not every secretive leveraged-buyout tycoon who can get the public to cough up $105 million to build him a new ballpark the way Eli Jacobs did.)

As for the ballplayers, they're good Americans too—devout instant yuppies, trying to consume to their full *GQ*-dream capacity. Sure they tend not to be very loyal. Sure they sell themselves to the highest bidder. Just like Harvard MBAs. You want them to be better than preppies? Have a heart.

What really matters about baseball these days is a whole generation of stunning players who emerged in the '80s on the heels of Cal Ripken.

What we have before us, if we can just see past our crise du jour, is the greatest infusion of talent and excitement since the black and Latin superstar bonanza of the '50s when the color line died.

This is one of those huge positive trends that get overlooked in favor of lots of tasty negative tidbits.

The entire decade of the '70s produced only eight rookies who are virtual certainties to be in the Hall of Fame: Carlton Fisk, Mike Schmidt, Dave Winfield, Robin Yount, George Brett, Andre Dawson, Eddie Murray, and Ozzie Smith. After that, it's a handful of weak maybes, like Dave Parker, Gary Carter, Bert Blyleven, Alan Trammell, Lou Whitaker, and Jack Morris. That's the whole decade. Pathetic. At least twenty-two players from the '60s—a typical decade—will be in Cooperstown.

The reason the '70s were tepid was that baseball was considered dull in the '60s. The Yankee dynasty was gone. Football and basketball were the boom sports. Naturally, a lot of ten-year-old Joe Namath and Bill Russell fans grew up to spurn pro baseball.

Then the pendulum swung again. By the late '70s, thanks to free agency and a run of fabulous World Series, baseball was glamorous again. The hot kids of the '60s had matured and taken over the high-profile roles: players like Rose, Ryan, Reggie Jackson, Johnny Bench, Tom Seaver, Jim Palmer, Rod Carew, Lou Brock, Steve Carlton, Gaylord Perry, Carl Yastrzemski, Joe Morgan, Tony Perez, Ferguson Jenkins, Willie Stargell, Phil Niekro, Rollie Fingers, Don Sutton, Catfish Hunter.

As a direct result, by the '80s baseball was attracting the cream of the youth crop again. Even Bo Jackson, whose physique and gifts seemed far better suited to the NFL, chose the long, healthy, wealthy career offered by baseball as his primary sport. (He probably wishes now that he'd made it his only sport.)

Appropriately, Ripken was a kind of point man. In '80 and '81, only Rickey Henderson emerged. Ripken arrived in '82 (28 homers, 93 RBI) and on his heels came Ryne Sandberg, Wade Boggs, Darryl Strawberry, Tony Gwynn, Dwight Gooden, Kirby Puckett, and Roger Clemens. Superior players like Lee Smith and Jeff Reardon, who may end up the all-time save leaders, and Julio Franco and Steve Sax, who may get 3,000 hits, haven't gotten their due after a decade of stardom —because there are too many bigger stars.

The true deluge came in 1986. In one season Jose Canseco, Will Clark, Ruben Sierra, Barry Bonds, and Bobby Bonilla arrived. Toss in a couple more names like Kevin Mitchell and Wally Joyner, plus Mark McGwire, who came up briefly that year. In baseball, it's just called the Class of '86. And the talent glut continues, lapping right over into the '90s. It's too soon to know who will endure, but you can't look better in your early career than Frank Thomas, Steve Avery, Ken Griffey Jr., Roberto Alomar, Dave Justice, Juan Gonzalez, and Barry Larkin. Sorry, forgot Cecil Fielder.

But of all the men who have blossomed in the last ten years, the exemplar—and the one who may have the largest lasting place—is Ripken.

Nine years ago, before anybody took him seriously, Ripken announced what he was going to do. "I'd like to play every game, every inning, every day for twenty years, like Brooks Robinson and Pete Rose. I'd like for kids to emulate me. To hear some kids playing and have one say, 'I'm Cal Ripken,' that would be the ultimate degree of success for me."

Act like Brooks, play like Pete. That was always the idea. How simple.

Ripken had prototypes in his own family. All he had to do was be as playful off the field as his mother and as tough on it as his dad. Just stand on the shoulders of others.

And over the years, as the son of a team coach, he's taken a page from each of the great Orioles he grew up watching and knowing personally. The result? An almost perfect baseball temperament.

He is gracious, self-deprecating, and a bit folksy like Robinson. To be exposed to Brooks (who might as well have been Cal's uncle) is to want to be like him. It's hard to grow up around Brooks and end up like Pete.

Cal is a conditioning freak and a student of the game like Jim Palmer. Like Palmer, Ripken plays other sports, especially basketball, year-round. Like Palmer, he talks the inside game constantly and picks the brains of his elders. (Ripken was voted the game's "smartest player" by his peers years ago.) And like Palmer, he lives by Cal Ripken Sr.'s mantra: "Not practice, perfect practice."

Ripken learned to sidestep the self-infatuations of celebrity by watching Eddie Murray, the "just regular" guy who welcomed Cal to the team and was a big-brother hero to him for years.

He even has some, though perhaps not enough, of Frank Robinson's arrogance. Ripken has the pride—the immaculate uniform, the erect carriage. But he's not a leader like Frank. His voice doesn't work right. His tone sounds whiny, not inspirational. It's Ripken's nature to be a little isolated and private. His mother would call it his moody streak. He's unselfish and wants the team to win. But, being a stoic, persevering Ripken, he can live without team victory. Robinson couldn't.

Despite all this, the player Ripken resembles most is one who is seldom mentioned, because their morals are so different.

Rose.

Both are slow, deliberate plodders who love ritual and abhor spontaneity. Both have an affection for baseball history and tradition that borders on a slightly embarrassing reverence. Both see themselves, almost entirely, as men defined by baseball and by their place in it. If Rose could have played until he was fifty, he would have. Ripken will try too.

Rose's father, a passionate small-time athlete, set the course for his son. So did Ripken Sr. Both of the old men were cussedly stubborn and proud of it. Both of the sons followed suit.

Rose barely missed a game for his first twenty seasons. He got in a marvelous rut from which nothing could dislodge him. No bad hop, no high slide, no inside pitch, no box seat railing was a threat to him. He'd seen it all so often that avoiding harm became tenth nature. The miracle was that he ever got hurt. He blended his whole soul, such as it was, to the shape of the game.

From the age of thirty-two through forty-one, for ten years, Rose missed only five games. Did it wear him out? At thirty-eight, he hit .331. At forty, .325.

That is why Ripken will shatter Gehrig's record: because Rose, with fewer physical gifts, has already shown the way and proved it possible. Rose started an 863-consecutive-game streak after he was older than Ripken is now. Once an example has been set for Ripken, he expects himself to live up to it. He's being honest when he says he doesn't think about whether he'll break Gehrig's record. He assumes he'll break it.

These guys think in decades. When Rose had barely passed 2,000 hits, I asked him if he'd get No. 3,000. "What about 4,000?" he shot back, years before anybody dared to express such an idea. Sounds a lot like Ripken's "every inning for twenty years" quote, doesn't it?

Whether Ripken catches Gehrig or not, an even more startling possibility exists: His current career totals—259 homers, 942 RBI and 1,762 hits—may only be half of his final statistics. Don't laugh. Sure, Vegas will offer you spectacular odds on this wager. But take another look at Rose's and Ripken's careers before you scoff.

Rose broke in at the same age as Ripken. Both won the Rookie of the Year award. Both were huge stars their first ten years. But in his second decade, Rose refocused himself, increasing his walks, his doubles, his runs, his runs produced, and his on-base average while keeping his batting average identical. In fact, his peak came from age thirty-two through thirty-eight. During that time, he hit .315 and averaged 207 hits a year. He even moved from leftfield to a tougher defensive position (third base) for four years. The season he finally moved to the old man's home—first base—Rose was so decrepit he only stole 20 bases.

If anything, Ripken may deteriorate more slowly than Rose. Look at his genes. At fifty-six, Senior can still outwork most Orioles. Ten years ago, nobody could keep up with the old goat. If Junior follows the family trend, he will probably get thinner, not fatter, as he ages. When he loses 10 pounds, down to 215, he'll really be a good ball-player.

Like Rose, Ripken has sanded off any edges of his personality that might interfere with a smooth pursuit of baseball greatness. He's a pleasantly boring fellow with no desire to surprise. He doesn't con-taminate his mind with too many hard ideas. He can play Brooks in public for years at a time without breaking out of character, but he also has a private streak of anger that runs through all the Ripken men and keeps him protected. Cal busts himself to do the right thing. But he can tell you to go to hell too. Few players have burned more umpires' ears than Junior. He just scalds 'em, then lets his image save him from getting ejected.

Ripken has an innate balance in his nature. He can be one thing, yet a bit of the opposite at the same time. He believes in being a role model and doing charity work. He's easy with kids and loves being a hero, just eats it up. But he's not the least like Steve Garvey. Junior isn't sold on his own con. He doesn't think he's a great man. He just thinks it's neat to be mistaken for one.

As with Rose, Ripken's core is his craftsmanship. That's where he hangs his hat. He's the old farmer who wears a starched white shirt into the field under his overalls and is furious if the ditch banks aren't mowed just right. Ripken just hates to screw up. Sometimes he's so mad he can't even talk when he does a thing the wrong way.

Failure? That doesn't faze him at all. Couldn't care less. He knows you can win only 60 percent of the time, or get hits three out of every ten trips. But doing a thing wrong—approaching the task incorrectly or being asleep at the switch—still makes him nuts. The guy is utterly responsible to his own sense of self-creation. And what he sees in the mirror is a "winner"—a cliché, but not a bad one.

He wants to beat you with his whole soul—then agitate you about it for a few days, just like an adorable thirteen-year-old.

Tell Ripken he's dull and it makes his day. He still thinks doggedness is his trump card in life. He's sure he can do some boring, self-improving thing more often than you can. And he's right. Fortunately, he doesn't think that makes him better than you. Just more wealthy, famous, happy, and lucky.

Winning doesn't make him feel guilty. Not even winning every time. Cal beat his brother Fred, one year younger, so relentlessly in childhood games that Fred (the best Ripken athlete, according to family myth) lost all his ambition in sports.

Never fear, Cal looks out for Cal (although, thank God, not as much as Pete looked out for Pete). Most of the thirteen-year-old is long gone from Ripken—lost somewhere back in the 21-game losing streak or his dad's firing as manager or the incredible tightness of Eli Jacobs's wallet. One used to worry that Cal would get worn out by all the fringe leeches with nothing better to do than hang on him all day. Forget it. Where performance is concerned, Cal can walk through them now as if they're not there.

He's got a job to do.

So don't listen when you're asked to mourn for baseball, to fret the spring away worrying about its future. Instead, remember the words of the prophet (James Brown) who said, "Some people don't want you happy, but they won't come right out and say it," and "Money won't change you, but time will take you out."

In baseball, the challenge for the greatest of the great—the long-haulers—is to stay happy in their hard, simple work though the world tries to tell them they are fools to care so much about a game so small. Their task is to ignore the money and take on man's meanest opponent—time.

Day after day, they resist insidious invitations to kick back and be less than they dream they can be. Take a day off, Cal, what the hell? Why bother to be different? Why try to find the absolute limits of your performance?

They are stubborn, ornery, almost bull-headed men. Not paragons, to be sure. But symbols, definitely. They are the part of us that sets our jaw, in defiance of common sense, and doesn't know why—yet feels better and more at peace for it.

Hank, Pete, Nolan, and Cal understand one another, though not one of them is a bit good at explaining himself. They all pull for one another, these fellows who can't imagine a better fate than to play every inning for twenty-five years and break every record they've been told is unreachable. They know their place in the scheme—in baseball terms, they'd call it their "role." Others would call it their destiny.

"Always hold to the difficult," another prophet (the poet Rilke) once advised. Cal Ripken has held to the difficult since childhood, where baseball is concerned. Now, at mid-career, all the pieces of the puzzle have come together.

Behind him is a string of clean, confidence-building accomplishments. First shortstop in history to have ten straight 20-homer seasons. Fewest errors in a season in history. Most assists in a year in AL history. Two-time MVP. Reigning Gold Glove winner.

Even the parts of his game that previously could not be calibrated, and so were not appreciated, are now coming into view. For years, baseball devotees swore, without proof, that Ripken had so compensated for his lack of speed with intuition and study that he was not only a flawless shortstop but stellar too.

Now, thanks to baseball's new phalanx of supernerds, we have "sabermetricians" who chart every batted ball in every major league game. We have Defensive Equivalent Games and Adjusted Range Factors. It may be bunk, but it's out there. (In this case, its name is Gary Gillette, who creates *The Great American Baseball Stat Book* for strange people like me.) Last year, according to Gillette, Barry Larkin was the only everyday shortstop who got to more balls than Ripken. In fact, Ripken supposedly gets to fifty more balls a year than the average shortstop.

Ripken has probably reached a level that eluded even Aaron, Rose, and Ryan. At this moment, he would win almost any voting on Best Player in Baseball; in fact, he won just such a (*USA Today*) poll of all major leaguers in mid-'91. Rose, a singles hitter and immobile fielder, never reached that level. Aaron lacked the flash to steal such an accolade from Mickey Mantle or Willie Mays, who had 50-homer seasons while Hank just drove in 120 boring runs. Ryan, despite the seven no-hitters and the 5,461 strikeouts (to date), has never won enough to be Best Pitcher. He still has no Cy Young Award.

Last season, thanks to all those newfangled statistics, you could actually prove the Ripken case. No player in baseball exceeded the average offensive production at his position by as much as Ripken. In fact, no one was close.

The average major league team got 54 RBI and 198 total bases from its shortstop position last season. Ripken exceeded that by 60 RBI and 170 total bases. For a rightfielder, say, to exceed the major league average by that much, he would have to have 150 RBI and 435 total bases.

Like Magic Johnson inventing the 6-foot-9 point guard, Ripken has created something equally "impossible"—a 225-pound slugger who can play shortstop for a decade. That he has become one of the best of all shortstops is ridiculous.

Just a year ago, Ripken was not getting such universal credit. Far from it. For three years, his hitting had slipped a notch, though his fielding was becoming nearly perfect. A tough-as-tungsten shortstop who fields .990 with 22 homers and 86 RBI a season—Ripken's numbers during his three-year "nadir"—goes straight to Cooperstown. Still, Cal was slowly dimming into a kind of invisible immortal. It seemed his satisfactions would be entirely those of the long haul and not the short term.

The public required many years to grasp the true stature of Aaron, Rose, and Ryan. The understated Aaron had to pass 600 homers to get out of the shadow of his generation of fabulous outfielders, including combative Frank Robinson and elegant Roberto Clemente. Rose had to pass Stan Musial in hits before the world came to his doorstep to chronicle the exploits of a slew-footed slap hitter. And Ryan had to pitch no-hitters (year after year) in middle age before he was forgiven for twenty years of .500 pitching.

For Ripken, the 1991 MVP award and the Gehrig chase, assuming it continues, should bring him similarly into focus. Already, June of '95 does not seem so far away. By next spring, the mania should be growing.

A full-blown Oriole revival may be too much to expect. But it won't be needed for Ripkenmania to build. After all, Rose, Aaron, and Ryan didn't play for contenders in their late-career days, and they finished their monuments to perseverance with the whole nation cheering them on.

For an America loaded down with troubles, real and imagined, cheering Ripken and the Gehrig chase over the next few years can do no harm. It might even be tonic.

Cal Ripken was raised by a strict family on the small-town values of rural Maryland. For him, the '60s and '70s might as well have been the '40s and '50s—when America was productive, self-confident, simplistic, and not too hip to have heroes.

A woefully malnourished child, he was never fed a drop of irony. He was raised to think that if you did not work for something—earn it and deserve it—you were really only stealing it. And what could such a prize be worth?

Cal Ripken Jr. would never make it in Eli Jacobs's world. But for the rest of the '90s, he may be good for more than baseball. He may remind us of the way we used to live.

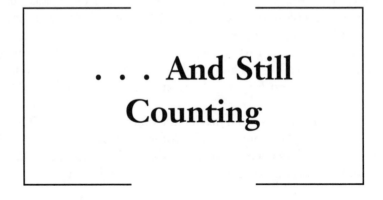

. . . And Still Counting

BALTIMORE, June 11, 1993—On Monday, Cal Ripken couldn't walk. Not in the morning. Not in the afternoon. His right knee was stiff and swollen from the previous day's brawl at Oriole Park at Camden Yards. Pain shot through the joint when he tried to bear his weight. When he left home for Camden Yards, he was hobbling badly.

"All day, I assumed I wouldn't play that night. I was sure the streak was over," said Ripken, who has played in 1,793 straight games. "I lived with it all day. Now I really know how I feel about it."

On Sunday, a wave of Seattle players bowled Ripken and Leo Gomez over as they tried to protect Mike Mussina in a bench-clearing beanball battle. The Orioles shortstop "heard something pop. Nothing like that's ever happened to me. Basically, I've never had an injury."

So Ripken told his wife, Kelly, he couldn't play. "She looked really sad."

"Couldn't you play one inning?" she asked.

"No."

"Or pinch-hit?"

"I wouldn't do that," he told her. "I just won't play."

"But the streak'll be broken."

"Yes," Ripken said, a little perplexed.

"I thought that's what you wanted," she said.

"You too?" said Ripken.

As he recalls this conversation, Ripken sits in the corner of the

Orioles locker room, his back against two walls. "That really struck me," he says, shaking his head. "People automatically believe that the streak has become me. Even the person closest to me in the whole world . . .

"I'm here simply to play. However things work out is fine. The streak just happened. I didn't ask for it."

An hour before Monday's game, after all-day ice treatments, Ripken still assumed he couldn't play. "I went back where nobody could see me to do some [exercises] to find out if I could give it a try." Ripken didn't know if he was risking a more serious injury by playing. But he was raised in the old school. Others were playing with bumps and bruises from the brawl. The team was on its first sustained winning streak of the season. The Orioles could use a Gold Glove shortstop, even one hitting .218.

"Once the game began," Ripken said, "it loosened up much better than I thought it would."

Ripken managed a single and two walks. In the ninth inning, with the Orioles ahead by a run, he made a highlight-film play in the hole to rob the leadoff hitter. "When I planted and threw off my bad [right] leg and nothing gave way, I figured it wasn't a serious injury."

By midweek, Ripken's knee felt "miraculously good. I must be a quick healer."

Still, streaks are in constant jeopardy. On Wednesday, Bob Welch's 0–2 fastball came at his head. Ripken threw up his hand. The ball grazed his left wrist and glanced off his jaw. Both were hit hard, but not squarely. His wrist could have been broken, like Chris Hoiles's last year, or his jaw broken, like Glenn Davis's this week.

Instead, Ripken never went down. Later that inning, he got revenge, clobbering A's catcher Terry Steinbach in a full-speed, forearm-to-the-jaw collision at the plate. The catcher knelt for several minutes, then sat with cold towels around his head in the dugout before finally leaving the game. Ripken never broke stride as his foot hit home plate, just in case Steinbach dropped the ball, and he jogged to the dugout.

"What's that guy made out of? Granite?" said a veteran Orioles official.

Let's face it, the Streak isn't going away. Ripken couldn't get hurt if he tried. And, lately, it seems like he's been trying.

Lots of people around the Orioles almost wish that one of these incidents had given Ripken a minor one-game injury. Almost. But not quite. "One day off isn't going to make any difference to Cal physically," says coach Davey Lopes. "Mentally? Only he can answer the question of whether the [mental] strain of the streak is tearing him down. People, like [television commentator] Tim McCarver and [Giants coach] Bobby Bonds, are saying things about Cal being selfish. To hell with those guys. They're not part of this organization.

"Cal doesn't need outside people telling him what to do. He's a man. He'll know. It's a tough situation," says Lopes, knowing that Ripken has hit only .242 with 19 homers in his past 866 at-bats. The thirty-two-year-old Ripken has been listening to "Snap the Streak" critics since he was in his twenties. They attributed his "bad" years— like 21 homers and 84 RBI in 1990—to his supposed physical or mental exhaustion. Then, the following season, Ripken won the American League's Most Valuable Player award.

Silence.

Ripken would like to produce that sweet silence again. In his scrupulously analytical—and stubborn—mind, he thinks his career progression as a hitter is perfectly logical. Hitters have career years when their mechanics and concentration are flawless. When one, or both, are out of sync, they have mediocre or career-worst years.

Ripken considers his range of performance in his twelve years to be normal for a hitter of his .275, 25-homers-a-year ability. Statistically, he's right. His best and worst years don't deviate from his median any more than Al Kaline's, Carl Yastrzemski's, Harold Baines's, or any roughly comparable hitter's.

Ripken thinks that in '91 all positive factors were aligned. In '92, his "focus" was ruined by his decision to negotiate an acrimonious $30 million contract during the season. This year, he thinks his mechanics and hitting luck have been bad. Until three weeks ago, when he returned to his pre-1991 stance. Now, basically, he thinks he's on the road back.

Who wouldn't hope that was true? Who really wants Barry Bonds to replace Nolan Ryan as the sport's most conspicuous player?

For a hitter who hasn't had a hot streak, Ripken's bad stats aren't that awful. He's one big typical-superstar month away from his normal numbers. But, after hitting worse than he ever has in his life for a full season and a third, the universal question about Ripken is obvious: Will he ever really get hot again?

If, by the dog days of August, Ripken is still a .220 hitter, even his friends will ask the same question. Cal, shouldn't you volunteer to take one game off? You've tried everything else. Why not get the mysterious powers of the Gehrig Streak (2,130 consecutive games played) out of your mind? Then come back and play the next thousand games in a row if you feel like it.

Ripken says he's thought about it. The day for such decisions could come even though it would cost him an enormous price in pride to give his harping critics such apparent vindication. Perhaps most important to Ripken, taking a day off would mean that his analysis of the entire situation was completely wrong. Honest self-analysis is the core of Ripken. For him to conclude, or be driven to the conclusion, that he's been wrong for all these years might do his confidence—his sense of himself—more damage than any streak. Nobody has the right to take Ripken's streak away from him at this point. But he has the option of taking it away from himself. Someday, he might. If he, not the world, decides that's what's best.

Let's hope that day never comes. It already feels too close.

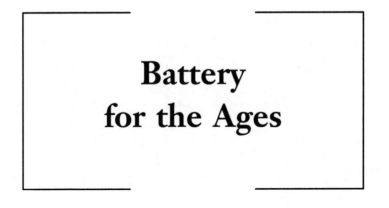

Battery
for the Ages

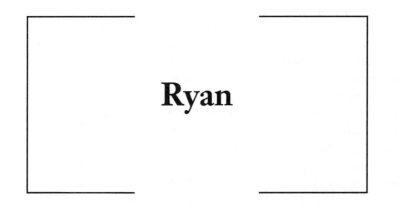

Ryan

SORRY, NOLAN

April 28, 1989—Nolan Ryan is a great pitcher. Nolan Ryan belongs in the Hall of Fame. There, I did it. It didn't kill me.

I give up. This month has been the last straw. When Ryan took a no-hitter into the eighth inning two weeks ago for the Texas Rangers and struck out 15, my knees—the knees of the Notorious Nolan Knocker—buckled. Finally, this week, came the knockout punch. Ryan, going for his sixth career no-hitter, was foiled with one out in the ninth. He "settled" for his eleventh career one-hitter with 12 strikeouts.

This is ridiculous. Ryan is forty-two—four days older than Dan Quayle.

I ignored his ERA title at forty. I pretended not to notice his strike-out crown last year at forty-one—his ninth, and second in a row. But fair is fair. The guy has worn me down and beaten me.

Okay, "Uncle." Nolan, you are an artist, a force of nature, a man who can be judged only on his own terms. You are not—oh, this is going to be hard—a grotesquely overrated .500 pitcher.

Each of us, in our private heart, carries a few opinions that are as perverse as they are deeply felt. We cling to them all the more because the world tells us we're crazy.

For two decades—ever since Ryan struck out more than 325 men in five of six seasons from 1972 to '77 and found a way to lose an average of 16 games a year in the process—I have hated him.

Not personally. The consensus is that Ryan's a sweetheart of a guy. Hardworking, friendly, dependable, and unpretentious. I have nothing to add. Except that, when I've been around him, I've found Ryan impossible to dislike. And I was trying.

I've long believed, and in general still believe, that only one statistic has any real meaning for pitchers: W–L. Forget the fluff. They give you the ball. You hold the game in your hand. They tell you to win. Either you do or you don't.

To make the point more precisely, it's how much you win relative to how good your team is. To me, a .500 pitcher on a .400 team is just as excellent as a .600 pitcher on a .500 team or a .700 pitcher on a .600 team. Over the long haul, a pitcher's winning percentage versus his team's record in its other games tells more than anything else.

For example, Jim Palmer's career percentage was 57 points higher than the good Orioles teams for which he played.

In other words, a .500 pitcher on a .500 team is a mediocrity and there's no way around it. To me, that was always Ryan. In his career he's gone 275–254. His teams in all the games in which he didn't get a decision over those twenty-one years went 1,420–1,403. In other words, they were practically as good as he was.

So how good could he be?

Only once in all those years did Ryan have the best percentage on his own team. In all (and this is stunning), forty starting pitchers on his teams have had better percentages than Ryan while only forty-three have been worse. On all those nondescript Angels and Astros teams, half the pitchers were able to do better than Ryan at what counts most: winning the game.

All these facts have not disappeared. But, in Ryan's case, I have finally come to believe that they must be, to a large degree, over-looked or forgiven. Because if you don't overlook 'em or forgive 'em, you can't call Ryan great. And that just defies common sense.

Let's be Ryan apologists and see where it leads. Perhaps home plate is just too small for what Ryan throws. Maybe a fastball that rises as much as his and a curve that drops as sharply just aren't going to intersect the zone as often as the less flashy pitches thrown by others. Also, hitters will take more of his pitches. Why? Because when you have so little chance of hitting, a walk looks good.

True, Sandy Koufax had the same two exploding pitches as Ryan, plus fine control. But let's not beat up Nolan with the pitcher who, for five years, may have been the best ever.

Perhaps the combination of immortal stuff and mortal control doomed Ryan from the start to walk more men than anybody in history: 2,456. If that's true, then Ryan has labored under a double burden all his life.

It's a law of nature in baseball that, for every two walks, a run will score. Don't ask how. The formula hasn't varied in one hundred years, either for teams or for individuals. Once on base, men in motion tend to stay in motion. Who can overcome 200 walks a year? It's only in the last five years, as Ryan has "slowed down," that he's shown normal major league control. And even that's not so hot.

Also, a wild pitcher's runs tend to score in bunches, in big innings, on the days when he's not his sharpest. That's Ryan. Untouchable one day. Then a certainty to allow a three- or four-run inning in his next start.

There's no evidence Ryan is a poor competitor. Players say the opposite. He can hold a lead in the late innings as well as most. He does not "want" to lose. He just does. It comes part and parcel with the great stuff–average control curse. Everybody takes Ryan deep in the count and tries to foul pitches. Everybody screams "big rally" as soon as he allows a walk and a scratch hit.

You can steal on him. Stats show that nobody ever helps this strike-out-popup pitcher out of a jam with a double-play grounder. And when Ryan aims the ball to avoid more runners, he becomes mortal. Big deal. Everybody knows. But almost nobody cares. Ballplayers hold Ryan in awe. Even if he goes 16–15 in heaven.

Ryan's only job, and he's always realized it, is to be the One and Only. He resembles nobody else. (The only pitcher in history within 20 wins, 20 losses, and 20 ERA points of Ryan is Eppa Rixey.) Will he pitch a no-hitter and strike out 18? Or will he find some ugly way to lose on bloops and walks, errors and steals, bad breaks and one line drive at the wrong time? Both, of course. Maybe back-to-back.

Nolan Ryan is something more fascinating than a star. He's a star who is star-crossed by the very nature of his spectacular talent. Most baseball fans have been smart enough to grasp that from the start and root for him.

Now, one more will.

NO, NO, NO, NO, NO, NO, NO

May 3, 1991—The only thing that can keep Nolan Ryan from pitching no-hitters until he's fifty is if his teammates injure him in one of their frenzied celebrations.

Come on, Rangers, take care of this guy. No more jumping by the dozen on his balding head. He's too old for that.

Of course, at forty-four, he is also too old to be getting better. But that's what is happening. And that's the real reason why the Ryan Saga is the best ongoing sports story of the '90s. The pitcher with perhaps the most frustrating career before age forty has now defined himself, probably forever, as the game's most inspiring testament to stubborn farmer persistence and sincere craftsmanship.

"My vocabulary is not that good," Baltimore Orioles manager Frank Robinson said when asked about Ryan's seventh no-hitter on Wednesday.

"The thing I admire is that he's a complete pitcher now. He's 150 percent better today than ever in his career," added Robinson, who ought to know because they were teammates in California in 1973 when Ryan set the all-time strikeout record of 383.

"He has a great repertoire now," said Robinson, who himself only hit 586 home runs. "He can throw four pitches and put all of 'em on any part of the plate. The hitter almost has no chance."

"I played against him and I was his teammate on three of his no-hitters [in '73 and '74]," said Orioles hitting coach Tommy McCraw. "Then he was just power. Strikeouts were his reputation. They were more to him than the game. He'd get ahead in the count, go for the punchout instead of just the out, and end up walking people and getting in jams.

"But he gradually learned how to pitch. Now he's awesome. You've got to marvel. It's not a pretty thought, but I swear it's true—he's getting better. Every year, a little better. He's gone from no control to good control and now he's finally got command of everything." Jack Nicklaus may have won a Masters when he was forty-six and Bill Shoemaker a Kentucky Derby at fifty-four but, with no disrespect to those fabulous moments, what Ryan has done since he's turned forty puts every other old-age tale in American sports in the shade.

George me no Blandas. Spare me Y. A. Tittle and Satchel Paige.

Forget the final chapters of Kareem. Gloss over Ray Floyd and leave George Foreman and Archie Moore aside. Ryan is way out there. He's going where no man has gone before. And he does it every fifth day.

This year he's on a pace to win his fifth straight strikeout title after his fortieth birthday. And he's done it with Dwight Gooden in one league and Roger Clemens in the other. Every year he ups the ante. In '89, it was 301 strikeouts. In '90, a no-hitter. And now another no-no, giving him as many as Sandy Koufax and Bob Feller, the next two on the all-time list, combined.

Finally, he even wins games, too. Since coming to the blah Rangers, he's 31–21. Ironically, later this year he will probably become the losingest pitcher of the twentieth century. He needs only 6 defeats to pass Walter Johnson (416–279 with awful teams). If Ryan has to hold such a bad record, it's nice he can set it at a time when the reasons for it have ceased to exist.

In baseball, nobody talks about anybody the way everybody talks about Ryan. Every dugout is transfixed, just as the Orioles and Mariners were in Baltimore on Wednesday, as scoreboards around America flash the word that "Nolan is at it again." Just "Nolan."

"Everybody on both benches is going, 'Come on, Nolan,'" said Ernie Whitt, thirty-eight. "It's reached the point where you can only emphasize positives about him."

When Ryan threw his last 93-mph heater past Roberto Alomar in Texas, one Mariner in Baltimore threw his hat in joy even though his own team was moments away from losing.

"I think now he might get in the Hall of Fame," deadpanned Mike Flanagan.

"The man is amazing," said Randy Milligan. "He's struck out everybody in this room except the trainer. He's even struck out our old coaches . . .

"You know, Ryan's not a power pitcher anymore. He's got a big curve and a change-up. He still has that hump on his fastball, but he's such a smart pitcher. You never guess what he'll throw. . . . Let me take that back about Ryan not being a power pitcher. That sounds dumb. He's a power pitcher and a finesse pitcher."

One side benefit of Ryan's night was that it upstaged Rickey Henderson's totally boring pursuit of Lou Brock's career stolen base record. By the end of Hank Aaron's chase of Babe Ruth, I was bored. For a year I yawned as Pete Rose crawled toward Ty Cobb. But the Rickey

watch—especially in recent weeks when No. 939 would not come—
was the worst.

It's gotten so bad that every time a pitcher approaches 300 wins or a
hitter gets near 3,000 hits or 500 homers, I crawl under a table. When
it's a Really Big Record, I lock the doors too.

Those of us who cover sports have perfected the saturation report-
age of utterly boring countdowns toward marks that everybody knows
are going to be reached. Could we stop now, please? Henderson came
into this season needing 3 steals to pass Brock. Since Rickey is thirty-
two and in better shape than Sheena Easton, that meant he had to
average one steal every two or three seasons to get the record. This is
drama? This is news, day after day? A lightning-bolt Ryan no-hitter is
news.

There's nothing boring in an Aaron, Rose, or Henderson. The
problem is phony enthusiasm over a purely symbolic event that's as
predictable as a sunrise.

Besides, the players who are being lauded are those who need a
boost least. Especially Henderson, the Vain King. How much more
whining do we need to hear about his sore calf or his insulting salary
($3 million) or how the A's ought to toss in a $200,000 Testarossa
because "it's the little things that count."

He got the day he deserved. He was thrown out twice. The A's gave
him a paltry Porsche. Brock was the real star. And Rickey, in character, told the crowd, "Today, I am the greatest of all time."

He's right, of course. And his deeds are worth a hundred times his
debits. But did he have to say it? Ryan didn't.

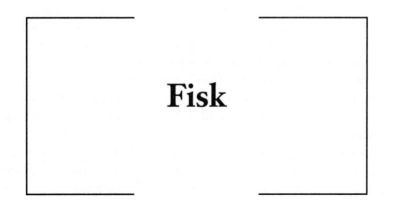

Fisk

DEION'S DUE

May 25, 1990—Call it the last stand of the dinosaurs. We may never see the like again, in any pro sport. So relish it.

On Tuesday night in Yankee Stadium, forty-two-year-old Carlton Fisk of the Chicago White Sox took twenty-two-year-old multisport multimillionaire Deion "Prime Time" Sanders of the New York Yankees to the woodshed for not running out a popup. And he did it in front of 24,142 witnesses.

Fisk said he blew his stack (causing a bench-clearing fracas) so Lou Gehrig could "stop spinning in his grave." He did it to honor what the Yankees once were. And to take a stand against what they, and many in sports, have become—a carnival of slipshod me-firsters. Fisk says, laughing, that he also did it for "truth, justice, and the American way." You wonder if he's kidding.

Fisk is profoundly anachronistic and proud of it. He's out of step with the times. And the times better watch out. It's not just that he's played in the majors in four decades or that he's caught 1,990 games, the most in American League history. It's not just that he stays at the park every night to lift weights for an hour and a half after the game. It isn't even that his starchy New England upbringing makes him seem like an endangered species of player.

Perhaps what sets Fisk apart is his antiquated notion that baseball is a calling, not just a silly game. Like a soldier, a cop, a priest, he reveres his forebears and is delighted to think he's worthy of them. What was good enough for Rogers Hornsby and Willie Mays is good enough for him. He knows how hard one game of baseball, properly played, can be, much less maintaining that high standard for twenty years.

In the third inning Tuesday, Sanders violated Fisk's idea of what sport should be. Sanders has been on the cover of *Sports Illustrated*, largely because of the way he returns kicks for the Atlanta Falcons, but partly because of his gift for selling himself with flashy jewelry and bragging quotes.

When Sanders popped up, he walked toward first base, then strolled to the Yankees dugout before the ball was caught. Imagine his surprise when there, behind him, bellowing, was the mammoth Fisk, who could bench-press two of Neon Deion.

"Run it out, you piece of shit," ordered Fisk, who's in his twenty-first season, to Sanders, who hasn't yet played in twenty-one big-league games. "Go on, run it out."

Sanders was nonplussed. Why would Fisk care if a player on another team didn't run out a popup? On his next at-bat, Sanders learned why.

Fisk stood and eyeballed him as he approached. Sanders muttered.

"What did you say?" asked Fisk.

"The days of slavery are over," said Sanders.

Normally, the introduction of a racial theme can alter the course of a debate. Fisk, however, wanted to make sure Sanders understood the nature of his complaint. It was not racial, but aesthetic. If Frank Robinson and Hank Aaron could run out their popups, so could Sanders—career average .234.

"Let me tell you something, you little [time-honored, but nonracial baseball epithet]," said Fisk. "There is a right way and a wrong way to play this game. You're playing it the wrong way. And the rest of us don't like it. Someday you're going to get this game shoved right down your throat."

The home plate umpire leaped between the two men. Both clubs ran onto the field. And everybody waltzed. After the game, Fisk refused to comment. But Wednesday in Baltimore he re-created the event.

Sanders has explained that his hero is Rickey Henderson and he wants to play in the same extroverted style. Beyond that, Sanders has not commented. "Rickey has earned the right to be animated," said

Fisk. "This guy hasn't. Maybe this will do him a favor and wake him up."

Until the day he retires, which may not be anytime soon, Fisk intends to continue to be a daily example of the way he thinks his game should be lived. "You can't measure everything he brings to our team," says Chicago manager Jeff Torborg. "He's just as productive as he's ever been. . . . He might do some things better now than in his days with the Red Sox."

Over the past two seasons, since he became forty, Fisk has hit 32 homers and driven in 118 runs in 628 at-bats—close to Jose Canseco ratios. Now that Fisk has had a metal plate inserted in his hand—broken in the same place in '88 and '89—he sees no reason he can't play every day. He hit .293 last year. This year, he's right around .290. The old man's done it despite a three-week sinus infection that's cost him 10 pounds. Of course, Fisk hasn't missed a game.

When the Red Sox let Fisk escape after the '80 season, he was thirty-three—an age at which almost every great offensive catcher has been, basically, washed up. This month Fisk played his 1,079th game as a White Sox, passing his Boston total. He's actually had more home runs (176–162) and RBI (616–568) as a White Sox—and in the same number of at bats.

Hitting well is the best revenge.

The highest compliment to Fisk is this: He can finally be compared to Johnny Bench without embarrassment. Both were born the same month. Yet Bench retired seven years ago! He's been in the Hall of Fame for two years. Now, their career stats are a shock. In 7,658 at-bats, Bench hit .267 with 2,078 runs produced. In 7,720 at-bats, Fisk has batted .271 with 2,009 runs produced.

Can they really be that close?

When Bench retired, he was assumed to be incomparably better.

This summer, Fisk may break Bench's all-time record for home runs by a catcher (327). Fisk needs 11. If he does, many will assume that Fisk just outlasted Bench. That's true. But it's also true that Fisk is just about as good as he ever was.

Look at all the skills—hit, hit with power, throw, field, and run. No catcher does any of them significantly better than Fisk at forty-two. Put them all together and the conclusion is stunning. If he can stay healthy, Fisk may prove he's still the best in the game.

Amazing what lifting weights until 1 A.M., and running out popups, can do.

JURASSIC PARK

June 30, 1993—For the past twenty-four years, including 2,226 games behind home plate, Carlton Fisk has stood out in the baseball world like a living statue. He is 6-feet-2, 240 pounds, but he seemed even bigger. He stood erect. He walked with an almost comic air of authority. And a decade of weightlifting had made his vein-bulging physique Ramboesque. He always spoke clearly and intelligently. For years, the block-letter sign above his locker said, "THINK." And if you didn't, you had to answer to Carlton.

Whatever was difficult fascinated him. The hardest position was the one he wanted. In all American games, the most grueling job, bar none, is major league catcher. It's not the most violent or dangerous. It doesn't require the most ability. But year in and year out, it is the most miserably unpleasant. Basically, you squat in the dirt all summer, sweltering inside a suit of armor on 90-degree nights, while trying to catch 90-mile-per-hour rocks that bounce off the ground toward your groin or ricochet off bats toward your knuckles.

For two dozen years, Fisk was a human bruise. He loved it. He hated it. He groused about it. He gloried in it. He called catching "the Dorian Gray position" because "on the outside, you look young, but on the inside, you're aging fast. You're afraid one day you'll take off the equipment and discover you've turned to dust." After saying that, he played another fifteen years.

Despite all his records and historic moments, his famous Foul Pole Homer in Game 6 of the '75 World Series, and his 351 homers as a catcher—the most ever—it was Fisk's face that left the most vivid memories. Nobody could look more disgusted than Carlton Fisk. Mention a gutless pitcher who wouldn't throw strikes or some showboat outfielder who didn't like to be brushed back and Fisk's face would become a mask of utter contempt. Then the revulsion would turn to amusement as he made some deliciously wicked aside about the miscreant. Only owners—as a group, but particularly his Red Sox and White Sox bosses—ranked so low on Fisk's scale that he couldn't manage a laugh. Perhaps that's because he knew they would get the last laugh.

The White Sox cut Fisk on Monday, days after he set the major league record for most games as a catcher. Just as well. They disgusted him. And with reason. He was surrounded by too many rich under-achievers, young enough to be his children, who were big on making money off card shows, but not so tough in a pennant race. He toler-ated an inexperienced manager who feared Fisk's authority in the clubhouse and kept him nailed to the bench the past two years in favor of Ron Karkovice. Ron Karkovice?

Above all, Fisk was disgusted with Jerry Reinsdorf. What an owner! What a perfect authority figure to despise. Imagine it, Fisk, the ulti-mate New England–bred purist, playing for a man who threatened to move the White Sox to the Sun Belt if Chicago wouldn't tear down venerable Comiskey Park.

For Fisk, who could more perfectly embody disrespect for tradition and the Demise of Baseball as We've Known It? For Fisk, the stakes are that high. He lost all perspective on his contract and playing-time disputes. He even ended up sounding shrill, aggrieved, and a bit greedy. Still, he made his stand. What other player ever made a public point of refusing to speak to his own boss—for two years—yet was so loved by the public that he could make it stick until he got the Big Record.

Yes, that's Carlton, an ancient shipwreck of a ballplayer, hitting .189 with one base stealer thrown out in 23 attempts, who could hold the most powerful owner in baseball at bay until he got No. 2,226 last week.

But that was last week. This week, Fisk, at age forty-five, is adrift and unlikely to find any lifeboat. He still wants to play, somewhere, but it's probably a fantasy. Hopefully, his acrimonious end will be forgotten. His first two years in the majors and his last two are irrele-vant—mere bench time. In between, he had the finest twenty-year run of any catcher who ever lived. Actually, he had the only twenty-year run. No other catcher ever held a regular job so long and with so little deterioration. (Bob Boone had a steady job for seventeen seasons.) In 1972, Fisk played in 131 games with 22 homers and 61 RBI. In 1991, he played in 134 games with 18 homers and 74 RBI. Over the entire twenty years, he averaged 120 games, 19 homers, and 65 RBI. Is that consistent enough for you?

Long ago, Fisk had a decision to make. He proved he could hit immediately. But where should he play? For his career, Fisk averaged 26 homers and 90 RBI with a .270 average for every 600 at-bats. At an easier defensive position, those numbers would surely have gone up. Fisk could stand down at first base for twenty or twenty-five years, get his 600 at-bats every year, hit 500 home runs, seldom break a sweat, and go into the Hall of Fame. Or he could squat behind home plate his whole career, hit only 376 home runs, miss nearly a thousand games from exhaustion and injury, and risk entering Cooperstown with incipient arthritis in every joint.

Fisk, of course, made the New Hampshireman's choice. He knew that a great defensive catcher who can handle a pitching staff and lead a team is worth as much as any slugger, even if that catcher is only a decent hitter. When the catcher in question can also bat as high as .315, drive in as many as 107 runs, and then hit 37 home runs at the age of thirty-seven, the choice is clear. For the good of the team, you have to strap on the gear and suffer.

So, Fisk did. And for twenty-four years, spoiled teammates and cheap owners let him down. Seriously, they did. In his whole career, Fisk went to one World Series—the one for which he'll always be famous. It should've been more.

Next time somebody says Fisk aged fast in his final years or that he seemed to feel the game owed him an unpaid debt or that, generally speaking, he was something of a grump by the end, ask yourself whether he had cause. No price was too high for Fisk. Did his teammates and his owners pay as much?

Once, Deion Sanders did not run out a popup. Even though Sanders was on the other team, Fisk was so furious that he ran after Sanders, cursing like a harpooner and threatening to fight on the spot, if Neon Deion didn't run. Sanders ran, all right, if only to get away from the 240-pound moralist. Next time up, Sanders muttered something about "plantation days" being over. Fisk stopped the game and gave Sanders another lecture, right at home plate, on how Hank Aaron and Willie Mays weren't too fancy to run out their popups and how there was only one right way to play baseball—"the big-league way." Sanders later said he appreciated Fisk's view.

The ice age is coming for Fisk. Or maybe it's a meteor that's about to hit the earth, or whatever it is that finally made dinosaurs extinct. For twenty-four years, you could watch him at Fenway Park or Comiskey Park. Now, he might as well be in Jurassic Park. Hopefully, Cooperstown will ask for one of Fisk's broken fingernails, snapped by a foul tip, in case anybody ever wants to clone the ultimate smart, stubborn, tough, clutch-hitting catcher. Of course, the next century might not know what to do with Carlton Fisk if it had him.

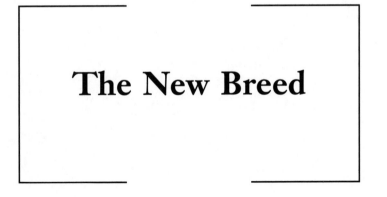

The New Breed

Frank Thomas:
The Big Hurt Begins

WEST PALM BEACH, Florida, March 19, 1992—The screaming of the children starts as soon as he appears from the dugout in his black White Sox jersey with No. 35 on the back. They call him the "Big Hurt" in Chicago. But these kids, running down the stadium aisles at life-threatening speeds, think they have a better chance for his precious autograph if they yell, "Mr. Thomas . . . Mr. Thomas!"

You see, Frank Thomas is polite. He signs autographs for free, believes in manners, and, when cornered for snapshots, cooks up a semi-genuine smile. The kids know this, just as they know everything imaginable about him.

Right now, he is baseball's Main Man—the biggest spring training attraction in Florida or Arizona. (Under the age of forty-five, at least.) If baseball has one player who'll be watched more closely than any other this season, it's Thomas. The questions are simple. Is he really this good? And can he get even better?

When was the last time a player, after one full season, was widely considered the best hitter in baseball? The most patient with the best eye and the least holes? The best in the clutch because he can fight off tough pitches? And the best at using the whole field—25 percent to left, 25 to center, 25 to right, and 25 percent in the parking lot?

This man can crank a 450-foot home run or take a pitch out of the catcher's glove and poke it down the rightfield line for a game winner. On purpose.

Last season Thomas hit 32 homers, batted .318, and had 138 walks (after breaking in at .330 for 60 games in 1990). And he got better as he went along. If there is ever another Ted Williams—a perfect blend of hitter and slugger—Thomas might be it. At twenty-three, he has the temperament of a veteran—studious, self-disciplined, calm, coachable, and utterly sure of himself.

Whatever happened to "too soon old and too late smart"? He skipped it.

Nobody in baseball can guess what the 6-foot-5, 240-pound Thomas may do if he stays healthy, keeps working hard, and isn't distracted by his new three-year, $4.3 million contract. Nobody has ever hit .350 with 50 homers and 150 walks, though Babe Ruth came close a couple of times. Thomas won't either. But he's the only player about whom you can even fantasize such numbers. Who knows what that autograph may be worth someday?

So "Mr. Thomas!" is what they scream. The kids dive on each other atop the dugout like they're trying to recover a fumble. They hang over the lip, sticking balls and programs toward Thomas for signing until, finally, one boy thinks he's being crushed and screams in real terror. The cops bust the whole thing up.

To understand the furor about Thomas, you have to understand his uniqueness. There are a couple of other hitters who may be as strong —Cecil Fielder and Jose Canseco. There is one, and only one, who is as patient—Rickey Henderson. Since Williams, there hasn't been a slugger, until Thomas, who has thrown down the gauntlet and said, "I never swing at a bad pitch." There are a few craftsmen whose all-fields, Charlie Lau–style technique is as good as Thomas's—like Wade Boggs and Tony Gwynn. There are a few other stars whose home parks suit them as perfectly as the new Comiskey Park—with its friendly power alleys—suits Thomas, who hit .371 at home. And there are a few other players who work as hard at improving as Thomas does with hitting coach Walt Hriniak, who critiques him on every batting practice pitch.

But the whole package? Nobody's close.

Perhaps best of all, Thomas is his own man at the plate, his own creation.

"I have my own style. It's nothing you can teach. It's always come naturally to me," Thomas said this week after an exhibition game. "It's hard to sit back and wait. It's tough to do, pick out a good pitch, in that little bit of time, lay off the bad ones. But that's always been my plan. If I can't get a good pitch, I don't swing. . . .

"The only thing I'd tell people is just don't come to watch me juice the ball over the fence. I'm a little picky, pesky hitter. I want to see a lot of pitches, fight off a lot of pitches. I'm trying to get a ball I can drive in the gaps. That's what my key is. Guys have to play me deep and toward the gaps, so a lot of my little weak hits fall in [down the lines].

"I don't go crazy over home runs. I want good-technique home runs. I concentrate on average and RBI. Those are what's important to me."

No one else will ever call Frank Thomas "a little picky, pesky hitter." So we might as well enjoy hearing him say it of himself. Also, it's nice, since Williams retired thirty-one years ago, to know that there's still one player who doesn't get excited about those tacky bad-technique home runs. Somebody's got to keep up the standards around here.

Sooner or later, some fool will try to change Thomas's approach because, like Teddy Ballgame before him, his ideas don't jibe with the thick-witted team-first patter that baseball loves to worship. Just wait, we'll hear it. He walks too much. He won't expand his strike zone in clutch situations to help the team.

What about it, Frank? Would you ever forsake 50 walks a year, not to mention that Ruthian .453 on-base percentage, to placate the Real-Men-Swing-the-Bat faction?

"That will never happen."

Oh, good. The line is drawn in the dirt. Let's all get on Frank's side.

Thomas isn't a perfect player. He's no base stealer and, at first base, though he gives an effort, he usually seems to be in some danger.

But he wants to be the Perfect Hitter.

The 240-pound Wade Boggs. Maybe that's why the gods put Hriniak, heir to Lau (creator of George Brett) and confidant of Boggs, at Thomas's side at this hour. Watching them take batting practice together is a trip. Hriniak's a piece of work to start with. He's been twisted several turns too tight and doesn't want to get loosened. Thomas, who seems imperiously nonchalant when he's not at bat, is every bit as intense.

When Thomas hits a 440-foot bomb over the centerfield fence, Hriniak says, "Don't lose your head, Frank."

Thomas takes the next pitch.

"Nice take," says Hriniak.

Finally, somebody has picked up the challenge again. A take-no-prisoners, make-no-compromises hitter. Hit for average. Hit for power. Draw a million walks. The whole nine yards.

Will Thomas go up a level and join the greatest of the great? Or will he come back a level and be just another excellent hitter?

"There are a lot of calculated guesses in this game," says Thomas, who prides himself on learning pitchers better than they learn him.

It's just a hunch, but let's guess that the Big Hurt will get even better.

Juan Gonzalez:
President Pardoned

BALTIMORE, April 6, 1993—President Clinton left Opening Day in Camden Yards Monday in the bottom of the seventh inning.

Someday, no one—not even the president of the United States—will leave a game when Juan Gonzalez is due up the next inning.

These days, the Rangers leftfielder is still the home run champion nobody knows. Relatively speaking. Someday pretty soon, however, he'll be the man people wait to see.

After all, no one wants to say they missed one of his 500 homers. Some even think Gonzalez, not Mark McGwire or Jose Canseco, will be the fourth man in baseball's 600 Club.

Monday, Gonzalez set a record crowd abuzz with two nearly identical signature homers. Both were liners to deepest left centerfield that skedaddled from point A to point B faster than the eye believes possible. It's fitting that Gonzalez now bats behind Canseco in the Rangers order. Jose hits flies that require FAA clearance. Juan may produce baseball's first sonic boom.

The wind-cheating rocket that Gonzalez drilled off Rick Sutcliffe in the third inning traveled 420 feet through a raw, flag-stiffening gale, landing in the Baltimore bullpen a few nanoseconds after the ball left his bat.

For the second home run, after Clinton's exodus, the wind was blowing even more briskly and the pitcher, Alan Mills, was throwing a lot harder than Sutcliffe. The Gonzalez drive was hit to an even deeper part of the Birds' bullpen. But the result was the same. They say that the greatest hitters turn the wind around. Both of Gonzalez's shots looked as if they had a 20-mile-per-hour tail wind, not a head wind.

President Clinton, who stayed an hour longer than most recent chief executives, can be forgiven for missing the second one. Not many fans outside Texas have caught on to Gonzalez's act. Last season, he slipstreamed behind McGwire all season in the home run race, then, on the final day of the season, hit his 43rd homer to lead the majors.

At the age of twenty-two.

When Gonzalez returned home to Puerto Rico, crowds lined the roads to greet him all the way from the capital, San Juan, to his hometown of Vega Baja. During the winter, he spoke to children at more than fifty schools. He also took courses in English and, yesterday, did a brave job of battling through long interviews in his second language. He seemed shy and tense, barely speaking above a whisper. But no question stumped him and every answer was apt. "I don't like cold weather," he said, "but it's my job."

Generations of Latin stars have failed to get their due in the United States, in part because American reporters seldom make much effort to beat the language barrier. So Gonzalez has decided to meet them 100 percent of the way.

That is fortunate for American fans because it would be sad not to get firsthand reports from Gonzalez on the special things he's almost certain to do. For example, only four other players have hit 40 homers before their twenty-third birthday. Their names are probably an accurate barometer of Gonzalez's future: Joe DiMaggio, Johnny Bench, Mel Ott, and Eddie Mathews.

Frightening as the possibility may be to the rest of the American League, the Rangers may also have a third slugger who'll someday be worthy of comparison to Gonzalez and Canseco. Dean Palmer, often hyped as the Next Mike Schmidt, hit two home runs Monday that were the kind that transform skeptics.

There are home runs. And then there are home run hitters' home runs. Both of Palmer's blows off Sutcliffe were the type that are nondescript outs for 95 percent of the game's hitters. On the first, Palmer tried to "hook" a fastball on the outside corner and pull it. Pitchers stay up late at night praying for hitters to try this. Say hello to a double-play grounder to short. Palmer's shot was gone from the crack, eight rows deep.

Next time, Palmer broke even more rules. He launched a curve to center into the same wind that'd killed every other comparable drive all day. Mike Devereaux climbed the fence but wasn't even close enough to reach.

Palmer already has 41 homers in 828 major league at-bats, including 26 last year in his first full season.

"Those are two strong young men to cut the wind like that," said Rangers manager Kevin Kennedy. "I talked to Jim Palmer before the game and he told me how hard it is to hit the ball out of here to left with the wind in this direction. He said, 'You have to go the other way.' I agreed."

Another fine intellectual theory torn to shreds by a couple of tall guys with doorway-size shoulders and 210 pounds of muscle.

"I see [Dean] Palmer as another Schmidt type. . . . He's going to be a super player," said Kennedy. "I told him that a few days ago. He's also like Schmidt [early in his career] in that he sometimes puts too much pressure on himself. He can hit to all fields. If he does, he has too good a stroke to hit .213 this year."

Yes, Palmer's career average is .213. He's the extreme example of the common flaw that runs through Gonzalez, Canseco, and almost the whole Rangers lineup. While Texas may have three men who can combine for 100 homers this season, they are all exactly the same type of hitter—free-swinging right-handers who are vulnerable to superior pitching. Precise pitching can make the Rangers look even more inept than most teams. Last year, Mike Mussina dissected the Rangers in Texas, pitching a 10-strikeout one-hitter in which he threw little but high fastballs and low change-ups—but in nearly ideal locations.

"They can be pitched to," said Orioles manager Johnny Oates. "Palmer has holes [in his swing]. Gonzalez has less holes."

No one will remember the day more vividly than Oates. "The president of the United States walked right into my office and he said, 'Where's the john?' " said Oates. "And I said, 'I'm right here.' " We have to excuse Oates. When you've been in baseball for twenty-seven years and it's Opening Day, you just get carried away.

Cecil Fielder:
The Baby Babe

September 12, 1990—The Detroit Tigers are hanging around the batting cage. A line drive streaks toward third base where a rookie, up for September, is not paying attention.

"Hey!" one alarmed voice screams.

The rookie lifts his foot just in time not to get hurt.

A few minutes later, another line drive. The same player is daydreaming. "Hey!" screams the same voice, saving the same guy's life. "Don't get hurt out there now," the Good Samaritan yells cheerfully. The rookie waves back, shamefaced but still in one piece.

When batting practice breaks up, every Tigers player avoids the fans along the box seat railing, just as almost every other major league player does. Sign one autograph, a mob will gather and you'll not only have to sign one hundred times, but you'll actually have to—yuck—shake hands and talk to the fans.

Even though no fan spots him or calls his name, the same Tiger walks directly to the box seats and takes a small boy's program and pen and begins the autograph session. He keeps signing for fifteen minutes until the police order him to stop and go into the clubhouse. At one point, the player realizes that two kids in the front row are getting squeezed by other fans. "Are these your seats right here?" asks the 247-pound Tiger.

The children are too awed to speak, but they nod. So the player moves down the row to prevent their seats from becoming a war zone; also he can answer questions from a new batch of fans.

"Did all that sushi make you strong?" asks one man, not expecting an answer.

"Yup. I'm going back for more," says the Tiger as he signs his name slowly, perfectly legibly—an artistic autograph in defiance of the sport's tradition of quick, sloppy blurs.

One boy walks away, not knowing who the lone signer is. Suddenly, as if shocked, he looks at his ball and yells, "I got Cecil Fielder's autograph!"

If you really want to know what a ballplayer is like as a person, don't just listen to him talk. Watch him when he's around other players. Or when he thinks nobody's watching him at all. At least that's what Sparky Anderson says.

The Tigers manager never dreamed that Cecil Fielder would hit 45 home runs—9 more than anybody else in the major leagues this season—or that he might become the eleventh man in history to hit 50 homers before this year is over. But he knew he had a team leader as far back as spring training.

"He has the same temperament as Alan Trammell," says Anderson, meaning that as high praise since Trammell always epitomizes sweet-tempered stability. "Players teach you about other players. Watch who they avoid, who they enjoy being around. That's part of the way you decide who to subtract from your club the next year.

"All the players liked Cecil from the first day. He is who he is. He doesn't try to be liked. He's just relaxed and comfortable being himself. We gave him about $3 million for two years. You lay out that kind of money and you find out right away who the jerks are."

Everybody knows Cecil Fielder's story now. But not too many know him. No player in baseball, until Fielder, had the self-confidence, or maybe audacity, to go to Japan—at age twenty-five—to prove that he was a star and not a part-time platoon player. In bits and pieces of four seasons with the Blue Jays, Fielder hit 31 homers in 506 at-bats. He didn't rebel. He didn't call names. He just left. And became a Hanshin Tiger—one who hit 38 home runs in 106 games.

In Japan he learned to hit soft slop and accept walks. When Detroit had the fiscal courage to make him another kind of Tiger, Fielder had his chance. "You just got to find out who you are. I got a chance," he says. "I had a lot of things to prove to myself. And you can't do it unless you play every day and relax. You have to let things happen. You can't worry about when you'll play again. . . .

"In spring training, I relaxed a little more. When I didn't get off to a good start, Sparky told me, 'I know you're going to hit.' I knew I'd play.

"The people who didn't think I could play the game," said Fielder earlier this year, "they can't take this from me."

Because Fielder is so wide, so ominous at the plate, and hits the ball so far—he is the first right-handed Detroit player to hit a ball entirely out of Tiger Stadium—it's often assumed that he must be macho. Actually, he seems the opposite.

"He's so polite and has such a nice family," says Anderson. "We tease him that he must have met his wife when he was a high school [basketball] star at point guard because that's the only way he could've won her. She's so beautiful, he couldn't get her now. She teases him about that too."

Of course, this may only be part of Sparky's plan to get Fielder to "come to spring training at 230 pounds next year." Typically, Fielder doesn't squawk at being asked to lose weight after one of the greatest offensive seasons in the last quarter century. "He's not real joyful about the idea," said Anderson, "but I promised we'd work it out together. Some guys can carry a lot of weight. It's a fine line. I don't want to get too smart for our own good."

Babe Ruth weighed 251 when he hit 60 homers. And Fielder is having a Ruthian season. Only one man, George Foster, has hit 50 homers since 1965. No player, including Fielder, will admit the symbolism of 50 homers. But that magic number—achieved less often in this century than a .390 batting average—seems to bedevil even the best of sluggers.

Since Willie Mays hit 52 in 1965, many of the greats have had a chance for 50 after Labor Day and then started to falter. Mark McGwire, Andre Dawson, Frank Robinson, and Harmon Killebrew (twice) got stuck on 49. Mike Schmidt, Dave Kingman, Willie Stargell, and Frank Howard made it to 48. After being ahead of 50-homer paces, Kevin Mitchell, George Bell, Hank Aaron, and Reggie Jackson came to a halt at 47.

"If he does hit fifty," says Anderson, "you'll never know, other than he might smile once while he's rounding the bases. This guy is going to hit thirty or more homers every year, but he will be the same person ten years from now."

As Anderson talks, a small, elderly Baltimore man approaches

Fielder and asks him some questions. As the fellow comes back through the Tigers dugout, he looks worried. "Cecil said he would come to our banquet this winter," he says. "Last winter, we invited Jose Canseco. He stiffed us and didn't show up."

Whether he gets his 50 or not, Fielder will be there. Anybody who watches him closely wouldn't have a doubt.

□ □ □

July 14, 1992—Since 1950, how many players have had more than 130 RBI more than once?

The answer is: two. One of them is Harmon Killebrew, who had 142 RBI in 1962 and 140 in 1969. The other man on this short list we'll keep secret a minute.

He's not Hank Aaron, Mickey Mantle, Willie Mays, Frank Robinson, Reggie Jackson, Mike Schmidt, Willie McCovey, Eddie Mathews, or Ernie Banks—although all nine of them are among the fourteen men with 500 home runs.

Need a clue? In his first full season in the majors, at the age of twenty-six, he had 132 RBI. In his second year, he had 133 RBI. This season, in his third full year, he's on a pace for 137 RBI.

That'd be 402 RBI in three years.

So, how good is that, how unusual? How many players have had 402 RBI in three consecutive seasons since 1950?

Answer: None.

Okay, okay, let's up the ante. Let's make this spectacular. How many players since 1950—including all ten of the 500-homer men mentioned above—have had 402 RBI in their three best seasons? Not three in a row. Any three seasons in their life.

Answer: None.

Unless, of course, our current star does it. If this fellow stays on course, he'll have more RBI in his first three full seasons than Hank Aaron or Mickey Mantle or Willie Mays or anybody else since the Korean War had in the three best years of his life.

Who is this demigod, you ask?

First, let's prime the pump a tad more. If our man—let's call him Cecil—does not drive in a single run in the last 75 games of this season, he will still have more RBI (340) than Mantle had in any three years in a row.

The baseball career most parallel to our hero's is that of Babe Ruth, who had his first 130-RBI year at age twenty-five. The Babe was supposed to be too fat to play very long. But he drove in 130 or more runs ten times in a thirteen-year span before—yes—getting too fat and fading fast at age thirty-eight.

Cecil Fielder is not Babe Ruth. But, in the world of RBI, he's the closest thing we've got. So why isn't he at the dumb All-Star Game tonight in San Diego? And why isn't anybody mad?

What does Cecil have to do to get his due? When has any player ever been so consistently snubbed? In 1990, Rickey Henderson beat Fielder for MVP, although Cecil hit 51 homers. Fielder was told it was because Rickey played for a winner. In 1991, Cal Ripken was the MVP, although Fielder produced more runs for a far better team. When he has the stats, the other guy gets it on "team play." When Cecil's team wins and the other guy's stinks, that doesn't count. Which way does this deal work?

Fielder may be the best player in baseball. He's on the short list, that's for sure. Yet AL manager Tom Kelly chose not to pick any backup first baseman for his All-Star team rather than take Fielder—who leads the majors with 75 RBI.

"Ridiculous," said Fielder's teammate Mickey Tettleton last week.

"It's an ugly situation," Fielder told the *Detroit News.* "Is it the city we play in? Is it that so few fans come to our games? . . . It's kind of petty stuff compared to the other disappointments of my career."

If Fielder ends his career with a case of paranoia, who could blame him? He scorched the minors and got ignored. Per 600 at-bats, he was on a pace for more than 130 RBI in A ball. In AA, he had 125 RBI in 597 at-bats. In AAA, he was right on a 125-RBI pace again. In bad circumstances as a part-time player for two years with Toronto, he still hit 23 homers in 349 at-bats—or 40 homers per 600 at-bats. He's wrecked pitching at every level. Nobody's ever stopped him or even slowed him. And he plays 160 games a season.

Yet, in the Jays organization, Fielder was blocked behind Fred Mc-Griff, who's very good but has never driven in more than 100 runs. Fielder had to go to Japan for a year, something no young player had ever dared try, just to get enough attention to land a full-time major league job back in Detroit.

For nine years as a pro, from the minors to Japan to the majors, Fielder has dwarfed every other RBI man in the sport. And n-o-t-h-i-n-g is more important than RBI. There is no flaw in him—no injury, no personality defect, no defensive liability, no laziness, no bad seasons. He is smart, funny, unselfish, modest, and beloved by teammates. He's an absolute total monster of a player and a prince of a guy. In fact, his son's name is Prince. Okay, in the last year, he's gotten grouchy on the subject of "recognition." But wouldn't you?

Yet Kelly left Fielder off the All-Star team and nobody outside Detroit has said "Boo." Much less "Boooooooo!!!"

Nobody knows how long Fielder's 260-pound body will hold out. He's played through a sore wrist this year and has "only" 18 homers and a .244 average. Maybe he'll fade as fast as Vern Stephens, the last man to have 400 RBI in three years in 1948–50.

But that's not what the record book says. Except for Stephens, every other man capable of 400 RBI in three years ended up a historic figure: Joe DiMaggio, Jimmie Foxx, Chuck Klein, Hank Greenberg, Al Simmons, Hack Wilson, Ted Williams, Lou Gehrig, and Ruth.

Fielder hasn't yet become the tenth man to join this club, but if he does, he'll have another special distinction. He and DiMag will be the only men to get 400 in their first three full seasons.

Clutch hitters are a special baseball breed. When they see men on base, it's as if the dinner bell just rang. They're ready to chow down. Last season, with the bases empty, Fielder had a slugging percentage of .433—barely mediocre. With men on, he slugged .601—not too far behind Ruth.

Some players live for pressure. Eddie Murray's career batting average with the bases loaded is .426 with 250 RBI. If Murray can maintain this clutch pattern for sixteen years, why can't Fielder do the same for a whole career? What evidence—even an iota—exists to suggest that Fielder, as long as he doesn't actually eat any of the bases, won't stay at this level indefinitely?

San Diego is chock full of superb players that the public probably does not yet fully appreciate. How many fans think of Roberto Alomar or Ruben Sierra as potential 3,000-hit men. How many think of Greg Maddux, twenty-six, as being ahead of Roger Clemens's victory pace or of Tom Glavine as having a touch of Warren Spahn about him? You can't look much better at twenty than Ivan Rodriguez or at twenty-two than Travis Fryman. Can Juan Guzman and Mike Mussina—who arrived only last summer—really be this close to the top? Yet nobody in baseball is as out of focus as Cecil Fielder.

Fifty-six players will be on display in San Diego, yet none of them
—not one—has done as much in the last two and a half seasons as
Cecil Fielder. In that time, he has been the best player in baseball. No
question about it. No arguments allowed. How can an All-Star Game
without him claim to be legitimate?

Barry Bonds:
Perfect Pedigree

June 6, 1993—Barry Bonds wants to know every nuance of anything that can happen in a baseball game. As the son of Bobby Bonds, he's been in a big-league clubhouse since he was three years old. His godfather is Willie Mays. Bonds has been a student of the game almost from birth, and he knows that while God may or may not be in the details, baseball definitely is.

This week, on his first visit to Joe Robbie Stadium in Miami, Bonds got acquainted with his environment. On a foul fly, the San Francisco Giants leftfielder made a cautious tiptoeing basket catch in the corner, then braced himself against the three-foot wall of the Giants bullpen. Frisco relievers yawned. Bonds had made another hard play look easy. So what? He has three Gold Gloves. At the moment, he is by consensus the sport's best player. He'll make $43.75 million in the next six years. He ought to catch 'em all.

Bonds's grab ended the inning, but he paused and studied everything. The fence, the warning track, the flags atop the stadium. Then he trotted to the dugout, chattering to his centerfielder, gesturing at the sky, telling the fellow what he'd learned about the swirling winds in this new National League stadium.

As Bonds jogged, his one gold earring glinted. His yellow wristbands, with his own picture on them, shone brightly. He grinned with innocent animation. In his joy over this obscure play, you could see why Bonds's old boyhood friends swear he's the sweetest, most harmlessly self-obsessed giggle-seeker you'd ever meet. At that moment,

Bonds was as happy as a bright, moody child from an affluent but difficult family playing endlessly with his favorite toy in the privacy of his own room.

Those who find Bonds incredibly delicious have a taste for craftsmanship. What, after all, were the odds that Bonds would ever have another similar play in this leftfield corner? And, if he did, who would care? The ball would, at worst, fall foul. When a man is batting .376 in June, when a fellow has a chance to win his third MVP award in four years, when a righteous dude might even have a shot at the Triple Crown or a world title or a season from which lifelong legend might be spun, why sweat the foul balls?

Just two innings later, another foul fly spun toward the same leftfield corner. This time, the ball was headed beyond the fence and into the bullpen.

Bonds sped across the grass, swift as a man whose father was a California long jump champion and whose aunt was a U.S. Olympic hurdler. Then Bonds hit cruise control, sensible for a fellow who has been on the disabled list only once. Finally, so fast it all seemed one gasp of motion, Bonds caught the ball, hit the waist-high fence, flipped upside down, then used his glove hand (with the ball inside) to do a handstand on the opposite side of the fence. For a split second, Bonds's toes pointed to the sky. Then, twisting sideways like a platform diver, he landed calmly on his feet in the bullpen. Ball in glove, of course.

Not one Giants player in the bullpen moved from his seat. Did they consider the play impossible and assume Bonds would let the ball drop? Did they figure that they, baseball mortals, could only screw up Bonds's work, so why get in his way? After all, Philadelphia Phillies star John Kruk has described Bonds's performance this season by saying, "He's making a mockery of the league."

Or, having gotten to know the Real Barry this spring, did his new mates hope that, if they stayed where they were, maybe he'd break half the bones in his body? After all, when the Giants went to Pittsburgh last month, Bonds visited the Pirates clubhouse to shake hands with his old mates. The Bucs gave him the freeze-out. Nobody got up. Card games didn't even stop. Think of it. Bonds put playoff money in every Pirates pocket for three straight years. By going free agent and becoming a Giant last December, he'd done no more than other Pirates before him.

Yet, by all accounts, he received not one "Hello." During the '92 playoffs, a Pirates coach said: "I hope Bonds hits a home run every time up the rest of the year. Then, after he's gone, I hope he never gets another hit the rest of his life. I wouldn't wish that kind of bad luck on any other player in baseball."

Like Father, like Son

Bobby Bonds is in a bad mood. He's glowering. He's doing his best to turn an idle conversation into an argument. He's looking for offense. He's ready to straighten somebody out with a sharp word or a full-blown lecture. Bobby and the world are in the forty-seventh year of a standoff.

During his career, eight teams decided they could live without Bobby Bonds. It's hard to hit 37 home runs and end up in another town the next year. Or 32. Or 29. Or 25. Or even 21. But Bonds did it. The teams Bonds left usually got better. Because they got so much in a trade for him, some said. Or because Bobby's abrasive personality left town.

Bonds is in a good mood. His eyes are soft and thoughtful. He wants to deepen the conversation. He loves candor. He's infatuated with trading anecdotes. He's a man who loves insight—a real hot-stove philosophizer. He even wants to talk all about Barry.

This change of mood has occurred in two minutes. What has caused it?

Bonds has discovered that the person he's talking to doesn't dislike him. That's all it takes. Bobby Bonds starts from the assumption that people who don't know him well probably assume he is a wrong guy. That's his rep. It is the same assumption—bad attitude, arrogant jerk —that his son now carries.

"Bobby went through a lot [during his career] and Barry has shared a lot of his dad's pain," says Giants manager Dusty Baker.

Bobby Bonds, the Giants first-base coach, sees it all happening again—this time to his son. In recent weeks, *Newsweek* has labeled Barry a jerk. *Sports Illustrated* billed him as the consummate shallow bore. The father finds it hard to believe the world is talking like this about his son. He looks up from his dugout seat and there, silhouetted against the rim of a great stadium, is the oldest of his offspring, born when Bobby was just eighteen. The boy has a gentle face—sensitive or spoiled or both—with none of the father's hard times written on it.

"Any father in the world would be proud to have a son like that.

And I'm leaving out baseball. Just the person," says Bonds. "Barry has maybe five friends—no, six—that he's known since he was a child. They really know him. He still sees them all the time. If any of them tell me he's changed, maybe I'll listen. But they say he's just the same. The rest? Those people don't know him. He's private. . . .

"Nothing bothers Barry," says Bonds, slowly. "He does not care what anybody thinks of him. There's no sportswriter who knows him or is going to know him."

The father then recites a dozen bad things—from drug abuse on down—that Barry has never done. In fact, many people feel Barry never has been less than a model athlete, model student, model son. If he isn't lifting weights or working on the martial arts, he's taking his wife, Sun, dancing or playing with their two young children, Nikolai and Shikari.

"His wife loves him, his mother loves him, I love him."

Barry Bonds is a chip off the old block, all right. Unfortunately, the chip is on his shoulder, just like it was on his dad's. If a father gets that chip knocked on the floor often enough—if he gets traded enough and bad-mouthed enough and goes as much as five years at a time without getting a job anywhere in the game—isn't it possible that the oldest son might pick up that chip and wear it like a family badge of honor?

If you grew up hearing your father constantly accused of not fulfilling his potential—specifically, of failing to be the next Willie Mays—then might not a dutiful son try to vindicate the father by vowing to finish the quest?

An extreme idea? Perhaps. But when Barry Bonds signed with the Giants, he said he was going to wear No. 24—"to honor Mays." The outcry at this dishonor was so loud that Bonds quickly said he'd wear No. 25, "to honor my father," whose first team was the Giants. The father, the son, and the godfather are pretty darned intertwined.

Exceptional as Bobby Bonds was as a player, with 332 homers and 461 stolen bases, he was usually found wanting. Too many strikeouts, too few RBI. Yet, ironically, after all of his son's awards, it's still Bobby who holds the best season marks in the family for hits, homers, and runs scored. Unfortunately, he never could hold a candle to Mays, who played next to him for seven seasons.

Now, throughout baseball this spring, you hear the same comparison everywhere: Bobby Bonds's son is the best all-around player since Mays. And it's true. Factually true. Since Mays, nobody has been able to blend the five basic skills—running, throwing, fielding, hitting, and hitting with power—as well as Barry Bonds.

Bonds also draws so many walks that he actually gets on base more than Mays did. And Bonds steals more. But Mays clearly was better. He had more power. He played a more important position (centerfield) and played it more spectacularly. And he had thirteen straight peak years, starting at age twenty-three. Bonds is only in his fourth megaseason, starting at twenty-five.

Still, make no mistake, the Barry Bonds of 1990 to 1993 is the only player in a generation to be statistically comparable to the Mays of 1954 to 1966.

Bonds probably won't come close to staying at this level for another ten years. But who thought we'd ever see another Mays? Even a diluted version. Even playing leftfield. Even for a few years.

Lessons Learned Young

Barry Bonds chokes up on the bat more than any other player in baseball, then stands closer to the plate than anybody else too. That's his key. Nobody else does it this way. Which pleases Bonds. He wore black high-top shoes when nobody else did. He loves it that only he, among serious power hitters, grabs the bat a full two inches up from the handle.

"I started choking up when I was a kid. My dad gave me bats that were too big for me," he says, telling the tale in the dugout where his father can overhear. "I remember a Bat Day, I think when he played for the Yankees [in 1975]. They gave away full-size major league bats.

"All the children of the players went down under the stands with these big bats. . . . We had to choke up so we wouldn't fall down [after a swing]."

A batter's stance toward the pitcher is sometimes his stance toward the world. Bonds crowds the plate and crowds the pitcher too. He's greedy. He takes the whole plate. He refuses to play by the unwritten rule that says the pitcher is entitled to his fair portion. His approach is overtly confrontational. It guarantees unpopularity. And, for him, success.

Bonds goes so far in making his challenge obvious that he is the only player in baseball who wears the equivalent of a padded plastic shin guard on his right forearm. In a sense, he carries a shield to ward off pitches. He's so close to the plate that, sometimes, when he checks his swing, the ball bounces off his arm guard. And he goes to first base —unhurt.

Bonds is also supremely picky. "When he was younger, he'd chase the high fastball and the slow curves in the dirt," says Baker. "Now, he's very selective. He gets a good pitch to hit or he doesn't swing. He's always ahead in the count."

The only time Bonds seems to revert to his bad old expand-the-plate habits is in the playoffs and, perhaps, in crucial late-game situations. Perhaps he can't stand the frustration of October walks because he wants the glory due a hero. Or maybe he wants approval after all. Or maybe he just gets tight. Whatever the cause, Bonds has chased too many high fastballs and low, slow curves for the past three Octobers, hitting .191 with 3 RBI in 68 at-bats.

Throughout his career, Bonds has shown no weakness against any sort of pitching. And he loves to hit with men on base. However, he has had one consistent flaw. All his numbers go down in what statistics mavens call "late and close" situations. His career slugging percentage is nearly 100 points lower in those spots. Maybe, when the stakes are highest, he starts to show how he really feels. He can't hide the truth from himself. He cares. Especially about how others think of him.

On the Edge

The Giants aren't going anywhere. The bus can wait. The flight back home can wait. It's almost midnight, but they are not going to leave their locker room. The Bulls and Knicks have a minute to play in Game 5 of the Eastern Conference finals.

There's only one TV and Barry Bonds has his chair in the front row. Lots of players make comments. But Bonds makes the most and the loudest. He doesn't really have a social knack. His comments don't quite blend. But then neither does he. Nobody in the room is dressed like Bonds. He looks like a hip Hollywood fashion show. Nobody else has a sweater covered with colorful geometric shapes and a new style of collar that looks a bit like a Nehru jacket. Nobody else wears their gold jewelry outside their collar. Nobody else has mustard-colored silk socks with little black animals stitched on them. Or shoes that look a bit like slippers. His shoes are, well, what the heck are they? They're the next cool thing, the cutting edge, the place where Bonds wants to be before everybody else, even if they might resent it.

"I like having Barry around," says veteran reliever Dave Righetti.

"You get eccentric behavior from a lot of exceptional people. Barry is just different. Lots of players have ability. What sets Barry apart is his belief in his power, his belief in himself. . . .

"The guys in Pittsburgh got it wrong," adds Righetti. "They think you have to go out, drink beers, go to dinner together, all that rah-rah college stuff. Barry doesn't do that. But then that's not his job."

Bonds fits in a big-league clubhouse about as much as his flamboyant, chic buddy Arsenio Hall.

Yet it also seems that Barry Bonds is finally home—to the degree that he can ever be. On one side, he has his weary-from-the-wars father. On the other, he has the hugs of his known-Barry-from-the-crib manager. Somewhere, lurking around the team, ghostlike, is the grouchy, abrupt Mays, so much like a Bonds in manner he might as well be part of the family.

The Bulls beat the Knicks at the buzzer. Everybody goes nuts. Bonds, the most vocal Bulls rooter, should be the happiest, right?

Barry says nothing. He slaps no hands. He disengages. Perhaps a commonplace response would be too ordinary—for a Bonds.

Mike Mussina: Under a Bell Jar

March 1993—Imagine that it is September of 1992 and you are facing Mike Mussina.

Mussina has now been in the major leagues for nearly a year and a half. He's been picking the brains of Orioles manager Johnny Oates, coach Dick Bosman, and veteran teammates Rick Sutcliffe and Mike Flanagan. As his remarkable 18–5 season has unfolded, he has added a cut fastball, which acts like a slider, to his rising fastball, his sinking fastball, his slow overhand curveball, his hard knuckle curveball, and his killer of a change-up.

He can hit the catcher's glove with all three fastballs and the change-up. That's called command. To have true command of four pitches is remarkable. Mussina can also hit some part of the strike zone consistently with both curves. That's control. A pitcher who has confidence that he can throw any of six pitches in any count should probably be declared illegal in all fifty states. Statistically, Mussina has as sharp control as any pitcher since World War II.

To make matters more difficult, all six of his pitches are thrown from an identical delivery and with the same arm speed. You can't tell one from the other until you pick up the spin on the ball halfway to home plate. All six pitches arrive at different speeds.

As a consequence, Mussina can practically calibrate his speed to the mile per hour. Think of his choices as 90 mph, 85, 80, 75, 70, and 65. We have a fellow here who can make the ball arrive at precisely the spot he wishes at exactly the velocity he desires and, in the process, make the ball go in any direction—up, down, in, or out; in any direction, that is, except straight. No one Mussina pitch is the best of its breed. Many men are faster. But, when it comes to a total, interlocking, analytical, merciless arsenal, the Mussina of September '92 is like a pitching equivalent of the Empire's Death Star.

Ironically, at this moment, Mussina may be more effective than if he were able to throw 5 mph faster. A 90-mph riser is an ideal speed—if it's in perfect spots. "He puts it right here, here, here, time after time," says Bosman, holding his hands at that ideal, forbidden-fruit level at the top edge of the strike zone. Hitters just can't lay off that heat at the letters. But they can't quite hit it solidly. That's why Mussina is one of baseball's best fly-ball pitchers. If he were faster, Mussina would watch hitters take more pitches or strike out after battling through long counts. Nothing is better than a one-pitch out. Jim Palmer made a career out of sneaky high smoke. Obviously, if Mussina ever loses his amazing control within the strike zone, he'll have trouble. But he's had control all his life. Palmer never lost it.

On the other hand, who knows if Mussina will ever be as sharp with as many different pitches as he was at the end of last season? Mike Boddicker never returned to the magical zone he found in 1983 and 1984, when he was Rookie of the Year, Most Valuable Player of the American League Championship Series, a World Series hero, a 20-game winner, an ERA champ, and the league's shutout leader all within eighteen months. Boddicker then was almost exactly as good—for two years—as Mussina is now. The following year, he went 12–17, lost his air of total command, and has been a .500 pitcher ever since. Without question, that could be Mussina.

Then again, perhaps what we have seen will merely become Mussina's norm for the next dozen years. In which case, he'd be Jim Palmer. History says both these possibilities are realistic. Boddicker or Palmer? Will it be 131 career wins and a sore shoulder or 268 wins and the Hall of Fame? Mussina even looks like a hybrid of the two—neat, black-haired, handsome, trim. For size, for speed, he's midway between them—a couple inches taller and a few miles an hour faster than Boddicker and an inch shorter and a few miles an hour slower than Palmer.

Mussina is listed at 6-foot-2, 182 pounds. Take an inventory of the Hall of Fame and you'll find that the ideal pitching size is 6-foot-0 to 6-foot-2 and 175 to 205 pounds. Big enough to generate power, but compact enough to have it under control. Cy Young, Walter Johnson,

Christy Mathewson, Grover Alexander, Warren Spahn, Tom Seaver, Nolan Ryan, Sandy Koufax, Catfish Hunter, Early Wynn, Robin Roberts, Don Sutton, Bob Gibson, Bob Feller, and countless others fall into this Mussina-like size range. Nevertheless, Mussina, who'll add 10 useful pounds with the years, seems a bit dainty, like a dapper misplaced Ivy Leaguer.

However, perhaps as compensation, Mussina also has an elitist's arrogance about him. He looks smarter. Smarter than who? Take your pick. Has any other pitcher in baseball gotten an economics degree from Stanford in three and a half years? Mussina also looks more intense, in a Top Gun way, than those around him. His father is a successful lawyer. He's never dreamed of failure. He's yuppie type A, all the way. Making the American League All-Star team only added to his poise. He's a slick, feline fielder with a quick pickoff move. Nobody bunts on him or runs on him. It all seems so easy for him. In high school, he'd catch the touchdown pass, then kick the extra point himself. Or dribble through the press, take a return pass, and hit the jumper. He has Sam Shepard's middle-distance stare, but with even more natural iciness.

He'll give you the firm handshake after he wins, but don't look for a hug or a slap on the butt. He doesn't specialize in buddies. He doesn't seem head-over-heels crazy about anybody. Oh, maybe himself, a little. But within reason. He carries with him an abnormal, distanced maturity. On the enthusiasm meter, he might as well be middle-aged.

His usual demeanor is well mannered, but sardonic. He enjoys the bleak and oblique black humor of the locker room. He functions well in a world where people routinely get hit by 120-mph line drives or 90-mph fastballs and where "going under the knife" may cost a man a $20 million contract.

He's the small-town Pennsylvania boy who passes as a polished preppie. He's the clean-cut player who likes heavy-metal Metallica. In spring training, before games are on TV, he grows a mustache and goatee. He'd look right playing rhythm guitar in the Smithereens. Then, the day after he signs his contract and he no longer has a reason to tweak management, he shaves; he seems more comfortable that way —hidden behind the appearance of being Just a Nice Boy. Mussina always seems to be one up on everybody, concealing a hole card. His own manager, Johnny Oates, says he's afraid to talk to the kid about anything except baseball because "I might say something dumb." Mussina doesn't want you to know what he's thinking. Or feeling.

Still, as you stand at the plate in September of '92, you figure he'd probably be pretty interested in throwing a perfect game. As he starts his windup—a precise, compact motion that seems to be a quick succession of checkpoints—you get the distinct feeling that you are a smallish person who has accidentally gotten in Mr. Mussina's way. He would never stoop to being rude. Nevertheless, you must be removed. Don't worry, this won't take long.

First pitch, knuckle curve at the knees. If you swing, you ground out to short. If you don't, strike one. You're either out or you're behind.

Second pitch, fastball, six inches above the belt. If you swing, you fly out. If you don't swing—although you probably will—ball one.

Third pitch, change-up at the knees. If you swing, you dribble to third and probably wrench your back lunging. If you take it, strike two.

Fourth pitch—this is it for you, buster. Mussina has better things to do than waste more than four pitches on one lousy hitter. Fastball. Right in your kitchen, up and in. In your face. On the black. It's the big pitch of the at-bat, so it's perfect. If you take it, you're called out. If you swing, you end up with half a bat, bees stinging your palms, and a popup.

You go back to the bench with only your bat handle for company. You can hardly wait to face this SOB for the next fifteen years.

But will he get fifteen years? And if so, will he mirror Seaver—or Sutcliffe? How'd you like the first fifteen years of your adult life to follow the progression of Sutcliffe's career: 0–0; 17–10; 3–9; 2–2 (traded in the off-season); 14–8; 17–11; 4–5 (traded during the season); 16–1; 8–8; 5–14; 18–10; 13–14; 16–11; 0–2; 6–5 (released); 16–15? He's been Rookie of the Year, Cy Young Award winner, and a guy who's been told by three teams that he was washed up. He's gone from winner to loser five times already.

Actually, Sutcliffe is the prototypical modern pitcher—a guy whose career is a manic-depressive's fantasy. Fans say glibly that so-and-so "should win twenty games this year." That's absurd. Their unspoken assumption is that good pitchers can easily leap to 20 victories in some years and will win 15 or more games for a decade or so at a time, just as the best sluggers seldom have a season when they fall below 20 homers or 75 runs batted in.

The record begs to differ. How many active pitchers have ever, at any time in their careers, had five consecutive seasons in which they won at least 15 games? The answer could shock you. Five: Roger Clemens, Dwight Gooden, Jack Morris, Frank Viola, and Greg Maddux.

In contrast, dozens of hitters are in the midst of long streaks of consistency. For example, Eddie Murray has had 75 RBI sixteen years in a row. It's commonplace for top hitters to reel off ten seasons that look like Xerox copies. Pitchers seldom do it three years in a row. Apparently, it's about five times harder for a pitcher to maintain career stability than a hitter.

That's why you don't want to touch Mike Mussina. You don't even want to breathe on him. And you don't want to let anybody else near him either. He'll have plenty of time to endorse products, make commercials, get married, change diapers, and cure cancer. He'll have plenty of time to become a fascinating personality and a fully human, normally flawed character.

But, for now, who really cares? For now, just let the man pitch. Let him find out how good he can be. No, that's not entirely honest. Let us find out how good he can be. Can this kid pitcher who has been so incredibly consistent for a year and a half become one of those truly great pitchers who can maintain form for five to ten years at a time? The last time an American League pitcher as young as Mussina posted an ERA as low as his was way back in 1976. The names? Mark Fidrych, then twenty-two, and Frank Tanana, twenty-three. Those names both bring a shudder. Both hurt their arms. Fidrych disappeared. Tanana transformed himself into a heroic but only modestly successful junkballer.

No one in American sports is more prone to inexplicable excellence, often followed by equally mysterious disaster, than a major league pitcher.

If a contending major league team is defined by its starting rotation, then that rotation is seldom better than its ace. Unless a team has one pitcher who carries its banner, encapsulates its style, and periodically calms its fears, it ain't goin' nowhere. If you have to ask, "Who pitches the first game of the World Series for us?" then you're probably not going to the Series anyway.

Everybody in baseball knows that the Orioles have one of the game's most promising kiddie rotations. But everybody in the game also knows something else: Mussina is the man. Once upon a time, the Orioles had Palmer, Mike Cuellar, and Dave McNally. However, in that group, Palmer clearly stood above the others. That's how Mussina's potential compares with Ben McDonald's and Arthur Lee Rhodes's. If the Orioles are going someplace big, the smart, skinny guy called Moose is almost certainly going to lead them.

"It's true there are going to be years when Mike doesn't win eighteen games," manager Oates told reporters in spring training. "But if he stays healthy, there are going to be a lot of years when he wins more than eighteen. I don't think for a second that that won't be the case."

The only young players worth watching are those like Mussina who're burdened with extravagant, improbable comparisons. If you're not the "next" Walter Johnson or Cy Young, you're nobody. So Mike Mussina must be the next Jim Palmer, the next Tom Seaver. Of course, he's only won 22 games in his life and he needs about 250 more to get in their class. But that's always part of the mountain that the great ones have to climb. Palmer beat Sandy Koufax with a shutout in the World Series when he was twenty. Think there weren't some expectations surrounding Palmer after that? When Tom Seaver was twenty-four—Mussina's age—he was Tom Terrific; he won 25 games for the Miracle Mets, helped capture the '69 World Series, and carried all of New York City on his back.

When we wish Mussina well, that does not include a wish that he be spared great expectations. If high hopes end up ruining Mussina, then he was going to be ruined anyway. Like that other Oriole perfectionist, Palmer, Mussina's already dreaming more than others can imagine. He's both instinctively self-protective and driven by an enormous disgust at mediocrity. Of the notion of failure, he has said, "I have never faced it, not at any stop. . . . I've just always been able to get hitters out."

If Mussina can go 18–5 with poor luck, what could he do with the breaks? This year, he may get thirty-five starts, not thirty-two. Since September 1 of '91, this man has allowed two or fewer runs in twenty-six of his thirty-eight starts. That's how you win 25.

Last year, he got sick in midseason and lost 10 pounds, plus some hop off his fastball; he never fully regained strength and spent two months experimenting with his between-starts regimen. What if he stays healthy? What if his off-season weight lifting gives him a tiny bit of extra speed? "He has better definition in all the right pitching muscles this year," says Bosman.

For that matter, how many games might Mussina win if his bullpen doesn't blow four saves for him in the late innings, as it did last year? One or two blown saves is the league average. What would he do if his run support were above the league average, rather than below it?

Whatever happens, Mussina's '92 season was no fluke. For a month, it rained almost every time he pitched, making him work off muddy mounds and through delays. Odd as it sounds, his best pitch in '91— his knuckle curve—never had its sharp downward break in '92. How many pitchers could dream of a 2.54 ERA in a season when their best curveball was temperamental all year?

The more closely you watched Mussina last year, the more eager you are for this season. Any young phenom can fall prey to the world, the flesh, and the devil. What makes Mussina different is not his vulnerability. It's the sense that, with normal development, he can get just a tad better.

Which means he could become the best.

At any one time, you could honestly make that claim for perhaps a dozen young pitchers. Still, there's a tiny list of finalists. Imagine that Mussina's name is in a hat with those of Steve Avery, Juan Guzman, Jim Abbott, and Cal Eldred. None of them has ever won 20 games or a Cy Young Award. But a couple of them will. Fate is going to pull out at least one of those names and, twenty years from now, stamp it on a plaque in Cooperstown.

If this seems extreme, consider a question: What pitcher in the American League had the best combination of stuff and control last season?

Only two pitchers in the league ranked in the top 10 in both fewest hits allowed and fewest walks (per nine innings). Those categories are usually mutually exclusive. If your pitches are extremely hard to hit, they should be hard to control too. The pitchers? Mussina and Clemens.

Actually, Mussina, a control pitcher with surprising power, allowed even fewer runners than Clemens, a power pitcher with surprising control. If Mussina "made it look easy," it's because he put fewer men on base than anybody in the league. That's been his calling card at every level.

So far in his career—and 328 innings over two seasons isn't such a small sampling—the league's on-base percentage against Mussina is .282. That would put him in the top 10 in the twentieth century, just behind Christy Mathewson, Sandy Koufax, Juan Marichal, and Walter Johnson and a bit ahead of Clemens, Seaver, Hunter, and Cy Young.

Go on and scoff. So far, in his two seasons, Mussina has had the seventh best control of any starting pitcher in the last fifty years. Last spring training, Bosman said, "I warm him up sitting on a stool. I put out the glove and I don't have to move it very often. It's pretty scary." By midseason, in an off moment, Bosman looked across the locker room at Mussina and said, almost to himself, "We're looking at the next Seaver."

Baseball has enough statistics to choke a goat, but Mussina's numbers are stunning. Not some of them. All of them. You don't have to be a student of the game to figure out their meaning. For instance, certain basic stuff is important. How do you pitch when you get in trouble with runners in scoring position? How do you pitch late in the game when you're tired? How consistent are you from start to start? Are your left-vs.-right percentages weak? Are you easy or hard to steal bases against? Do you fade at the end of a long season? The answer to all of these is: Mussina has been fabulous.

With runners in scoring position, he reaches back for something extra—a .175 batting average, second best in baseball last year.

Most pitchers flag as the game goes longer. Mussina gets better and is at his very best after 105 pitches (.143 average). Last season he pitched into the ninth inning eighteen times in thirty-two starts—the highest ratio in baseball.

Even more remarkable than Mussina's stamina is his consistency. Because of his control, his simple mechanics, and his intelligence, he almost always gets off to a good start. He understands that the best pitch in baseball is a good fastball in a good spot. (Not a great fastball in a bad spot.)

Because of that consistency, Mussina had the highest percentage of "quality starts" in the American League last year—twenty-four of thirty-two. As unbelievable as it sounds, he's pitched only two poor games (in forty-four starts) in his season and a half.

Mussina also shows no nagging minor weaknesses. Despite the Orioles' poor-throwing catchers, Mussina shuts down the running game as well as anybody in the league, including left-handers. Twice in September he made the swift Milwaukee Brewers look helpless. As for left-handed hitters, Mussina's screwball-like change-up has rendered them harmless. Left-handed hitters had *one* home run and 17 RBI in 422 at bats last year. That also should not be possible.

For those who follow the Orioles with a neurotically intense level of attention, Mussina is an obvious symbol of the whole team. Perennial contenders are usually built around people named Clemens or Morris or Dave Stewart, who win 90 to 100 games over a five-year period in their prime. A few, like Palmer and Seaver, turn those five years at the top into a whole decade.

Mussina has already proved that he can be brilliant. A 2.54 ERA and a .783 winning percentage are so good that few fans can fathom how rare such a combination really is. For example, Robin Roberts never had an ERA that low. Warren Spahn and Catfish Hunter did it only twice. How many times did Jim Palmer win 13 games more than he lost? Only once in his whole career. How many times did Seaver, Clemens, Gooden, Spahn, Palmer, Hunter, and Roberts have a percentage as high as .783? Once each. Bob Gibson and Steve Carlton never got that high.

The question is not the happenstance of Mussina's final record in 1993. Any pitcher can lose enough 1–0, 2–1, and 3–2 games in an unlucky year to turn a 20–10 season into 15–15. The question is: Can Mussina keep pitching like this? Can he keep holding the league to a .239 batting average—a Don Drysdale level? Can he keep walking fewer than two men a game? Is his ludicrously wonderful career ERA of 2.63 just a cruel, misleading joke? After all, only one pitcher since 1920 has had a career ERA under 2.75 (Hoyt Wilhelm).

Does this slim young man have shoulders broad enough to start thirty-five games, work 250-plus innings and win 20 games several times? Or will the effort break him in fairly short order? Is he Boddicker or is he Palmer?

And are the Orioles, largely depending on his fate, contenders or pretenders?

There's no sky quite so clear as the sky in St. Petersburg. At least the chamber of commerce claims to have the stats to prove that the town leads the world in sunny days. So it's hard to watch the Orioles in their spring training home at Al Lang Field and think that your sight is foggy. Everything seems so crystalline. Everybody is so optimistic.

Especially about Mussina. Most of the time, the Orioles like to stay mum about him. They know he still has one more year to sneak up on people. Well, the dumb ones, and maybe the press and public outside Oriole Land. Why undercut his last year of normal life before he becomes BIG? However, if pressed, they admit he's Superman.

"He's got the whole package," said Sutcliffe during spring training. "He combines intelligence with ability and desire. The best thing is to watch him between starts. Nobody works harder. After he finishes pitching, he heads to the weight room for an hour and a half. After everybody else has gone, you see him running three and a half miles around the lake.

"He has a ton of friends in this clubhouse. But he's different. It's his confidence. On the mound, he's eight feet tall and bulletproof."

These days, Mussina is still trying to figure out how a twenty-four-year-old man who is eight feet tall and bulletproof should present himself to the world.

"I don't know what my 'normal season' is yet," he says.

It's pointed out that, perhaps, he'll have a solid, comfortable career like Boddicker's, with 130 wins and several million dollars in the bank.

"I'd like to win 230," he says, semijoking. "If I'm still with this club, I could chase Palmer [for the all-time team record of 268]. Do you think Jimmy'd come out of retirement again [to protect his record]? I'd be thirty-seven. What'd he be, fifty-five?"

Mussina tries on different stances toward his growing stature as though they were suits of clothes. Wouldn't you? One minute he says, "You never know when it's going to end. If I break, we might be knifing it tomorrow and who knows when I'll be back or if I'll be back." A minute after that he says, "I'm retiring in two years after that first arbitration year." He's totally joking. But he's also relieving pressure by telling himself that if he can just keep this balloon from popping for a couple of years, he'll be in control of the game—at least financially, even if it still controls him emotionally.

You have to read between the lines to get Mussina's true view of his own big picture. Asked about a statistical oddity, Mussina says, "It's too early to know what that means. We're looking at one season, plus two months. We have to wait thirteen and a half more seasons."

The theme that always recurs in a Mussina conversation, no matter how hard he tries to submerge it, is the vastness of his self-expectation. Tell him that, so far in his career, he's been one of the half dozen best control pitchers since World War II and he says, "Who's ahead of me?" Told the hallowed names, he not only does not look impressed, he looks genuinely perplexed. "I thought I walked a lot of guys last year. A lot more than I walked in the minors."

After a decent spring training start, in which he gives up one run in three innings, wins the game, and strikes out four men—all with the knuckle curve he's polishing—he says, in passing and without emotion, "I stunk."

"You stunk?" a writer asks.

"If I'd given up a run and three hits in seven or eight innings, that would be okay," he says. "They had a lot of Triple A guys in that lineup I'd never heard of. . . . I don't go out there to pitch okay. I go out there to pitch good. Or rather to pitch 'well.' . . . Things are a touch different this spring. I'm working on my curveball, not just trying to get outs. Maybe I'm not taking it as seriously as I should."

That is rather doubtful.

What will he do differently in his next start?

"Try to get everybody out."

By and large, the Orioles try to help Mussina by giving him room. Don't touch him. Let him stay in his bell jar of perfectionist concentration. They bite their tongues. Don't jinx him. One more year like last year—but with thirty-five starts, no blown saves, and some run support—my Lord, how many would he win, how far would he take us? It's a dream, they know, but the pennant is always a dream. Except when it comes true.

Bosman comes back from the bullpen in St. Petersburg after catching Mussina's workout between starts.

"How was he?" asks Oates.

"He had the best stuff I've ever seen him throw," says Bosman. "He had me very uneasy just trying to catch him. His fastball explodes late and now that knuckle curve is breaking hard. I was just trying to keep the ball off me."

When the catcher's main concern is trying not to get hit, how's the batter going to get a hit?

When something seems too good to be true, it usually is.

But not always.

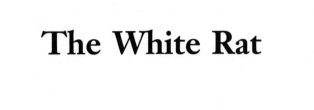

The White Rat

Our Casey

June 1990—Everybody in baseball says the same three things about Whitey Herzog: He's the best manager in baseball or else the first name mentioned on a very short list. He's the most abrasively self-confident and outspoken executive in the sport. And, whether he's in the middle of a controversy or a pennant race, he seems to have a better time than everybody else.

Once, between the fifth and sixth games of the World Series, Herzog was asked if he'd be available for interviews during the off day. No, he said. Not unless you're in a fishing boat or on a golf course.

Which would it be? Fish or play golf?

"Both," said Herzog. Fish first, then golf. Maybe 36 holes if the sun stayed up long enough.

Herzog's life is one long extra-inning game. When you need only five hours' sleep a night, when the U.S. army says you have an IQ of 140, when everything about the world fascinates you, when you're the kind of man who laid every one of the 18,000 bricks in his first home with his own hands, then you just naturally can't sleep much later than 5:30 A.M. Why sleep when being awake is such a kick? Herzog can always sit in that big, quiet house he designed himself and read until Mary Lou, his wife, wakes up.

"Mary Lou bought that game Trivial Pursuit for Christmas," says Herzog. "We got the family around. But we had to stop playing. I knew all the answers. Every damn question."

Herzog barely graduated from high school. He preferred skipping class so he could hitch rides with truckers, hang out in burlesque houses, and watch the St. Louis Browns. But Dorrel Norman Elvert Herzog—a man in search of a nickname since birth—shocks people with his knowledge. Even Mary Lou, who has known him since they were kids, was impressed by his prowess. "She was amazed," he says, grinning. "She said, 'Where'd you learn all that stuff?' I told her, 'Whaddaya think I been doing down here all these years while you've been sleepin'? I read everything.'"

"Whitey has a special place in our game, like Casey Stengel once did," says Frank Cashen, general manager of the New York Mets and Herzog's archrival. "A few of our prominent citizens can, shall we say, scratch themselves at inopportune times and get away with it. Whitey can."

And Whitey does. Herzog the manager is revolutionary enough—preaching such heresies as "Relief pitching is more important than starting pitching" and "Speed beats power." But it's Herzog the cocky, self-reliant White Rat who fascinates people most.

Nobody else seems able to survive managing. Earl Weaver, Gene Mauch, and Dick Williams, recent managers who resemble Herzog the most, have all retired—none contentedly. Cheerful Sparky Anderson ended up in a hospital with "total exhaustion." Billy Martin flamed out, too.

By contrast, Herzog, the St. Louis Cardinals manager, is in beaming health and bumptious spirits. "Talk about a man who enjoys life," says Royals public relations director Dean Vogelaar. "I've never seen anybody who can go as hard, twenty-four hours a day, as Whitey."

And talking every step of the way.

Since Weaver retired, Herzog has become baseball's annual best bet to add a quotation to *Bartlett's*. He once called the Oakland Coliseum "a graveyard with lights" and still refers to Candlestick Park as "a toilet bowl with the lid up." A hint of what he says in private after a few beers may be gleaned from what he says in public. "I'm not going to second-guess Dallas Green. All I'm going to say is that he just traded his best pitcher for a sack of garbage." He deliberately got thrown out of the seventh game of the 1985 World Series, telling umpire Don Denkinger, "We wouldn't even be here if you hadn't missed the fucking call last night."

"Whitey doesn't care whether people like what he says or not," says

Milwaukee general manager Harry Dalton, chuckling. "With him, it's 'I think it; therefore, I say it.' "

Herzog has built contenders for fifteen years with raw materials that other teams discard: mediocre pitchers who are lucky to go six innings and swift glove men who can't hit a ball to the warning track.

"You look at the Cards year after year and say, 'They're not that good.' But damn if they don't keep grinding it out for Whitey," says Cleveland general manager Hank Peters, a forty-year front office veteran who first hired Herzog for a nonplaying baseball job in 1963. "He has the confidence to evaluate and the courage to act."

Herzog's St. Louis teams hit the fewest home runs in baseball. And his starting pitching staffs have been almost pathetic. How on earth did he win three National League pennants in the '80s? Except for a couple of legendary bad breaks—Denkinger's blown call in 1985 and Jack Clark's ankle injury in 1987—he would probably have won three world titles in the past eight years.

Nobody knows exactly how Herzog got the better of the New York Mets in the '80s. They had the talent. He got the rings. No wonder Peters says, "Whitey Herzog is the best judge of talent I've ever seen."

No setback seems to outflank Herzog's capacity for personnel improvisation. That's why 1990 may be a typical Herzog season. He has lost his All-Star catcher (Tony Peña) to free agency, and his bullpen star (Todd Worrell) isn't expected back from elbow surgery until midseason. In a situation where most managers would be expected to fail, it's assumed that Herzog, until proven otherwise, will find some ridiculous way to succeed.

Herzog creates the impression that he can bully, finesse, or laugh his way through anything. On the first day of spring training this past March, after the thirty-two-day lockout, every team scrambled to work out at the earliest date. Except the Cards, who began a day later than everybody else. The three-week spring was wonderful, said Whitey, far superior to seven weeks. "Shit, we just come down here in February so the general managers can play golf."

Herzog is the only man in baseball history who has held every significant job in the game—big-league player, third-base coach ("I was the best ever"), head scout, farm director, general manager, and manager. He may know more baseball—firsthand and at more levels—than any man who has ever lived. Whether he does or not, he acts like it. One former colleague says, "He's one of my favorite people. But you just have to understand that his ego is bigger than the stadium."

"I'm not as stubborn now as I was," says Herzog. "I had a lot of Dutch in me. But when I *know* I'm right and someone disagrees with me, that's when I have a problem with him. Because when I know I'm right, I almost always *am* right."

Backing up that confidence is a commanding ballpark presence. His white burr-cut hair might as well be a rooster's comb, announcing his arrival. His hands are enormous. He also has the comfortable belly that he wants. He has had that thumbs-at-the-waist farmer hip cock mastered for years. But you need some heft, some ballast to pull off the look. Friendly, solid, but daunting.

The man has been a ham, a hot dog, a dude ever since his mother started sticking him in amateur hours to sing. He loves to play a role to the hilt, hiding behind it all the time. Check out those old '50s black-and-whites from his playing days; nobody in *Damn Yankees* dressed that sharply, not even the Devil. Although his eight-year playing career was mediocre, he could run and throw with the best and got more money than Mickey Mantle coming out of high school. Ted Williams even said that Herzog had one of the best swings he had ever seen. Too bad he couldn't hit a slow curve with a canoe paddle.

Back then, Satchel Paige nicknamed Herzog "Wild Child." Now his style is shameless middle-American gothic. That's as it should be. He has boxed the compass and returned to his origins, as few men even dream of doing. Today, he lives just forty miles from the small town of New Athens, Illinois, where he was born and raised.

"My bedroom now is bigger than the whole house I grew up in," he says, not so much proud of now, or ashamed of then, as surprised at how little difference it seems to make to him. The house is big and comfortable, with a confident, sweeping progression to the rooms, all of which are understated by jock standards. The memorabilia and awards are there, the signs of wealth and celebrity, yet the overall impression is unpretentious.

Herzog has an enormous sense of self, but not an enormous sense of self-importance. He may be a showman and a shoot-from-the-lip go-to-hell guy, but he also respects and enjoys other people. And he doesn't think baseball is the whole world.

Perhaps that's because he has seen so much of it. "My family didn't have much money. They had to scratch," says Herzog. "My mom had to be a house cleaner." Some boys have a paper route. "My route was the whole town." He didn't just work in a funeral home; he dug the graves, then drove the hearse. Whether mopping the brewery, mowing lawns, or fixing water pipes when it was ten degrees below zero, no job was too hard for him. Nothing was as bad as taking a pick into the mines, as his forebears had. New Athens had two lumberyards, a foundry, a brewery, a shoe factory, thirteen grocery stores, "and sixteen taverns, to make it all bearable," according to Herzog, who remembers his father as a good-hearted man who drank a lot, never took care of himself, and died when he was forty-eight. "I never asked my dad for a dime."

In those days, Herzog lived to play sports. And to get out of New Athens. Both of Herzog's brothers spent most of their lives in their hometown. That suited them but not Whitey. Four years after he left to play in the minors, Herzog passed through New Athens on a team bus. He told his teammates who'd be sitting where on the street, who'd be sitting on which stools in which bars.

"Every one of 'em was right where I said they'd be," recalls Herzog. "Still are, unless they're dead."

When one of Herzog's teams has a bad year—and his Cards have followed all three of their pennants with losing seasons—his response is unique in baseball. He shrugs, fishes a little more, and starts planning for next year. Why make everybody miserable?

"I really enjoy managing. In July of 1979, the Royals lost fourteen out of fifteen. Our pitching fell apart. In two weeks, I gave only two signs, because we were always behind by five or six runs so fast. The writers brought me a half gallon of Scotch with a nice note. They thanked me for not being a jerk. I could've locked the clubhouse, blown up at everybody. I didn't. I managed my ass off that year to keep us in the race until the last week."

Herzog got fired after that season. "It's no big deal. The way to make more money is to get fired. The first time I got canned [in Texas], our friends wouldn't come around, because they didn't know how to act. So Mary Lou and I threw a party."

How does Herzog get away with such a laid-back style? For one thing, he's as tough on the inside as his coal-mining and farming ancestors. He may look like a big old kindly bear these days, but nobody has forgotten the Garry Templeton incident in 1981. The shortstop, then considered a future Hall of Famer, gave the finger to the hometown fans who were booing him for jaking. Herzog grabbed him with both hands, dragged him into the dugout, and had to be pried off him by other players.

"Templeton doesn't want to play in St. Louis. He doesn't want to play on turf. He doesn't want to play when we go into Montreal. He doesn't want to play in the Astrodome. He doesn't want to play in the rain," Herzog said the day after the fight. "The other eighty games, he's all right."

Templeton was lucky that Herzog traded him to San Diego instead of Tokyo. Everybody said the Rat's anger had gotten the better of his judgment when he dealt Templeton for Ozzie Smith. Funny thing: Templeton's career withered immediately and it's Smith who'll go to the Hall of Fame. Herzog's mystique grew.

The manager has only four rules: Be on time. Bust your butt. Play smart. And have some fun while you're at it, for Chrissakes. Transgress the big four, and you'll hear about it plenty. "People say you've never had your ass chewed out until you've been chewed out by me," he says flatly. "I let 'em have it with both barrels. Then it's done. I don't have a doghouse.

"My door is always open. But a lot of guys come in thinking they're gonna tell me off and leave wishing they'd never come in."

Herzog has a way with a harsh word. Asked if Willie McGee reminded him of a young Mickey Rivers, he answered, "Yeah, except Willie doesn't play the horses, he shows up on time, and he can throw." At his first press conference in Texas—never having managed a pro team anywhere—Herzog said, "This is the worst excuse for a big-league ball club I ever saw."

On the other hand, when the players earn Herzog's respect, he reciprocates. He always arrives at the ballpark four hours early so he can post the lineup *before* his players arrive. Then they know where they stand and can prepare properly from the moment they arrive. (Sometimes, Billy Martin, when hung over, wouldn't post his lineup until *after* batting practice. His players had to guess who should hit with the regulars.)

As usual, Herzog has sensible ulterior motives for arriving so early. Casey Stengel taught him "to bullshit with the writers" every day. He got the message: They can dig up their own stories or you can write their stories for them.

Patting backs and taping ankles, Whitey fills every notebook every day and doles out off-the-record quotes and background info like a

master White House propagandist. Thus, his version of reality domi-
nates the coverage of his team as completely as any other recent manager's. Herzog is one of the few who understand that either the manager controls his team through the media or the media sense a vacuum
and gradually take control from the manager.

Herzog even invites reporters into his dugout in spring training.
What's to hide?

"You see why I let him hit," crows Herzog when one of his pitchers
hits a home run. "I had to talk that man into goin' up there." Next
time the pitcher is due up, he snaps, "Sit down. I can't stand to watch
you hit another one. It's embarrassing to my other players."

The stars he cajoles and instructs, nagging about technique. "Re-
lease that split-finger right from the ear, like a catcher. Don't reach
back." The humpty dumpties, the guys who make a living by sitting,
are his buddies. "Whitey handles role players especially well," says
Duke Wathan, now the Royals manager but a role player for Herzog
in the '70s. "He keeps making small talk, finding out about your family, doing his Casey Stengel imitations, making sure you understand
how he plans to use you and where you fit. He's very honest. He never
sugar-coats to pacify a guy."

Once, Herzog shocked a scrub, Tito Landrum, by walking up to
him in mid-game and apologizing for not having him in the lineup.
"The last time we faced this [pitcher], you hit the ball hard three out
of four times up," Herzog explained.

"That was two years before," said Landrum. "Even *I* didn't remember."

Herzog, like Earl Weaver in his day, can stay with one team indefinitely, because every clubhouse grievance is aired and then usually
forgotten. Very few managers have been smart enough or glib enough
to flourish in such an atmosphere of candor. It works only as long as
the manager, in a pinch, has the personality to intimidate any of his
players.

Also like Weaver, Herzog has little fear of eccentrics or hard-to-
manage players. Herzog didn't care if Amos Otis wouldn't talk or Hal
McRae dressed like a third world insurgent. He traded for Darrell
Porter *after* his cocaine problems became public and won a world title
with him as series MVP. Herzog's tolerance finally snapped when he
discovered that he had about seven heavy cocaine users. Even then, he
didn't get rid of them all and didn't trade Keith Hernandez and Lonnie Smith until he was convinced their play was being hurt.

In trades, he sought out Joaquin Andujar, Jack Clark, and Pedro Guerrero, supposedly the head-case trifecta. To Herzog, they were invigorating. What better way to spend an off day than to have a star player slam on the brakes, pull into a Porsche dealership, point to a $92,000 item, and say, "I'll take two of those. One for me. One for my wife."

"That guy had at least ten cars. Couldn't get out of his own driveway," says Herzog. "He went broke. But a great guy."

Only direct, no-bullshit dealings appeal to Herzog. He once proposed a trade to Harry Dalton by saying, "How'd you like to win the pennant this year?" When they finished swapping players, both the Cards and the Brewers were so vastly improved that they met each other in the next World Series.

"Whitey's one of the few guys who know how to make a trade," says Frank Cashen. "He's very frank, not trying to be sinister like some [executives] who think they're in the CIA. You ask Whitey, he tells you. And you can believe what he says, including what he says about his own players. He's a bright, inventive guy who doesn't waste time beating around the bush."

Perhaps the nickname White Rat—given to Herzog in the '50s because he resembled a former player with the same moniker—is unintentionally appropriate. Perhaps it is synonymous, in a baseball sense, with benevolent dictator. In other words, a rat, yes, but a *white* rat. Sharp teeth and a mean bite? Sure. But this rat, who never pretends to be anything else, is one you laugh with when he steals the cheese—even when he steals it from you.

Put it all together and you have the Autocrat of AstroTurf—the man who may be the prototype of a twenty-first century manager. Herzog's success has been predicated on a central guiding idea of a new way to build a modern team. The '80s Cardinals were a concept with several parts—none of them entirely new, all of them the culmination of trends that had been building since the '60s. First came the notion that speed and raw athletic ability are preferred at every position over any other virtue, even at the expense of power or baseball savvy. Herzog didn't invent the bunt, the steal, the hit and run, or taking the extra base at every chance. Ty Cobb did all of that. Also, Herzog didn't conceive the all-out running attack, with six or seven thieves who steal at any time. Chuck Tanner did that in Oakland in

1976. And the Dodgers had five switch hitters in one lineup long before Herzog put six slap-hitting switchers in the same batting order.

But Herzog put it into one formula: the Runnin' Redbirds—a team that could lead the major leagues in scoring while being dead last in home runs. He realized that players who aim at the middle to top of the ball, instead of at the middle to bottom like power hitters, have the advantage of turning modern pitching theory on its head. "Keep the ball low" is an adage that has been chiseled in stone since the home run age began. However, a knee-high strike only fuels the Cards' game.

Herzog also realized how team speed in a big park can turn a mediocre starting pitching staff into a good one. His starters allow lots of hits but few walks or home runs. They may not strike out many hitters or pitch complete games, but they get lots of double-play grounders.

Herzog claims only one true radical idea as his own: "Start with the closer. Build your bullpen first, then worry about your rotation. . . . I was the first to look at it that way. My job is to put us in a position to win come nut-cuttin' time."

The old sport of baseball is so afraid of new ideas that few teams have followed any of Herzog's principles. One, however, did—the hopelessly desperate Baltimore Orioles, after they lost 107 games in 1988. "No question about it. I'm a great admirer of Whitey," says O's GM Roland Hemond, who put his fastest and best defensive players at every position, sacrificed power, and put the franchise's best young arm (Gregg Olson) in the bullpen, not in the rotation. The Orioles broke the major league record for fielding percentage. Great defense rekindled team morale. Hapless pitchers suddenly became mysteriously decent. Olson was Rookie of the Year. And the Orioles showed the third greatest one-season improvement in the history of baseball (32½ games).

When a manager has such a looming personality, when he is the public focus of the franchise, it tends to diminish the stature of the team's potential charismatic leaders. In crises, the top dog is in the dugout, not on the field. That can be a slight disadvantage in a playoff or in the Series and may be part of the reason that Weaver and Herzog each have only one world title to their credit. Sparky Anderson and Tommy Lasorda may not be as tactically acute, and their teams do not exceed expectations as consistently. But Anderson and

Lasorda teams are not psychologically dominated by good old Sparky and Tommy.

If Herzog has a weakness as a manager, it is that his moods become his players' moods and his fears become theirs, too: Call it the Gene Mauch Syndrome. Last season and right into last winter, he seemed fixated on his club's inability to sign either Bruce Hurst or Mike Moore as a free agent in the 1988–89 off-season. As the '90s begin, Herzog has his doubts and, as with everything, does not bother to hide them. True, he was hailed for extracting 86 wins from the Cards last season and keeping them in the pennant race until Labor Day, when injuries to relief ace Todd Worrell and centerfielder Willie Mc-Gee caught the team right at the kneecaps.

Still, Herzog has big-picture worries about the shape of his team. The Cards overall speed isn't what it used to be. "The league is catching up with us. Defense against the running game is better," he says. "Our club doesn't manufacture runs like it used to." Will the Cards be shuffled again?

The White Rat will think of something. He always has. And even if he doesn't, so what? He's already a man who has left more than a mark on his game; he has left a truly personal signature. "I'll retire when it's not fun anymore. Right now, I couldn't be happier. If I get fired here, that'll be the end of it, anyway."

All fates await Herzog with equal promise. He has made his life the way he made that first house—one brick at a time. And that is why it is so solid. He is almost entirely self-created.

When, in his autobiography, *White Rat*, Herzog writes about his own children—smart, educated, normal—he winces, because they remind him of kids in general. "I think we had it better then," he writes of a time when he had nothing. "For kids today, everything is organized. Everybody tells them where to be, what to do.

"One time, we built an airplane on the roof of the shed behind my cousin's house. We modeled it after one of those balsawood jobs with the rubber-band motor, only we used an inner tube from a truck tire as a motor. We wound that sucker up, and I jumped in and hollered to let it go. Went right off the shed and landed on my head. I was lucky I didn't break every bone in my body."

Herzog has been making crazy airplanes ever since, making them his own way, flying them himself as he damn well pleases, and never worrying whether he lands on his head. He takes the chance, he takes the ride, he takes the credit, and he has the laughs.

For all of that, Herzog has never maintained that his dream occupation is baseball manager. "Perfect job?" he says. "Ski instructor." His only avowed goal on snow is to go in a straight line as fast as possible.

Maybe.

Or maybe Whitey Herzog just wants to see if he can break every bone in his body.

The Hell with It

July 8, 1990—They say you can't fire the whole team, so you have to fire the manager. Nobody told Whitey Herzog.

On Friday he fired his team.

Technically, Herzog resigned. But it amounted to the same thing.

The White Rat got sick and tired of watching the St. Louis Cardinals play baseball in a way that offended his sensibilities and injured his enormous pride, so he quit—with a flourish of dignified self-recrimination worthy of a disgraced British prime minister.

"I'm totally embarrassed by the way we've played. We've underachieved. I just can't get the team to play," said Herzog. "Anybody can do a better job than me. . . . I am the manager and I take full responsibility."

Translation: They quit on me. Now I'm quitting on them. Get me a new team.

The White Rat shouldn't receive more than about fifty offers—twenty-five as general manager and twenty-five as manager. Some teams will offer him both jobs, a pay raise, and team stock.

Whitey Herzog, even with his team in last place, is the most respected mind in baseball. What Earl Weaver was, Herzog is. Honest, funny, tough, smart, just mean enough, and with a cat-o'-nine-tails for a tongue. "They say you've never had your butt chewed out until you've been chewed out by me," he has said.

That Herzog would fire his entire club will probably only reinforce the general high opinion of his judgment. Herzog stuck with his team for a more than honorable period as it gradually eroded, due to age and tight purse strings. As the Cardinals were losing Jack Clark and Tony Peña to free agency, Herzog begged for replacements. He even asked for the right guys—Mike Moore or Bruce Hurst before the '89 season. He got nada. So he won only 86 instead of, maybe, stealing another division pennant.

This year, with Peña gone, Todd Worrell out for the year, Ozzie Smith showing age, and others showing signs of complacency and me-firstism, Herzog brought back John Tudor from the bone-yard and traded one of his gamers, Tom Brunansky, for large Lee Smith.

Desperation.

Helped by a little bad luck, the face-lift failed spectacularly: last place.

Herzog built the Runnin' Redbirds of the '80s, who won three pennants. And he stuck around to watch them lose their morale and start to bicker. Why should he hang around for the last act, like Weaver with the '87 Orioles and Sparky Anderson with the '89 Tigers?

"You didn't want to go through five more years of this aggravation?" Herzog was asked in a phone interview Friday.

"That's part of it," he said. "I just didn't think it looked like it was going to get any better."

"Will you answer the phone if other teams call?"

"I do answer," said Herzog.

"Are you tied to the Cards if you got an offer you wanted?"

"No," said Herzog. "Anything like that you want to write is okay."

Whitey's not in a hurry. He's not even sure he's coming back. But he's definitely the prize free agent of '90.

Could Herzog, at fifty-eight, stay out of the game permanently?

Probably not.

Baseball needs Herzog far more than he needs it. Who else claims his ideal job is "ski instructor."

For years, Herzog has been perhaps the only manager or coach in pro sports who could say, "I manage because it's fun," and make you believe it. And he always swore that when it wasn't fun anymore, he'd dead-flat quit and head to his bass boat and the ski slopes.

Herzog had only four rules. Be on time. Bust your butt. Play smart. And have some laughs while you're at it.

The Cardinals broke the rules.

So Whitey canned 'em.

Good for him.

May he get the team of his dreams. Or a job in Vail.

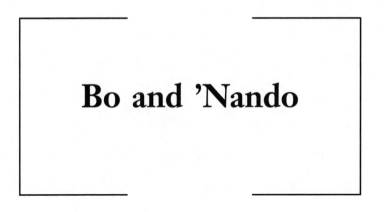

Bo and 'Nando

What Bo Knows

DEVIL'S BARGAIN

March 19, 1991—Until he arrived, no man in American athletics had ever played both of his nation's most popular sports so well. He broke ground that had barely been trod before he arrived. The whole country asked one question. Was he better as a consensus All-America halfback or as a slugging American League outfielder?

Then, at the peak of his powers, his career came to a sad and sudden end. One day, he was a big-league Most Valuable Player. Then, seemingly overnight, he was forced to retire. He ended up running a Christmas tree farm and baseball camp in Charlottesville. By fifty-five, he was dead.

Bo Jackson's luck, terrible at the moment, will have to get a lot worse before his career becomes as pitiable as that of Jackie Jensen.

The only time Jensen wasn't running for long touchdowns for California in the late '40s was when he was passing for long touchdowns. The coach of the San Francisco 49ers said: "Jensen blocks like Molotov, runs like Truman, and passes like Manville." To this day, Jensen is the only man who was All-American in football and MVP in the majors. For the Red Sox, he had 667 RBI in a six-year period.

Then, in a rush, his golden life fell apart. Jensen's marriage to ten-time national springboard diving champion Zoe Ann Olsen broke up. Next, an incurable fear of flying forced him to quit baseball in 1961 at the age of thirty-four. From there, it was downhill.

It's not time to say, "Bo knows tragedy." However, if any athlete needs our best wishes right now, it's the only man in history to be an All-Pro in the NFL and an All-Star in the major leagues.

Yesterday, in a shocking announcement, the Kansas City Royals released Jackson. Between now and Friday, any team can have him for $1.

So, do you think Bo Jackson has avascular necrosis of the hip or not?

In recent days, the sports media have been buzzing with rumors that Jackson has this rare and probably career-ending condition in his right hip. Jackson says he doesn't. His personal doctor agrees and adds that "there has been no collapse of the hip." Even the Royals aren't claiming they have a medical name for the injury—originally diagnosed as a dislocated hip—which Jackson suffered in an NFL playoff game January 13 against Cincinnati.

No, the Royals are saying something much worse. They're saying that they don't think Jackson's athletic future at age twenty-eight is worth $1.

Remember, the Royals have in the last two years spent tens of millions of dollars on free agents such as Mark Davis, Storm Davis, Kirk Gibson, and Mike Boddicker. Yet they won't risk a one-year, $2.38 million deal to keep Jackson around and see if he heals by next spring. Doesn't that tell you how certain the Royals are about Jackson's future?

"Don't count me out," says Jackson.

Nobody who has seen him run 92 yards from scrimmage or hit a Nolan Ryan pitch 461 feet would dream of it.

Yet, at the moment, the sports world feels a chill. Did Jackson fly too close to the sun? Should he have followed the Royals' advice—the Royals' pleading, really—that he play only baseball? Was it an act of heroism or hubris for Jackson to sign with the Los Angeles Raiders, then refer to his NFL career as "a hobby."

When Jackson was first injured, should he have taken his condition more seriously? A Raiders doctor has been quoted as saying that Jackson was supposed to stay on crutches. Yet, one week later, Jackson was on national TV on the Raiders sideline, walking without crutches. Did he aggravate his injury?

Jackson's injury has come at a moment when he is both at the peak of his fame and yet has not accomplished much of lasting substance in either sport. He has done amazing individual deeds and has had isolated games as memorable as almost any other player's in either sport. Yet his contributions have been lightning flashes, not sustained performances.

In baseball, Jackson has had hot streaks, but never a full, healthy season. The only thing he has ever led the league in is strikeouts; in four seasons, he drove in more than 78 runs only once. In his sport of choice, Jackson was as consistently amazing as he was amazingly inconsistent.

Perhaps the perfect Jackson moment came last July when, in Yankee Stadium, he hit three consecutive home runs—then disabled himself for five weeks while trying to make a diving catch. As always, he annoyed teammates by waiting until he was completely healthy before returning. But when he did, he made news—hitting a home run in his first at-bat to tie the major league record for most consecutive home runs (four).

Dazzling streaks, comatose slumps, more strikeouts per at-bat than any player in history (638 in 1,837) and a .250 career average. That is Jackson's baseball legacy at the moment.

In the NFL, he was the only man to have two runs from scrimmage of more than 90 yards. He gained 2,782 yards in 515 carries as a part-time player for a magnificent 5.4 yards per carry average. Yet he never led the Raiders anywhere. Sometimes, he couldn't even keep Marcus Allen from taking his job.

Bo Jackson made a choice. Some would say a devil's bargain. He wanted to create a superhuman persona; he wanted to be the only man in America who could star in two major professional sports at once. And make it look easy. His uniqueness brought him incredible fame—probably disproportionate to his deeds. In salary, and in worldwide visibility through his Nike commercials and his autobiography, he hit the jackpot too.

Now we will find out if he also has to pay a huge price for his enormous prize—a price in pain, disappointment, and unlived potential. Bo Jackson, the most celebrated athlete in America, has, in one day, become perhaps the most pitied as well.

SUI GENERIS

March 12, 1992—Would Herb Score have won 300 games? Would Tony Conigliaro have hit 500 home runs? Would Ernie Davis have approached Jim Brown's achievements? Would Len Bias have extended the Celtics dynasty?

Those all are plausible questions.

What is the comparable lingering question that fans will ask about Bo?

Assuming Bo Jackson's future includes both a hip replacement and no more pro sports, what has the finest two-sport athlete of this generation left undone?

The answer may be: Not very much.

Bo did what Bo knew how to do and he did it spectacularly—for about as long as could be expected of a player who was injury-prone in two sports.

Let's not get this wrong—Jackson isn't lucky in any sense. When you have avascular necrosis at age twenty-nine, that's nothing but a rotten break, no matter how rich and famous you are.

However, Jackson's fans are probably, in some sense, fortunate. They got to enjoy the best of their man, something we can't say about most other superb stars whose careers ended too soon.

Bo wasn't a Career Achievement kind of guy. He was a Best Picture type. If he were a director, he'd be Orson Welles shooting *Citizen Kane* right out of the box, then perhaps never matching it.

Not a line of stats or a row of championship banners. Bo will never be in anybody's Hall of Fame, unless Madison Avenue has one. He was more a film clip phenom—the ultimate "let's go to the videotape" creation.

Bo Jackson once ran halfway up an outfield wall. After a pretty good catch. Nothing special. What made the play an international hit was that Bo nonchalantly defied gravity by jogging vertically until he was horizontal. Then he came back to earth casually, never losing his balance or his hat. He used the wall like a drag racer uses a parachute. Just be glad he didn't decide to run through the wall.

Then again, if he had, it would have been pure Bo. "Jackson Runs Through Wall (and Goes One-for-Four with Two Strikeouts)."

Nobody ever got more mileage out of two long touchdown runs—neither significant in NFL history—than Bo. "Most runs of 90 or more yards from scrimmage: two." That's Bo's big record in pro football. Two plays. But you've seen Bo turn left end and hit the jets up that sideline—turning the five-yard stripes into blurs—so many times that you can practically re-create the Raiders' blocking scheme in your mind's eye.

When Bo knocked over somebody (not his specialty), he didn't just hit him. He knocked Brian Bosworth mohawk over teakettle on national TV and exploded the image of the Boz in a split second.

In Kansas City, they still show you where Bo's titanic home runs landed, even though he had only 112. He even hit 'em into the water fountains—to the opposite field. With Bo, there was always a twist. Not just into the fountains. But in the "wrong" direction. What if he'd ever gotten all of one? He said he never quite did.

Baseball folks can show you the warning track where Bo heaved a ball that put a runner out at the plate. He stood right there. You never saw a throw like that in your life. So what if the only category in which Bo ever led the league's leftfielders was errors?

As long as there's baseball, fans will talk about Bo, walking back to the dugout after a strikeout, putting the bat over the top of his helmet, and snapping it in two. With ease. After that, who was surprised when he broke a bat in two just checking his swing?

Funny, Jackson struck out more frequently than all but one other player in history. The new breed of stat freak has even determined that he hit the ball on the lowest percentage of swings of anybody. But, in the TV age, who cares? People have always wanted to break a bat over somebody else's head after a strikeout, but who else would do it to himself?

Even the best athletes generally lost all self-control when describing Bo. Because he was the rarest of all locker room types—the guy who could do something nobody else could imagine.

"God doesn't make athletes like that anymore," gushed White Sox Carlton Fisk after Jackson's sad announcement on Tuesday that he had probably played his last major league game. "He never did before. Probably never will again."

Jackson was the ultimate spectacular one-shot artist. And, luckily, he got to take his shots. At the ages when most baseball players have their best seasons—twenty-five, twenty-six, and twenty-seven—Jackson was playing major league ball. His 32-homer, 105-RBI, All-Star Game MVP year in 1989 was worthy of being called his personal "best." Although the rest would probably not have been too shabby.

Jackson's career wasn't meant to be an arc. It was a rocket blast. Straight up and, perhaps inevitably, straight back down. He wasn't built to last. Even in baseball, the soft game, Jackson was hurt every year. In his four full seasons, he missed 162 games. A tumbling catch on grass disabled Jackson for a month. Of course, he came back and hit a homer in his first at bat.

Maybe Jackson knew himself—and his limits—better than the rest of us. Maybe five years of total stardom was the role that suited him best. Who says he'd have had a long career in either sport? And who can say that he would have been truly great—rather than simply breathtaking—in either sport, even if he'd focused on it entirely?

Go ahead and feel sorry for Jackson the man, because of all the pain in his hip. And hope that the doctors can, as they say, fix it for practical everyday purposes with a hip replacement.

However, for Bo the athlete and Bo the public figure, don't shed too many tears. Some, yes. But not the whole bucket. He made more money per RBI and TD than any man who ever lived. He got as much worship as his huge athletic ego could want and more than the modest private side of his nature enjoyed.

What's saddest for Jackson is that he really loved playing games. He always wanted to do something special, find a moment that suited him and fly to the moon—with everybody else on board.

That's the part of Jackson that still dreams. "Realistically, [Monday] could've been my last at-bat in the major leagues. I know that," he said. "[But] if there's going to be someone to come back and perform on the professional level after a hip replacement, it'll be me."

Regardless, we'll always be able to remember Jackson at his peak—snapping bats, going deep, pounding the Boz, breaking the long one, and smiling with utter self-confidence into our living rooms.

This was not an athlete whom nature intended to grow old slowly, losing a bit of his raw majesty each year. That wouldn't have been Bo Jackson. Sad as it seems, we must now hope that Bo knows one last thing—when to go.

MIRACLE, MAN

BALTIMORE, April 21, 1993—No athlete ever has been such a wonderful shell of himself as Bo Jackson.

When you play major league baseball one year after getting an artificial hip, you don't have to resemble your old, legendary self very much to discover that you have suddenly become a new and equally legendary self.

Of course, it doesn't hurt that legend if you hit a home run in your first at bat back in the major leagues. But then that's Bo. He lives to amaze.

"I never doubted that the [rehabilitation] work was worth it and I never doubted myself. Where there's a will there's a way," said Jackson Tuesday night, sitting in the Camden Yards visitors' dugout. "Who originated the word 'expert'? I wouldn't judge someone else until I had walked in their shoes."

Someday, it will take a lot of words to explain why a man with a .249 career batting average and less than 2,600 yards rushing in the NFL could have been the most famous athlete in America for several years. By then, Deion Sanders, and who knows who else, may have made the concept of a two-sport pro athlete seem almost plausible.

But what Jackson is doing now will never require much explanation. No matter what medical marvels become commonplace in the next century, people will always intuitively grasp the willpower, self-confidence, and audacity needed to play in the big leagues with a prosthesis. It's one thing to hit or throw a ball a little farther than other people can. It's another thing entirely to do something much of the medical community says is impossible.

Of all American athletes in his generation, perhaps Jackson had the ideal background for doing the nearly unthinkable. He'd had a lot of practice. Once, when Jackson came to this city, he caught a fly ball on a dead sprint in Memorial Stadium and ran halfway up the leftfield wall. He kept going vertically until he was horizontal. Then, without so much as a nod to gravity, he cruised back down the wall.

"Does it surprise me that he's come back? Him, no. Nothing he does surprises me, not since I saw him run up the wall," said Orioles manager Johnny Oates. "That can't be done. I know because I went out and tried it a few days later. That was embarrassing."

Jackson never gave much thought to such deeds. He just did them. If he got mad after a strikeout and felt like snapping his bat, he put the miserable two-pound twig over the top of his helmet and cracked it in half. People gasped. Yet, at such times, Bo always acted as if he hadn't done anything special. When he hit a 430-foot home run to lead off the 1989 All-Star Game, he said his big thrill of the night was watching a squadron of F4s fly over the park.

These days, Bo Jackson isn't much of a ballplayer. At least not compared with Bo Jackson. But he is a ballplayer. And that alone makes him just as much an object of awe among his fellow pros as any of his former feats. Frankly, Jackson is glorying in these comeback days—gloating, really. Why not let him?

As recently as two months ago, you couldn't unearth a baseball insider who thought Jackson would make the White Sox roster. He walked with a slight limp. He'd lost his speed. He had trouble opening his hips to pull the ball. Nobody knew if he could slide into bases or make outs in the outfield without reinjuring himself.

All this came on the heels of two years of nagging from doctors and pundits telling Jackson he'd be wise to give up his arduous athletic life and accept his fate. Avascular necrosis and a hip prosthesis mean The End.

Jackson, however, is a spectacularly stubborn Alabaman. He hates to be told—anything. All the anger that he felt at his freak NFL-injury-gone-wrong was funneled into his rehabilitation.

"It might be amazing to some people but not to me. I don't sit here thinking about it," said Jackson, who must give a mass interview in every city the White Sox visit, even though he is now a platoon out-fielder who will bat only about 250 times this season. "I knew [I'd be back] after the surgery. . . . I knew when I ran around the house playing with my kids."

That form of bravado is only half of Jackson's story. The other half is, well, it's bravado too. Ask Jackson how hard he worked to get back and, basically, he says Samson couldn't have done more.

"It was twenty-four hours a day. There was a certain way to walk, a certain way to sleep, shower, get in a car," he said. "If there was rain or snow, I couldn't go outside. . . . How hard was it? If you combined all the years I played sports—twenty-three years into one year—that's how hard."

The last nag gnawing at Jackson was that he risked serious injury if he tried to perform like a normal baseball player—with a certain element of sane recklessness. "I can slide left, right, on my stomach."

When did the doctor give him that green light?

"It wasn't left up to the doc."

Bo Jackson is living life his way. If there's an ugly episode down the road—and nobody denies there could be—Jackson says the game is worth it.

Perhaps that is the part of Bo that few knew. Beyond the awards, the records, the millions, and the worldwide commercials, Bo just loved to play games. Why two sports all year round? More games. More challenges. More fun.

Some are mystified that Jackson can accept his new stature so easily —that's to say, not very much stature at all. Since his dramatic first-at-bat homer, he's gone 4 for 13 with no RBI. Even though starting leftfielder Tim Raines is out until Memorial Day, Jackson plays only against left-handers. For now, his role is not likely to expand beyond platoon and pinch-hit play.

It's a new self-deprecating Bo who meets the baseball world these days. He wears it well. Jackson is thirty and seems to want to be closer to people—less a national figure and more a likable man. "I'll never be as fast as I once was," he said Tuesday night. "But I guarantee I can outrun anyone here with a microphone."

In a sense, Jackson can see the end of the long tunnel of fame and pressure that he's been in since he went to Auburn to win the Heisman Trophy. He has to visit thirteen American League cities this season. In each, he'll have his dugout comeback media circus. Then he'll be free. Finally, he'll be just another ballplayer, unburdened by great expectations and armed with an ironclad excuse for any conceivable failure.

"I've reached the goal I set," said Jackson, the superstar who now is ecstatic to be one step up from a scrub. "It's kind of fun this way. Let somebody else be in the limelight for a while."

That way, Bo can do what he probably loved best all along. Just play.

Won't Fade Away

VALENZUELA SYNDROME

May 20, 1989—Sometimes, we don't even get to say goodbye. Looks like it's going to be that way with Fernando Valenzuela. At twenty-eight, the best southpaw of the decade appears washed up. Last year, he was 5–8 and missed the World Series with shoulder pain. This season, he's winless and reduced to junkballing. The Los Angeles Dodgers have all but ruined him. They didn't mean it. They just didn't know then what everybody's learning now: The faster you rise, the faster you fall.

By contrast, how much phase-in are the Angels giving Jim Abbott? Not a day. That's about how much the Mets gave Dwight Gooden and the Royals allowed Bret Saberhagen, and they're both showing signs of wear already. Before the Angels get too excited about Abbott's first career shutout this week, they should consider the long-term cost of denying him a year to experiment in the minors plus a sub-225-inning season in the majors to let his arm mature completely.

Are you paying attention, Orioles? After you draft Ben McDonald, all 6 feet 7 inches of him from LSU next month, don't rush him to the majors at twenty-one. He'd probably be good right away because, like Abbott, he's precocious and poised. But if you'll just put him on the slow track for two years, he could be great for a long time.

Valenzuela should be a lesson for a whole generation. He pitched eight shutouts at the age of twenty, including five in his first seven major league starts, and took L.A. to a world title in '81. But now it looks as though he's over the hill—ten years too soon.

Even rivals feel pity when they see Valenzuela, who's allowed 60 runners in 35 innings and has an 0–3 mark and an ERA of almost 5.00. "His fastball was just floating up there," said Kevin Mitchell of San Francisco. "The guys were coming back to the bench saying they couldn't believe they couldn't hit him," said Pete Rose after a good Valenzuela game.

How slow is Fernando? When utility man Mickey Hatcher pitched in a Dodgers blowout recently, the radar gun clocked him at 82 mph —the same speed as Valenzuela, who sometimes can't get to 80. This is the man whose fastball once set up 1,448 strikeouts in seven years.

The Dodgers have tried to excuse themselves from guilt. They blame the screwball, although Valenzuela calls that the dumbest of theories, claiming his scroogie is easier on his arm than his curve. They blame Valenzuela's stretched anterior capsule on those 255 straight starts at the beginning of his durable career. Finally, the Dodgers hint that the culprit is Fernando's tummy. They make much of his winter workouts—with 10-pound weights.

"I really thought my career might be finished," said Valenzuela in spring training. "I was ready to say that I was lucky to pitch eight seasons in the majors, smile, and call it quits." Now, however, he buys the fitness spiel and says he feels great, although "I know it will take a long time to come back."

Perhaps the saddest part of the story is that Valenzuela still thinks all this was virtually inevitable. "It would have happened anyway," he told Steve Dilbeck of the *San Bernardino Sun*. "It was a lot of years. I pitched a lot of games. And it's not the innings, but how many pitches. I know why it happened—I threw a lot."

That's both exactly true and terribly misleading, according to statistician Craig Wright and Rangers pitching coach Tom House, who have coauthored a book called *The Diamond Appraised*. Their work includes a study of the endurance patterns of pitchers since '76.

That's 1876.

Their conclusion is that innings worked before the age of twenty-five (especially tough, late-game innings) burn up a pitcher's career at double or triple speed. Almost without exception, those like Vida Blue, who were workhorses before twenty-five, suffered truncated careers that produced little after age thirty. Burned-out pitchers such as

Frank Tanana, who become reborn as junksters, are as rare as they are courageous.

As usual, some wise men guessed long ago what Wright and House now seem to have proved. Earl Weaver preached this doctrine twenty years ago. His rule of thumb was that a young pitcher should stay in the minors an extra year. Then, use the prospect as a long reliever or spot starter in a low-pressure rookie season. Finally, once he's in the rotation, protect him from excess complete games for a season. That's a three-year phase-in. Two examples of maximized careers: Mike Flanagan and Dennis Martinez, who were decelerated for two seasons each and are still winning at ages thirty-seven and thirty-four. If Storm Davis, 16–7 at age twenty-six, has a dozen more useful years, he'll be another sample of a Weaverized pitcher.

Being a superstar at age twenty-two or younger seems to be the real killer. Twenty-four complete games at twenty-one erased Mark (the Bird) Fidrych. If you can just stay in college or the minors long enough to avoid a monster 250-inning season until you're a little older —such as Jim Palmer (twenty-four), Don Sutton (twenty-four), Steve Carlton (twenty-five), Nolan Ryan (twenty-five), Tommy John, (twenty-seven) or Gaylord Perry (twenty-seven)—you have a far better chance to win 250 games. To survive tons of innings before twenty-five, you better have perfect mechanics and the incredible lower-body strength of a Tom Seaver. How Bert Blyleven survived is still a mystery.

Among current pitchers, Greg Swindell of Cleveland may have been brought along most smoothly. Abbott and McDonald should move no faster. Also, by the luck of being a late bloomer, Orel Hershiser, thirty, may pitch until 2001.

In sports, it's sad when knowledge comes too late. That's the case for Valenzuela, who looks to the sky on every pitch but probably won't find succor. However, it's not too late to preserve the next generation of pitchers. Young phenoms don't come along very often. Luckily for them. When we see an Abbott or McDonald who's in imminent danger of being too good too soon, we now know what to do: Tell 'em to remember Fernando's fadeaway.

SO CLOSE

ST. PETERSBURG, Florida, March 13, 1993—Every morning, Fernando Valenzuela gets up late and has breakfast in the Hilton Hotel coffee shop about 10 A.M. He sits alone, modestly dressed and dignified, always wearing sunglasses and carrying a purse. Being a superstar celebrity in L.A. for a dozen years is bound to leave some mark.

The once great pitcher and the red-haired, pregnant waitress always discuss whether he would like his ham and mushroom omelette with American, Monterey Jack, Swiss, or Gruyère cheese. Fernando, a perfect gentleman who speaks nearly perfect English, usually prefers Swiss. If anybody recognizes the medium-size fellow with the comfortable double chin and tummy, you'd never know it. Most days, nobody says a word to him. One day, one man, without breaking stride or making eye contact, said, "Good luck, Fernando."

"Thank you," said the man who, for ten years a prisoner of room service, would have had to sign a hundred autographs if he dared to eat a meal in public.

In the big, airy gazebo breakfast room, Valenzuela dines slowly, thinking but not reading, his table bathed in the morning sun. He looks out the window a great deal. About 100 yards from his seat is the pitcher's mound at Al Lang Field, spring training home of the Baltimore Orioles.

Fernando is this close, so close, to being back where he belongs.

On Thursday night, Valenzuela walked up the mound once more in a major league uniform, pitching for the Orioles for the first time. He hadn't shaved since breakfast and his stubble beard made him look older than thirty-two.

Of course, some never believed his age anyway. When he broke in with the Dodgers in 1981 at nineteen years of age, he made veteran hitters look like fools. So everybody joked that the kid owned a phony birth certificate.

If only Valenzuela had really been three or four years older, maybe the Dodgers wouldn't have incinerated his career and left the best of him in the past before he ever reached his twenty-fifth birthday. But he was so good, so legendary, so unbelievable, that they could not keep from abusing him with overuse. And Fernando was too polite, too dedicated, too in love with the game to say, "No."

Maybe you don't remember, but once upon a time, Fernando Valenzuela was baseball. For an entire season, the game revolved around him, and him alone. Nobody today approaches the mythic stature that he had in 1981. These days, baseball has nothing half so rare as Fernandomania was then.

At the age of twenty, Valenzuela was the Dodgers' last-minute Opening Day starter and pitched a shutout. He then won his first eight starts, seven with complete games, and had an ERA of 0.50. Some wondered if he would be the best pitcher who ever lived. His 90-mph fastball sawed off bats in right-handed hitters' hands. His screwball was far better—almost unhittable. His big-time curveball paralyzed left-handed hitters. His control, his craftiness, his eyes-to-the-sky windup, and his spooky poise unnerved older players. He was chubby as a dinner roll, yet he could field, hit, hit home runs, bunt, and, basically, do everything. Except explain himself.

Which made him all the more wonderful. He was a miniature, in-fant Ruth.

That year, Fernando started the All-Star Game. He was Rookie of the Year. He won the Cy Young Award. He was the hero of the post-season. His Dodgers beat the Yankees and were world champions. In a strike-shortened season, he tied the rookie record for shutouts with eight. He was the best player in baseball.

You tend to forget.

Because the innings wore him out. About 275 of them per year. Before he was twenty-six, he'd won 99 games. Then he hit the wall. Now there's a name for it. Fernando Syndrome. Because of the way he crashed and burned—14–14, 5–8, 10–13, 13–13, 0–2, and, finally, Out of the Majors in 1992—people began to study the record books. For every inning you pitch—over 250 per season—before you are twenty-five, you shorten your career radically. Great. Now we know.

Every young pitcher for generations can thank Fernando Valenzuela.

But what about the real Fernando?

As he took that mound on Thursday, he was surrounded by the lowest expectations. Many assumed the Orioles had signed him only to cover their PR fannies because the organization was under fire from Mexican rights groups that were outraged over racist comments made earlier this month by an Orioles scout. Valenzuela's fastball had been so unimpressive in early workouts that some Orioles, though wishing him well, found him a comic figure.

On his first pitch, Valenzuela announced himself. Chris Hoiles's mitt cracked and the radar gun said 83 mph. Not very good. But not bad either.

Valenzuela battled through two melodramatic innings. After a lead-off hit, he struck out Derek Bell on a screwball and jammed Joe Carter into a double play. In the second inning, a single, a double that barely missed being a home run, and a hit loaded the bases with no outs. "He was almost down to his last pitch," said manager Johnny Oates when the count on Pat Borders was 3–0.

If Valenzuela comes back and wins 10 games for the Orioles this year, folks will talk about what happened next for quite a while. If his arm doesn't bounce back, if he gets shelled the rest of March, it'll be forgotten.

Fastball, strike. Cut fastball, checked swing, strike. Screwball below the knees, strike three swinging. Then, a jamming fastball, another double play.

That's pitching.

That, also, is only two shutout innings and just 38 pitches.

"My arm feels good. . . . It's really hard to believe I'm back," said Valenzuela. "I try not to put too much pressure on myself. . . . But I was nervous."

When were you last nervous on a mound?

"Probably the 1981 World Series. . . .

"Last year, when nobody called me [to try out for a major league team], I started thinking. But I figured, 'They probably don't know how [good] my arm feels.' So I pitched in the Mexican League." There he went 17–13, then followed that with an even stronger showing in winter ball.

"He's a good story," beamed Orioles GM Roland Hemond. "He had a better fastball than I was told," said Oates. "Can his arm bounce back?" asked pitching coach Dick Bosman. "There are still a lot of questions."

If Fernando Valenzuela should read this story, sitting by the window at breakfast, perhaps he will hold in mind these words from his catcher, Hoiles: "I heard all the reports about him being washed up and his time being in the past. Well, he had some giddy-up on his fastball. And he had a good cut fastball. That's a real good screwball. He impressed me. I think he has at least one year left in him, if not more."

Maybe, someday, Fernando Valenzuela's face will be so familiar again that he'll have to go back to ordering room service.

BACK IN THE SUN

TORONTO, July 27, 1993—When John Olerud came to bat against Fernando Valenzuela here in SkyDome on Wednesday night, you needed a cup of coffee to make sure you were sober. What have we got here, a split-screen hallucination? The scoreboard said that Olerud, playing in his 100th game of the season, was batting .403 and that Valenzuela had allowed three runs in his last five starts—a 0.65 ERA. Wasn't that Valenzuela's ERA a dozen years ago at the height of Fernandomania?

Some stories seem too good to be true. So one or both of these tales will probably turn out to be a summer night's dream, not a lasting reality.

Still, fans can't blame one another for fantasizing. It's time to say the words, not so much because we really believe them yet, but because there's no point in denying ourselves the pleasure any longer. Maybe Olerud is the next Ted Williams. Maybe Valenzuela is the next Luis Tiant. There, wasn't that fun?

Again on Wednesday night, Olerud and Valenzuela lived up to their fabulous seasons. In the first inning, Valenzuela was neck deep in trouble—one run in, men at the corners, and only one out. His nasty screwball got a double-play grounder out of Olerud. In their next meeting, Olerud got a measure of revenge, lofting a towering home run—his 20th of the year—barely over the rightfield wall.

Naturally, in their last two meetings of the night the wise old left-hander walked Olerud. He knows a player on a lifetime rampage when he sees one. After all, once upon a time he was one. Still, one of Olerud's walks led off a two-run seventh inning that tied the game and ultimately cost Valenzuela a win.

Valenzuela finally left with two outs in the eighth inning, knocked out by an error. Three of the four runs off him were built around jam-shot flares off the handle. When Johnny Oates took the ball from Valenzuela, he said, "You pitched your butt off." True. But fortunately, there's plenty left.

While Olerud is big news, Valenzuela's return sometimes feels like profound news. Is his career becoming a magical yarn worthy of Gabriel García Marquez's mystic realism? Valenzuela seems to have shed his past life as a Dodger, including his severe shoulder miseries. Can a man just go off and return with a new skin, a fresh start?

Valenzuela submerged himself in the Mexican league for two years, pitching tons of innings there. No surgery. No fountain of youth. No new regimen. No radical rest and rehab. Nothing, really. Fernando was gone. Now he's back. That's it. Of course, Valenzuela discusses his comeback cordially. But, thank goodness, he really explains nothing.

Tiant also disappeared from baseball's rather narrow radar screen for two years, then came back at the same age (thirty-two) as Valenzuela. Though never as overpowering as he'd been in his 1.60 ERA season, Tiant had *seven* excellent Bosox seasons, including three 20-win years. Could Valenzuela have 50 or, like Tiant, even 100 wins left in him? In March, nobody thought he had 10 left. In St. Petersburg, if you saw an Oriole doing what looked like an imitation of a left-handed seal trying to throw a beach ball sidearm, it was probably somebody making fun of Fernando again.

They ain't laughin' now. Valenzuela's arm strength has increased every month. His command, especially of his screwball, has gone from poor to good. He still walks too many. He's not spotting his fadeaway like he once did. But his new cut fastball is so precise it makes up the difference. Valenzuela has not merely won with guile but demoralized foes so badly they hardly seem to want to bat for fear he'll mess up their minds for future games.

The Orioles now call Valenzuela "Freddy" after Freddy Krueger in the *Nightmare on Elm Street* horror series who keeps coming back and back.

If you want a lift, look at the league leaders these days. There's a tall, lean kid who's flirting with a .400 average, a .500 on-base percentage, a .700 slugging percentage, 100 extra-base hits, and 400 total bases. Where have you gone, Joe DiMaggio? Maybe to Canada. Did Joltin' Joe ever have a better year than this? For another smile, just look at the pitching leaders. There, in the top 10 in ERA, shutouts, complete games, and lowest batting average against is the eminent screwballogist from Sonora.

Maybe it's too good to last. But who cares? Clip the newspaper. Circle the names. Laminate the stats. It's true today.

The First
Worst-to-First

The Bums
of Summer

March 1989—How do you enjoy a bad baseball team?

No, that isn't quite it. Let's try again.

How do you enjoy a very bad baseball team?

Okay, okay, so that's not exactly the problem either. Let's give it one more go.

How do you enjoy one of the worst baseball teams in history?

There, that's more like it.

Once more, it's time to say, "Goooood moooourning, Baltimore Orioles." Say, can we keep that rotation of Jay Tibbs (4–15), Mark Thurmond (1–8), and Jose Bautista (6–15) intact?

Yes, THEY'RE BACK.

The team for whom every day is Friday the 13th.

The team that makes you wonder, "If Joe Orsulak is the answer, what could the question possibly be?" (Unfortunately, the question is "Who had the Orioles' highest average last year?")

The team that began last season with 21 consecutive losses—a new record for this solar system.

The team that responded to the ignominy of its 107-loss year by trading a Hall of Famer—Eddie Murray—for nothing. Okay, for George Bell's minor league brother, Juan, plus spare change.

The team that, with enough ill luck, could break every major league record for futility this season.

The team that gave a spring training tryout to anyone who could walk. And some, like Bob Horner, who could only waddle.

The team that has amateur theater companies changing the script of *Damn Yankees* so that Joe Hardy is now an Oriole.

Before figuring out how to enjoy this version of a baseball Foreign Legion, we have to see the Woes for what they are. Soon enough, we'll explain why they're still worth watching and how to do it—a Michelin Guide to a season in purgatory. But for now, let's take off our rose-colored glasses and gaze awhile at the Carthage of the American League.

What we've got here is a whole roster worthy of Dick Stuart, the first baseman nicknamed Dr. Strangeglove. Stuart once admitted, "I got a standing ovation in Pittsburgh when I caught a hot dog wrapper on the fly." This season's Orioles first baseman may be Larry Sheets, who misjudged four fly balls in the same exhibition game last spring. One fell to his left, one to his right, one behind him, and one in front of him. There were witnesses. It made the papers.

The worst Washington Senators and St. Louis Browns teams now have company. What Babe Herman once said of himself could apply to any Orioles outfielder from Pete Stanicek to Ken Gerhart: "I never got hit on the head with a fly ball. On the shoulder a few times maybe, but never on the head."

These late-'80s Orioles have been outscored by 400 runs over the past two seasons. To watch them is to understand the emotional distress of Richie Ashburn when he played for the Mets at the end of his career. "I don't know what's going on," the former batting champion said, "but I know I've seen it before." That's how manager Frank Robinson feels almost every day.

Without Mike Boddicker, Fred Lynn, Don Aase, and Tom Niedenfuer—the competent veterans of 1988 who were dumped near the end of last season in salary-saving trades—is there any limit to how far this club could fall?

The plan is to go with youth. But this spring the Orioles also called in a platoon of emergency veterans, most of whom had been presumed dead for years. Horner, Al Holland, Kevin Hickey, Mark Thurmond, Dickie Noles, Ken Landreaux: Is this the cast of a George Romero movie? Some of them had been out of the majors so long when they reported to camp that they should have been given an autopsy instead of a physical.

Now is the time for all good Orioles fans to realize that this season could be even more amazingly bad than 1988. Yes, this could be The Year. Has any team ever started a season with only one player in its entire organization (Cal Ripken Jr.) who's definitely a major leaguer? Be honest. Would any other Oriole, if he had a bad spring training, be certain to make any other team in baseball, even the miserable Atlanta Braves? Probably Dave Schmidt. Maybe Sheets or Phil Bradley. But none of 'em for sure.

One hundred and twenty-one.

That's the number to keep in mind if Ripken ever gets hurt. If he goes down, then Marvelous Marv Throneberry, Choo Choo Coleman, and Elio Chacon are in big trouble. Who's going to give them free rubber chicken dinners to recall the exploits of the '62 Mets if the '89 Orioles break their record of 120 defeats?

Actually, as truly awful teams go, the Orioles are a marvel of potential interest. They show teasing promise of being the most fascinatingly atrocious team in at least a generation—yet maybe, just maybe, they could fool everybody and be the most improved team in baseball in 1989.

After all, former Yankees manager Lou Piniella really did become so depressed one day last September that he was heard to say, "I'd trade our pitching staff for the Orioles' right now."

Rookie pitchers are the most unstable isotopes in baseball. And, brother, do the Orioles have rookie pitchers. Last year, at various times, it was Oswald Peraza, Jose Mesa, and Curt Schilling who were supposed to relieve the gloom. Mesa had a fastball. Peraza had a splitter. Schilling had a sinker. All had solid futures predicted, at least by the Orioles front office. Instead, they were terrible. That's how it goes with rookies.

Now it's Pete Harnisch, Bob Milacki, and Gregg Olson—not to mention several other supposed "prospects" in the system—who are being touted as legitimate causes for hope. Harnisch has a fastball. Olson has a curve. And Milacki has a change-up. Too bad they can't all stand on the mound and alternate pitches.

Fact is, these three saviors have a combined big-league record of 3–3. On a staff that has no stopper in either the rotation or the bullpen, these children could be shell-shocked by June. It's easy to imagine them paralyzed on the mound while facing some hulking slugger, shaking off sign after sign as the young Lefty Gomez once did until his catcher came out to demand an explanation. "Let's wait awhile," said Gomez. "Maybe he'll get a phone call."

At the moment, the Orioles are like the player of whom it was said,

"He's turned his life around. He used to be depressed and miserable. Now he's miserable and depressed." Certainly, the Orioles have turned themselves around—or at least inside out. Few teams have ever turned their fate over so completely to players with negligible major league experience. Of course, bad teams always go for face-lifts. "We've got a whole bunch of new players," Ozzie Smith once said of his Padres teammates, "but I don't think they're the right ones."

At least the Orioles have reason for hoping they've got "the right ones." The greatest pleasure, or pain, in watching the Orioles this season will come from observing the development, or the destruction, of Harnisch, Olson, Milacki, and Schilling. Also, three of the better players anywhere in AAA last season—outfielder Steve Finley, third baseman Craig Worthington, and shortstop Bell—will surely be force-fed. Unfortunately, none is a sure thing.

If the last two seasons proved anything, it's that a desperate team can be a bad place for a rookie of moderate talent. Pitchers like Eric Bell, Jeff Ballard, and Bautista, as well as outfielder Brady Anderson and outfielder/second baseman Pete Stanicek, actually had presentable first seasons—or would have had if they had been hidden on a confident 90-win team, like the Orioles used to be. Instead, they were asked to be leaders, not role players.

Burleigh Grimes once said, "The older pitcher acquires confidence in his ball club. He doesn't try to do it all himself." These days, Orioles pitchers see no rational reason to trust their teammates; so they often try to do it all. That's why they don't survive to become veteran pitchers. Even Sandy Koufax claimed he never found success until he learned to try to make the batter hit the ball instead of missing it.

The dark side of a clean sweep is the risk of destroyed confidence. The glorious possibility, however, is that you cleanse years of bitterness and bad blood in a few months. That's what the Orioles have done. Five years of Baltimore depression and sad memories have been expunged in a year or so.

The names most closely associated with the Fall are all gone: the late owner Edward Bennett Williams, general manager Hank Peters, and farm director Tom Giordano. Nobody left in the Orioles clubhouse blames anybody else for the sorry state of affairs. Last year, this team came to training camp with sulkers like Lee Lacy, depressed veterans like Scott McGregor, million-dollar-a-year has-beens like Terry Kennedy, and talented fellows like Boddicker, Lynn, and Murray, who admitted openly that they felt like hostages. At least the air in the Orioles clubhouse is no longer full of tension and frustration, guilt and recrimination. Perhaps it's easier to restore a dilapidated house if you weren't there to see how all the damage was done—and by whom —in the first place.

And look at it this way: The Orioles shouldn't have too tough a time getting off to a better start this April. They'll almost have to be ahead of their '88 "pace" for months.

Won't they?

No matter how well the Orioles rebuild, even if their fondest hopes are realized for their young players, this team will lose, and lose badly, for the next two to three years. So, for both the Orioles and their followers, an appreciation of the virtues of defeat is now essential.

"Losing, rather than winning, is what baseball is all about, and why, in the end, it is a game for adults," Roger Angell once wrote. We all know that the best teams still lose 60 or more games a season and that even a great hitter fails two-thirds of the time. It is obvious, but also absolutely central, that if you can't cope with constant, unrelenting, inescapable failure, you just can't play major league baseball. It will eat you alive.

So the Orioles might as well start learning to cope. At least now, with their proven talent dispersed in trades, they will have their dignity restored: Instead of being mysterious, sulky, overpaid veteran underachievers, as they've perceived themselves for several seasons, the Orioles can think of themselves as lovable underdogs. That's one reason why trading Murray, even for less than equal value, was important psychologically.

Right now, the Orioles are an almost ideal lousy team. At least for a connoisseur of bad baseball.

First, they have a truly great player. Cal Ripken Jr. is not merely an almost certain Hall of Famer but, if he stays healthy, a first-ballot pick. Like Brooks Robinson back in the early '60s before the Orioles won a pennant, Ripken is worth the price of a ticket; you can watch the entire game through him. He's also as clean as a Brooks tooth, so he makes a fine hero for a child.

Those who followed the Washington Senators for many years know how essential it is to have one Mickey Vernon, Roy Sievers, Harmon Killebrew, or Frank Howard who can win a batting title or home run crown and do it with decency and humility. One superb player can give a whole team, even a bad one, a tad of dignity.

Next, the Orioles have reached a point where only a masochist could possibly feel any real pain at their defeats. After a certain point —and 107 defeats is well past that point—a team simply can't be taken seriously. If you don't laugh along with the misfortunes of a team like these Orioles, or the old '50s and '60s Senators, then it's your own fault; you're just stubbornly refusing to get the joke.

Anyone who grew up on Bill Veeck's Browns in the '40s or Joe Garagiola's Pirates in the early '50s or Roger Craig's Mets in the '60s or Nate Colbert's Padres in the '70s or (as in my case) Cookie Lavagetto's perennial last-place Nats in the late '50s knows that a bad team—loved for its effort, its suffering, and its eccentricities—is a civilized, charming pleasure. Even as a nine-year-old, I knew there was nothing sad about rooting for a Senators team that lost 99 games. So what if Chuck Stobbs lost 20 games? I thought he was a "stylish left-hander" because he was the most stylish left-hander my team had. So what if Eddie Yost batted .250? He could walk. In my memory, Julio Becquer will always be a great pinch hitter, the biased opinions of the record book be damned.

Anyone, especially any child, can root for a champion. What's tough about loving perfection? Miss Universe always gets a date. It takes conviction, maybe even a smidgen of character, to root for Herb Plews or Billy Ripken. Lessons in handling daily frustration, or matching our ambitions to our abilities, aren't learned from World Series winners.

The worse a team, the more fortitude it demands of us. For example, holding a marriage together might seem easy after rooting for Baltimore to protect a late-inning lead. W. B. Yeats said, "Hearts are not had as a gift but hearts are earned / by those that are not entirely beautiful." Or, sometimes, by those, like the Orioles, who're pretty ugly.

Even the worst teams reward us with moments we would never suspect. Who was the only pitcher to strike out 21 men in a major league game? Tom Cheney of the Washington Senators. I heard all sixteen innings on the radio as a child—except for the twelfth, when my mother made me eat the fastest dinner in American League history.

Who could forget Jim Lemon hitting three homers in one game off Whitey Ford with President Dwight Eisenhower in the stands? Or

Camilo Pascual striking out 15 men on Opening Day? Or Sievers tying the American League record by hitting a home run in six consecutive games? The sixth came in the seventeenth inning off Al Aber of Detroit into the leftfield beer garden. The temperature was 98 degrees. I don't need to consult a record book, any more than I would to recite Sievers's entire statistical line for the 1957 season: 152–572–99–172–23–5–42–114 –.301–.579. No child was ever harmed by filling a spiral notebook with game-by-game stats on Rocky Bridges—in the exhibition seasons.

To the student of bad, heroism can be relished even in the perverse, like Ed Fitz Gerald of the Nats breaking up Billy Pierce's no-hitter with two out in the ninth. Or was it a perfect game? To this day, some of us know why Mickey Mantle would never race Pedro Ramos in the 50-yard dash. And it wasn't because he was afraid he'd pull a hamstring.

No sport demands as much patience and taste for deferred gratification as baseball because no other sport makes you wake up as an underdog every morning for six months. Right now, the Orioles all know the long, arduous schedule they are on. Baltimore's new stadium will be ready by 1992. The Orioles are expected to be worthy occupants by then.

Anyone who can't wait isn't a real baseball fan and should be forced to face it. Aligning oneself only with winners, with the beautiful, with what is safely acceptable at the moment, is called "front-running"; it's the trait that players spot quickest and despise most in fans (or reporters). Even if they later grow rich and vain, ballplayers seldom forget the early ingrained lessons about enduring the long season, riding out agonizing slumps, maintaining confidence when surrounded by lost faith, and always adjusting your game to compensate for your inescapable flaws.

Fans of bad teams occasionally do some learning, too. That's useful in a nation where front-running is an epidemic disease. Front-runners get divorced or declare bankruptcy as fast as possible—so they can "start fresh." Front-runners respect Donald Trump and spend "quality time" with their children.

Those bad teams that manage to be genuinely charming are often distinguished by a touching blend of earnestness and self-deprecation. Who can fail to be amused, yet moved, by those midseason postgame Orioles interviews in which Rene Gonzales, or some such dedicated fellow, makes it heart-wrenchingly clear that he believes, from the depths of his heart, that, despite his .215 career batting average, he is just about to find his comfort zone and tear up the league? We almost gasp at humanity's capacity to deceive itself completely; yet we love it, too.

When a pathetic team understands its plight, yet fights against it with good grace and humor, it becomes truly adorable to its fans. The early Mets weren't loved out of perversity. They handled themselves properly, especially old Casey Stengel, who said during an intrasquad scrimmage, "Take those fellows over to that other diamond. I want to see if they can play on the road."

Those around such teams have an obligation to grasp the spirit of the thing and get into harmony with it. Last spring, for example, after the Orioles lost their 20th consecutive game, I slipped Frank Robinson a lapel button that said, "It's Been Lovely but I Have to Scream Now." He burst out laughing, then put the button in his office drawer. Despite his plaque in the Hall of Fame, he grasped the attitude his new situation required.

Listen to the tone of the young Jimmy Breslin writing about the '62 Mets: "They lost an awful lot of games by one run, which is the mark of a bad team. They also lost innumerable games by 14 runs or so. This is the mark of a terrible team. Actually, all the Mets did was lose. . . . They lost with maneuvers that shake the imagination."

Anything can be endured so long as the wound is not salted with hope. The Orioles won't have that problem for at least another year or two. In the meantime, games at Memorial Stadium can be watched with a soul-cleansing dispassion—not an attitude that a fan would want to adopt indefinitely, but salutary in small doses. These are the days to appreciate the Orioles' foes. Even the Yankees. Even Rickey Henderson. Okay, maybe not Rickey.

In a sense, a season without expectations is a less obsessive and, perhaps, more gently enjoyable experience than the nightly agonies of following a team that's "in contention." Naturally, being human, we much prefer agony. Still, if wisdom and serenity are going to be shoved down our throats, maybe we can stand it for a little while.

The sanguine baseball fan knows, of course, that his game, more than most, is not about the final score. It's about the stories along the way. Yes, just like life, where you know the final score before you start. Death wins. So what? Let's play.

The tales when you're not very good are just as wonderful, in their way, as the ones when you're a star. "This boy is wild low," scout Fresco Thompson once reported to Branch Rickey. "He doesn't have enough stuff to be wild high."

Wilfred Sheed, the author, said he loved the way you could "read around baseball" without ever getting to the game at all. If you're watching properly, day in and day out—focusing on the psychology, sociology, humor, pageantry, and humanity of the game—you may be able to read around the Orioles, too. No, it's not as exciting as '79 or '83. But baseball in its all too human form has its pleasures as well. It sure as hell wasn't the 1927 Yankees who gave us the line "If the crowds get any smaller, they'll have to put fractions on the turnstiles."

So why not go out to Memorial Stadium to see if Larry Sheets can catch a hot dog wrapper or Joe Orsulak can bloop and bunt his way to .300? Find out if fireballing Pete Harnisch can overcome his goofy little windup and his stubby legs. Maybe, by September, you'll even get to see the American League debut of the one and only Texas Mike Smith. Or is that the one and only Mississippi Mike Smith?

If all teams were competent, baseball would be poorer by half. Or, at least for the Orioles' sake, let's tell ourselves it's so.

The Thing
with Feathers

March 5, 1989—The Baltimore Orioles are the worst damn team in baseball. But they're one of the happiest, too. For them, spring training still symbolizes hope and the dream of a distinguished future. For them, this is a time of joy and enthusiasm, not scandal and recrimination.

Not one Oriole, you see, has ever dated Margo Adams. That privilege is reserved for the lucky Wade Boggses of the baseball world.

Not one Oriole has been called a drunk by Rickey Henderson. Only rich Yankees have that pleasure.

Not one has sued his agent for millions. You have to make millions, like Keith Hernandez, to do that.

Not one is threatening to leave town if his enormous contract isn't renegotiated, à la Darryl Strawberry.

In a spring full of baseball horror stories, the Orioles, who lost 107 games last season and might lose even more this year, are—odd as it seems—an emblem of what's best in baseball. They're not under arrest or in drug rehabilitation. They don't drive 125 miles per hour or, like Professor Oil Can Boyd, tell a teammate he ought to seek psychiatric help.

Why, at last report, none of these Orioles has even met Steve Garvey, let alone borne his children. The Orioles are probably the only team that still buys *Penthouse* for the pictures. And gets embarrassed.

You have to know how to play baseball before you can use that skill to get yourself in trouble. And the Orioles are still very busy learning.

Someday, no doubt, they will go the way of all big leaguers. As manager John McGraw said long ago, "One percent of ballplayers are leaders of men. The other 99 percent are followers of women." For the moment, however, the Orioles' primary passion is still the double-run-down defense.

The Baltimore jerseys here don't even have names on the back, only numbers. For two weeks, all players had to sign in when they entered the training room—"Just like *What's My Line*," said one coach—so the trainers knew whose arms they were kneading.

At the moment, however, in this lush fantasy world called spring training, the Woes are still a team of children. They're all hope and, for a few more weeks, little reality. All future and no past to live down. Everywhere they look, they see new friends to make, new lessons to learn. Old enemies and old sorrows are unknown to them. When, over the past two years, they traded or cut players named Murray, Lynn, Boddicker, Kennedy, McGregor, Dempsey, Flanagan, Shelby, Martinez, and Davis, they washed away the franchise's collective memory.

Only the Ripkens remain, and they might as well be the three monkeys who neither see nor speak nor hear evil.

"You can tell this team is very inexperienced," said former Oriole Jim Palmer, looking at fifty players sitting on the grass listening to a lecture. "They all have their hats on. A veteran would know this is a sun [tan] opportunity."

The Orioles are so green it's sweet. When rookie pitcher Bob Milacki met Palmer, he stammered, "Nice weather we're havin'." Rookie Gregg Olson couldn't even manage that much savoir faire: First, he did a double take when Palmer stuck out his hand and said, "Jim Palmer. Glad to meet ya." Then Olson sat on a dugout step and, wordless, stared at Palmer for fifteen minutes.

The Orioles could easily have eight rookies on their Opening Day roster. "It's refreshing," says Cal Ripken Jr., who was depressed in recent years by the veteran negativism around him. "What we have here is enthusiasm. They're all in a hurry to get a career. There's no ragging or complaining. With veterans, the only fun is winning. Now, even a bunt drill can be fun when you see somebody grasp the concept."

"Attitudes have been very good. We've gotten a lot of work done," says Frank Robinson, who was hired as manager 6 games into the Orioles' historic 21-game losing streak to open the 1988 season. "I've always enjoyed working with young people, teaching them and talking baseball. It's a pleasure to watch someone get better and better until he's a bona fide big leaguer. . . . All a teacher wants is for them to listen and try."

Can the Yankees' new manager, Dallas Green, say as much? He's already made a couple of cracks—hopefully in jest—that Henderson won't forget soon. First, when Henderson reported to camp later than Green wished, Green asked, "Does Henderson know how to read?" Then, when Henderson said "too many [Yankees] got drunk too often" last season, Green struck again, saying he knew how players would have handled Henderson in his day. "Let them go kick the crap out of him. . . . Truthfully, it's between [the players]," Green reportedly said.

Spring training has already been so discombobulating for everybody —except the meek and gentle Orioles—that Dallas Green, in answering a question this week, broke the Triple Negative Barrier, a verbal feat neither Casey Stengel nor Yogi Berra ever managed.

"I was never not optimistic that it wouldn't," Green said.

Baseball shouldn't be that complicated. But, for the high and mighty these days, it almost always is.

Mea Culpa

Some time ago, an impostor, using my name, wrote a story titled "The Bums of Summer" for this magazine. The noble Baltimore Orioles were the subject of this villainous fabrication. At the time, I took no legal action. I even accepted the odd compliment for this forgery. But now, I have retained counsel, hired a private operative, and am hot on the heels of the perpetrator.

I've even bought a mirror.

Oh, me of little faith.

Let's get this mea culpa out of the way so we can move to the interesting stuff—like Rene Gonzales and Mickey Weston. No, the Orioles are not "one of the worst teams in history." No, Orioles fans do not need "a Michelin Guide to a season in purgatory." No, Kevin Hickey doesn't need an autopsy more than a physical. And, no, this is not the team for whom every day is Friday the 13th.

Rather, it has become the club for whom every day is April the 1st.

Midseason's a good time for authorial repentance because the Birds are still far enough from The End that they could come to grief. But who really cares if they fade? ("If lovin' you is wrong, then I don't wanna be right.") For what they've already done, they've earned all the apologies they can get, including mine. Okay, so I said nice things about them, too; and I've written about them for fifteen years. But it's a pleasure to beg forgiveness under such circumstances.

What's so special about the 1989 Orioles? Why is it so much fun to be wrong about them? Sure, everybody loves an underdog. But this is more than that. All around the sports beat, normally stiff-necked types enjoy groveling before the Birds' success, boasting about how mistaken they were, adding, "I love 'em."

Part of the phenomenon is the sheer magnitude of the club's reversal. Before this season began, the Orioles tempted us with the possibility that they could, with enough bad luck, be the worst team ever. After 107 losses in '88, why should 121 be impossible?

Now, they tempt us again, with an even more beguiling possibility: They could be the most transformed team in history. No club has ever improved by more than 33 wins in a single year; conceivably, the Birds could. No team has ever gone from being the worst in the game to finishing in first place the next. The O's could. As usual, the miserable, no-good, rotten truth will probably be right in the middle.

But maybe not.

For adults, the ability to make even a small emotional commitment to the Orioles—to answer the question "Are they for real?" with a firm "Yes, I think so"—is almost a litmus test of the ability to show irrational faith in something that ought not be possible.

The cynic thinks he knows what will happen before it happens. The past will repeat itself. Hope is useless. The rich will get richer. Why get out of bed?

The child sees a world of wonder, full of novelty. Anything might happen. He might learn how to blow soap bubbles, then chase them and smash them with a big hammer. He can barely remember any day that's repeated itself. He wakes up singing and tries to escape his crib.

Cynicism is just a mask we wear to protect the aging child inside. Given a chance, we would all rather tear away that disguise, at least for a while, and be childishly, ridiculously joyous. At the moment, the Orioles have become an excuse to reclaim some of what is left of our innocence—the part of our nature that is enthusiastic, pliable, even gullible. As long as the worst team in baseball (last year) is in or near first place, the laws of diminished wonder have been revoked.

One of the oldest and most basic themes in literature is rebirth—by which we mean a return to a state of youthful, freshened spirit. Start over. Try again. Forget the past. Forgiving sins is akin to forgetting them. But how, we ask, can that rebirth begin? Where does it start? The usual answer, from Shakespeare to the man in the street, is with a radical change of heart, a change of soul. "Nothing is but thinking makes it so," says the poet. "If I could change my attitude, I might change my life," thinks the common man.

That's why the Orioles, for a little while, have a kind of aura around them that extends beyond sports. They are not winning because they bought free agents or made marvelous trades or hired a genius for a manager or developed new Hall of Famers in their minor leagues. In fact, they bought nobody, they traded away a Hall of Famer, they kept the same old manager, and they unveiled no new magnificent stars.

Hard as it is to believe, idealistic as it sounds, the Orioles basically just changed their attitude.

They didn't do it this year. They did it last year—in the depths of a 21-game losing streak to begin the season, a streak that may have been the worst national humiliation any team ever suffered.

Then, the team's gentle old general manager, Roland Hemond, and its twice-fired manager, Frank Robinson, and its bright young farm director, Doug Melvin, made a lovely, radical decision. Since things couldn't possibly get any worse, they decided to run the team exactly the way they'd always wanted to run one. Get rid of all the players who, for whatever reason, weren't happy. Trade them or give them away. Look for players—young ones, troubled ones, discarded ones—who wanted a fresh chance or a first chance. If playing for the worst team in baseball sounded like a great opportunity, you were what they wanted.

Hemond, Robinson, and Melvin didn't denounce players like Eddie Murray, Fred Lynn, Mike Boddicker, and others when they left. They weren't evil people. Some, in fact, had been at the heart of wonderful Orioles teams, like the 1983 world champions. It's just that the marriage didn't work anymore. They needed fresh starts of another sort—with better, older, richer teams.

Like a young family that makes do with simple pleasures because they can't afford expensive ones, the new Orioles were built around the commodities that baseball values least. In other words, the kind of guys you can't trade if you already have 'em, but can always get more of if, Lord knows why, you want 'em:

Fast outfielders who may hit fairly well, but without power (Mike Devereaux, Joe Orsulak, Steve Finley).

Control pitchers not thought to have the raw stuff to be either starters or stoppers (Jay Tibbs, Brian Holton, Mark Williamson, Jeff Ballard, Kevin Hickey, Mark Thurmond).

Veterans who had failed in some way (Phil Bradley, Mickey Tettleton, Bob Melvin, Larry Sheets).

And young prospects with talent who had not matured as fast as expected or who had nagging flaws (Brady Anderson, Randy Milligan, Jim Traber, Bill Ripken, Craig Worthington). Add one humble superstar (shortstop Cal Ripken Jr.) and one gifted No. 1 draft choice (relief pitcher Gregg Olson). Mix in Al Jackson and Tom McCraw, a couple of smart, assertive black coaches—the kind many teams don't seem anxious to get. Bring back fired manager Cal Ripken Sr. as the third-base coach, out of decency.

What have you got?

Something the Orioles hardly dared to hope for—clubhouse chemistry.

Translated, that means everybody knows they need help from everybody else to survive in the majors. The pitchers need the fielders. The hitters need to be platooned. The regulars need rest. The bullpen has to be a committee. And everybody—even Cal Ripken Jr., whose reputation as a hitter had slipped—feels he has something basic to prove.

Hemond, Robinson, and Melvin knew that they would have a hustling, hungry team because they had players who'd be crazy not to hustle or act hungry. What they did not know—and are still afraid to believe completely—is how well these disparate, flawed parts seem to blend together into a pretty dangerous team.

At the technical level, the Orioles offer a fascinating puzzle to purists. The sources of their improvements can be measured. Many fewer errors by the whole defense, many more catches by the outfield, and many fewer walks by the pitching staff add up to a lot fewer runs allowed—about one a game.

And although it is usually overlooked, the Orioles offense, for reasons almost invisible to the casual baseball eye, is almost as much improved as the pitching and defense. Many more walks, a higher team average (at the expense of power), many more steals, and more extra bases (thanks to speed) mean more runs scored—also about one a game.

Perhaps in other sports the general public would not have quite so firm a grasp of what the Orioles were doing. Baseball, however, is not only most open and inspectable of games but also an addiction for many of its fans. They know, or can find out quickly, the personal odyssey of every player. Here was a team with twenty-three scrappy wanderers who needed a home. When they started to win, they got hugged.

But will it continue? And for how long? How much of this is enthusiasm, synchronicity, and luck? Will Gonzales, a utility infielder, continue to get two-out, sudden-death, game-winning bloop hits against the New York Yankees? Will Weston, a twenty-eight-year-old career minor leaguer, keep on shutting down teams as he did the Oakland A's in his debut?

Having been so dramatically, if happily, incorrect once, I suppose I'm honor-bound to make a fool of myself again.

Yes, barring lots of injuries to pitchers, there's no reason the Birds won't continue to play in the style to which they've become accustomed. Defense and speed don't suddenly disappear. Morale should not disappear quickly. Presumably this is not a team that needs to be in first place, or even in a pennant race, to maintain its intensity. For every overachiever like Tettleton and Ballard, who have been ridiculously hot, there are several players, statistically long overdue, who could pick up the slack when they cool off.

That's more than enough predictions from such a suspect oracle.

More to the point, or at least our point, does it really matter whether the Orioles continue to amaze us? Isn't it enough that they have already made us wonder about the limits of renewed wonder? If the O's can do what they have already done, then how much might we accomplish ourselves with a similar change of attitude, a comparable rebirth of enthusiasm and willed innocence?

The Orioles have already reached a point where all that stands between them and the impossible—finishing in first place—is an entirely plausible amount of good fortune. If other American League East teams continue to play poorly . . . If the Orioles stay healthy . . . If a few key Baltimore players perform fairly well . . .

All the truly incredible and inspiring work has been done already. What could not be imagined, could not be rationally discussed, and was never even dreamed of by the Orioles themselves in April is now a perfectly reasonable possibility. Everybody talks about it.

In gamblers' argot, the Orioles have put the impossible on the board.

And how did they do it?

By enduring the worst losing streak of their generation with considerable personal dignity. (Their clubhouse in the worst times was more civil than some teams' in normal times.) By shedding their past without vilifying it. By finding people who were anxious to do the hard job at hand. By recognizing their mutual interdependence. By enjoying each other, focusing on their limited strengths and laughing at their obvious weaknesses.

If the summer heat melts the Orioles' wings, it would be a shame to see the moral of their tale as some baseball equivalent of the myth of Icarus. The Orioles have not flown too close to the sun. Rather, they have shown us how close, and even reachable, a star can be.

Reasons to Believe

March 1990—Major league ballplayers love detail. When they tell a story, there are seldom any capitalized Truths. Big thinking gets you the horselaugh in a world of such relentless reality testing.

Big leaguers also have a sixth sense for spotting a telling detail—in technique, in temperament, or even about a whole team. Maybe all those years of spotting the spin on a curveball help you recognize dishonesty in a passing expression on a manager's face. Maybe picking up signs flashed in a blink before every pitch helps you spot panic, or confidence, as it flows soundlessly through a whole team.

Plenty of fans have the knack for watching carefully, too. Like players, they can't always explain why they know what they know. So many games, so many plays. But what's a photograph except a sea of dots? Enough of them make a picture. That's how we see a team's season: an ocean of details that finally form a portrait.

Last summer, fans asked one question before all others: Are the Orioles for real? In other words, have the details formed a picture yet? Month after month, we kept asking, listening to games on the radio, watching on TV, studying box scores, and charting the flow of the averages as the weeks went by. Baseball isn't just for the ballpark. You never know when you'll suddenly see the picture.

Every follower of the Why Nots has favorite moments from a season in which lasting baseball lore was created by a team that won no title and set no major records. The '89 Orioles weren't baseball's best team. Their final 87–75 record was only the eighth best in the majors.

But there may never have been a club that had a better attitude or surpassed reasonable expectations by a greater margin. Evidence, you ask? Only two teams in history ever improved by more than the Orioles' 32½ games—the '03 Giants and the '46 Red Sox. And the Sox should not count. They got Ted Williams (123 RBI), Bobby Doerr (116), Johnny Pesky (.335), Dom DiMaggio (.316), and six of their seven best pitchers back from World War II. Guess they probably would improve. But only a half game more than the Orioles!

So let's rewind our minds to Opening Day of 1989 and, as a new season approaches, relive nine innings of memory that will always seem lit from within.

Finley's Catch

On Opening Day, Steve Finley, on his first play in the majors, ran full speed into the rightfield fence and disabled himself for three weeks.

But he held the ball.

Finley's catch was not particularly acrobatic. If no fence had been there, it would have been a normal full-stretch, in-stride, sprinting catch.

But the wall was there. And Finley simply ignored its existence. He hit the fence shoulder-first a millisecond after the ball stuck in his glove. Had he struck one of the metal poles that support the fence, Finley's career might have lasted only one play. Instead, he got lucky, took a standing eight count, and tried to exchange a high five with a teammate. That's when he discovered he couldn't raise his arm above his head. Even so, Finley stayed in the game until the end of the inning.

To a man, the Orioles insisted Finley's play "set the tone for the whole season." How can such exaggeration be taken seriously?

Sacrificing your body can be inspirational. And, on a team with nine rookies in key roles, one youngster needed to show the others how to play fearlessly. If Finley was not daunted by seeing President George Bush in the stands, the division champion Red Sox on the field, or Roger Clemens on the mound, then others might find their courage too. Finley's play certainly foreshadowed the rookie heroics of Gregg Olson, Bob Milacki, Craig Worthington, Randy Milligan, Mike Devereaux, Pete Harnisch, Dave Johnson, and Brady Anderson. (Wheeew!)

Still, Finley's play—at least within the Orioles clubhouse—was seen as far more important than these factors would indicate.

Why?

A team has to have a reason to think that it can improve. It's not enough to get in shape, have team meetings, and preach optimism. That's all nice. But something more tangible has to be added to the mix. A ball club needs a guiding idea as to its own identity. In '88, the Orioles had no source of pride, nothing to hang their hats on, no firm ground as a starting point.

In 1989, the Orioles had defense.

In baseball, defense isn't supposed to be very important. Not compared with pitching and hitting, anyway. But at least it's something. And because defense gets so little respect, it's easy to acquire. Shake any tree and "glovemen" fall out.

Only one executive in the 1980s believed that defense (and the speed that usually goes with it) was enormously important and vastly underrated. Only one man made it a cornerstone of his teams: Whitey Herzog, the manager of the St. Louis Cardinals. By an interesting coincidence, the Cardinals—probably the best all-around defensive team in history—were the only franchise in the '80s to reach the World Series three times. Almost nobody noticed. Except Roland Hemond.

Ask the Orioles general manager point-blank if he consciously rebuilt the Birds along the lines of Herzog's Cardinals, and he says, "Yes. Absolutely. I have great respect for Whitey." Hemond may be the only baseball man who has recognized the stolen Herzog's two key ideas: (1) Great defense turns poor-to-mediocre starters into decent-to-good pitchers; (2) a great bullpen is the most important factor in modern baseball. Ergo: Sacrifice starting pitchers and slow sluggers—the sport's traditional glamour guys, like Walter Johnson and Babe Ruth—for firemen and leather wizards.

When the Orioles won on Opening Day—5–4 in eleven innings on a bloop hit by a rookie that a slow Red Sox outfielder couldn't quite reach—the Birds decided to take the lesson about defense to heart. After all, 1–0 is a lot better than 0–21.

They went on to compile pathetic statistics in most sexy categories and mediocre ones in the rest. Batting: 12th in the American League. Slugging: 11th. Hits allowed: 13th. Strikeouts: 14th.

But the Orioles had the best team fielding percentage in the history of baseball. Sometimes, fielding percentage can be a meaningless statistic because slow, clumsy players—like the infamous Zeke Bonura—can play "flawlessly" while actually missing everything. However, the Orioles had exceptional team range throughout the outfield and at third base. Both the Ripken brothers, Cal Jr. and Bill, have above-average range for middle infielders. Couple all that with adequate catching and the surest hands (statistically) in history, and you have one of the best total defenses ever.

Baltimore's Opening Day victory was noted nationally with amusement and, perhaps, a touch of relieved sympathy for the team. I heard the score on the evening TV news along with half a dozen other sportswriters. Everybody laughed. "Guess that means they'll only lose 106 this year," I think I said.

The Otter Arrives

The hard breaking ball started at Dave Parker's hands, then almost picked off his front kneecap as he swung pathetically and missed the pitch by a foot. Parker didn't bother to glare out at the mound as he walked back to the dugout. When you strike out on a pitch that almost hits you, you don't do much talking. Dave Henderson came next, and he looked even worse. He thought the curveball would arrive knee high, so he figured he had to swing. By the time he finished flailing at the Yellow Hammer, the horrible downer, the pitch was one inch away from the dirt. He'd misjudged the amount of break by a foot. Finally, Mark McGwire was paralyzed completely. His front foot did a silly tap dance and his knee did the shimmy as the big slow curve froze his whole nervous system. The pitch bisected the heart of the plate to end the game as McGwire stood, bat on shoulder.

Gregg Olson had struck out the side in the Oakland Coliseum to beat the American League champion A's, 2–1. You can't send word around a league much faster than Olson did that night. He might be pudgy and look like his nickname—"the Otter"—but that curve of his was an Outer. And his fastball was almost as good.

In the history of the major league draft (which began in 1965), the Orioles had never had a pick as high as the No. 4 player. So, when they took Olson in the summer of 1988, it was a historic moment. The Orioles, so consistently good for so long that they never got first dibs on great prospects, had a chance to grab a player who ought to be a star.

The Orioles also had to decide whether to make the 6-foot-4, 211-

pound Olson a starter, which he'd been in high school and the first half of his college career, or keep him in the bullpen. Hemond, operating on the Herzog agenda, decided to keep him a reliever and bring him to the majors as fast as possible. That's another pet Whitey theory. "You're either capable or you're not. Experience means nothing." Who says relievers should be old, mean, and nerveless? What the Cardinals did with Todd Worrell at twenty-five, the Orioles did with Olson at—gulp—twenty-two years old. They made him the ace, the star, the closer, the psychological linchpin of the team.

Only one rookie (Worrell) ever had more saves than Olson's 27, and only one reliever had more saves at a younger age.

Until Olson arrived, the Orioles were a charming spring oddity. Just a few days earlier, the team had nosed into first place. The day after that, Milacki (helped by four double plays and a thrown-out base stealer) had pitched a shutout in which he faced only twenty-seven batters—the minimum. And the day before Olson fanned the side, Jeff Ballard had won his fourth straight start, this time in Anaheim as President Bush (an Orioles fan) shook players' hands in the bullpen. However, all this could be a mirage. A brainy lefty with a new sinker like Ballard and a big stubborn right-hander with a straight change-up like Milacki were helpful, but not so special. The league might figure 'em out. It was also pleasant that A's castoff Mickey Tettleton was hitting a few home runs, that every Orioles outfielder of '89 was better than any Orioles outfielder of '88, and that the Birds had won five games against former 20-game winners.

But the coming of Olson, for as long as he could remain untouchable and allow others to assume subordinate bullpen roles, made the Orioles a potentially different team.

Some fickle fair-weather types started listening to the occasional Orioles game on the radio again.

Joe Carter's Bunt

Joe Carter is a slugger, a free swinger, not a finesse guy. With the winning run on third and two outs in the ninth inning, he's the last guy in the world you'd expect to drop down a bunt for a hit. If he fails, it looks like he chickened out, abdicated responsibility for his cleanup role. Against a journeyman pitcher like the Orioles' Mark Williamson, a star like Carter would look doubly dopey if he popped up a bunt. Swing, fool!

But Carter bunted. Perfectly. Chugging out of the right-hand batter's box, he barely beat it out.

When he crossed the bag, the Orioles lost the most brutal sort of game: 1–0 in sudden death. First baseman Milligan lay on his back in the infield dirt for a minute after the game ended. Not a good omen. A superb performance by Milacki, wasted. A chance to beat Cleveland ace Greg Swindell, squandered. A five-game winning streak, snapped. And the team's league lead down to one game with a night flight back to Baltimore on the docket. Let's see. Who's pitching for the Rangers tomorrow night? Maybe we'll catch a break.

Nolan Ryan.

A bad team becoming a good team is a fragile thing. Almost every spring, two or three clubs threaten to make the leap. Yet, since World War II, only fourteen teams have improved by 25 or more wins in one year. The ones that make the great transformation tend to get remembered. The 1969 Miracle Mets. The 1980 A's, who played Billy Ball. The 1984 Cubs, who finally finished first.

Such teams are extremely prone to lost confidence and sudden, disastrous losing streaks. Often, one spooky game starts the catastrophe. Baseball mythology has it that surprise teams usually collapse around the 50th game or the 100th—either you swoon in June or the dog days of August get you.

How would the Orioles respond to their first morale-slaying loss of the season?

For fans, it was painful to tune in Monday night's game after watching Carter's bunt on TV the previous day. But by now, 45 games into the season, the Orioles' struggle to stay above .500 (they were at 23–22) and in first place for as long as possible had become a question of faith. Might as well watch the carnage. It's been a great ride. Too bad it had to end so unluckily. Damn stupid bunt.

Ryan, the hottest pitcher in the league, threw Tettleton a change-up.

The Froot Loop Kid hit it into the rightfield bleachers.

Ryan threw Larry Sheets his best low fastball. Sheets hit it even higher into the same bleachers.

Ryan threw Cal Ripken his best knee-high curveball. Ripken golfed it into the leftfield stands for another home run.

Sure, Ryan struck out ten. But the Orioles became the first team in years to hit three homers off him in one game.

Would such a game have any carryover effect, you might ask?

Before they cooled off, the Orioles won 8 games in a row—that's 13 of 14 in all, with the only loss on Carter's bunt. Yup, it sure upset 'em. If the Orioles weren't scoring six runs in the first inning in Detroit, then Milacki was pitching a two-hitter or Tettleton was becoming the first American League catcher since Rudy York in 1938 to have 13 home runs before the start of June.

The insanity reached its apex in Yankee Stadium. Over the radio I heard Jon Miller say, "It's outta here! A grand-slam home run for Steve Finley! And the score here in the top of the third inning is Baltimore 11, New York 0."

I almost drove my truck off the road. The division lead was 5 games.

The Ripken Way

On this night in Memorial Stadium, the Orioles and Toronto Blue Jays met for the first time in '89. The season was really beginning. By the ninth inning, the Orioles, the worst team in baseball in '88, had introduced themselves quite thoroughly to the Jays, the favorites to win the American League East.

Tony Fernandez, the Jays shortstop, slap-bunted the ball past the charging Orioles third baseman. What followed has become my favorite play from my favorite season.

Shortstop Cal Ripken chased the ball down the leftfield line. Without looking toward the infield, Ripken slid across the grass, like a runner coming into second base. He barehanded the ball in mid-slide, then, still canted at a 45-degree angle, threw perfectly to second base as he collapsed face-first into the grass. Fernandez hurried back to first with a single, instead of a double on a bunt.

At that moment the score was Baltimore 16, Toronto 3.

Considering those circumstances, Fernandez was hustling. But Ripken's play came out of some other league. Or species. Ripken, playing in his 1,161st consecutive game, could have sprained his ankle, wrenched his back, or thrown out his shoulder. His team was 13 runs ahead. With 89 more games to play. It was a ridiculously wonderful, totally meaningless play. And one that, perhaps, no player had ever even tried before. Such a slap bunt is a freak play. Who'd plot a ploy to stop it? Or improvise a method in a split second? Ripken, the headiest player of his era, would. And, last season, in the year of "Why Not," the entire Orioles team probably would too.

For once, an entire team performed, from Opening Day to Closing Day, with the same level of commitment, alertness, and indomitable stubbornness that Cal Ripken always provides.

The Ripken Play epitomized the team's evolving style. Do the mundane, and do it at full throttle, without asking about rewards. Just do it. Ahead by 13. Down by 13. That's how habits are formed. In baseball, over 162 tedious, jet-lagged, nerve-racking games, you become your habits. Frank Robinson's only rule of managing was: Play the game right. The way the Orioles once played it for more than twenty years in a row.

The night after Ripken made the play, the Birds and Jays eyeballed each other in earnest. With the score 1–1 in the eighth, the Memorial Stadium press box had its game face on. This was no longer a colorful feature story. It was the biggest story in baseball, by far. The season's halfway point was only a week away and the Orioles' division lead was so big—7½ games if they won this one—that they could probably lose a dozen games in a row and still be in first place. The O's were so inspired and improved, and the division so weak, that they threatened to become the first team in history to go from worst to first in one season. There was a new song out, and the biggest crowds in Orioles history turned out to sing it every night. "Can you believe where we are today? You see it just don't matter what no experts say. . . . It's really happening. . . . Come on, O's, we can win this thing. WHY NOT?"

The "Why Not" part was usually pretty loud.

When Ripken—yes, the same guy from the night before—took a curveball from John Cerutti into the leftfield bullpen in the bottom of the eighth inning, the game was already over (final score, 2–1) before the ninth inning began. Why? Because Olson was going to strike out the side. Manny Lee. Nelson Liriano. Junior Felix. Just like Parker, Henderson, and McGwire.

Why not, indeed?

The next two nights, the Orioles lost, 11–1 and 16–5. Oops.

Guess it's really baseball, not fiction, after all. It seemed so unfair or, perhaps, wonderful that the Orioles were going to have to play all 162 games with the world watching and judging.

Foul Is Fair

When foul balls start becoming sudden-death game-winning hits, then everybody knows that the game is afoot. This was the weekend when the general public got the message. Many Orioles fans remember Mike Devereaux's home run on Saturday night July 15—a hooking drive that almost everyone but the umpire thought was foul—as the most dramatic single swing of the season. The final score was flashy: 11–9. The opponent was worthy: the California Angels. And the Orioles, who never led until the game ended, trailed by three runs as late as the eighth inning. However, I liked Sunday's game better. Every team has a few hellacious comebacks and a few ridiculously good breaks in any year. In fact, statistically, the Orioles did not have as many late-inning comebacks in 1989 as the average big-league team. Nonetheless, when Mickey Tettleton's probably foul ground ball was called fair just eighteen hours after Devereaux's gift home run, the Orioles seemed to have the Fates on their side. The Orioles even seemed to anticipate such omens. When Tettleton's smash down the first-base line picked up—maybe—one molecule of white chalk on its trip into the rightfield corner, the Angels defense reacted slowly. Meanwhile, Cal Ripken, a Clydesdale base runner, gambled all the way and scored from first to win the game with his "speed."

The Angels seemed almost too stunned and furious to argue. Actually, it may have been lucky that California's explosive manager, Doug Rader, had been ejected before this game ever began for screaming obscenities about the previous night's injustice. Rader might have been cerebral hemorrhage material.

Teams in pursuit of miracles need to believe in their own magic. At some point, circumstances must offer them raw material that they can interpret as divine baseball intervention. Otherwise, the tough losses grow in memory. Devereaux's homer and Tettleton's double, with their double impact, seemed to make up (with interest) for a game that the Orioles had lost a month earlier to the Yankees. On that bizarre night, a routine New York fly ball in the ninth inning disappeared into a pea-soup fog and was not retrieved until a 1–0 Baltimore lead had become a 2–1 Yankee victory.

The illusion of luck, magic, and mystery always helps a team bond. These guys aren't two dozen nuclear physicists; they're delighted to buy into any myth or ritual that's helpful.

For instance, as the season progressed, the Orioles became obsessive about shaking hands after victories. Every player made a serious attempt to shake hands with every other player. That's 276 handshakes, not factoring in the coaches. No wonder it sometimes seemed that the Orioles might be out in the infield giving each other skin until midnight.

"We believe in really shaking hands and looking people in the eye," said Bill Ripken. "It takes a while. I don't know who started it. Maybe Cal Junior."

"After one game Craig Worthington bumped into me and said, 'Don't give me a dead fish [handshake]. Look at me,'" said coach Al Jackson. "Now he and I bump into each other so hard, we almost knock each other down. You've got to eyeball each guy and say something [specific] to show you really appreciate what he did."

For fans, watching the Orioles shake hands and make their little hip quips of appreciation became a ritual too. On most teams, you notice which players seem to like each other. On the Orioles, everybody seemed to like everybody else. Such deliberately crafted conceits can start to become reality.

Within days, the Orioles needed all the camaraderie they could get their hands on. On July 21, in the 94th game of the season, with the Orioles holding a 7½-game division lead, the worst possible thing happened. Gregg Olson walked to the mound in the Oakland Coliseum on the first night of a fourteen-game road trip with the Orioles leading, 2–1. It was the same mound from which he'd announced himself so brilliantly.

This time, he walked four straight men, threw a wild pitch, and simply handed the game to the A's. The team's psychological security blanket had come unraveled. And the Orioles fell apart.

Milligan's Swing

The radio reception on Mount Desert Island off the coast of Maine wasn't very good, even if you were just trying to pull in Ned Martin's gravelly version of a Boston Red Sox game. Too many hills surrounded our vacation rental for the signal to make its way easily to the old kitchen radio. That romantic, flickering, fading reception was even more infuriating because it was the fate of the Red Sox' opponent that concerned me. Or, you could say, obsessed me.

A grown man does not cancel his family's summer vacation just because he doesn't want to be out of touch with a baseball team that's in a slump. In particular, a man doesn't do such a pathetic thing if for twenty years he's written about games, particularly baseball, for a living. Enthusiasm for one's work is all very nice, but if you let it spoil your two weeks in the Maine woods, you are a sick puppy.

Like a lot of people, I had become a sick puppy.

When my vacation came due, the timing was perfect—perfectly awful. On my first morning in Maine, the *Bangor Daily News* informed me of Olson's disaster. There may be such a thing as knowing your subject too well. The Orioles had lost only two games in a row. But I told my wife that, conceivably, they could lose every game on the rest of their road trip. "Whatever it takes to lose, they'll do it," I said. "That's just how it works." In the midst of Eden, I suddenly found myself in hell. For ten days, I refused to pay outward attention. A few calls to a New York score tape, sure. But sometimes I didn't even bother to find out the score until the following afternoon. I knew they'd lost and that they'd lose again. Just as they knew it. Blow a 4–0 lead? Why, of course. Lose eight games in a row—one shy of the A.L. record for most consecutive losses by a first-place club? No question about it.

When the Orioles finally won a game, it was because the Royals, also choking in a pennant race, forced them to take it in the thirteenth, courtesy of an error, a wild pitch, and a perfect peg that sailed over an uncovered base.

After that win, the Orioles made sure they lost. One day they walked ten men. The next, they made four errors. The day after that, they lost a doubleheader. Quicker than you can say, "Life's a bitch and then you die," the Orioles had lost 13 out of 14 games, and their division lead was 1 game with 57 to play. They were still in first place (at 54–51) but were already doomed.

I listened to every pitch of the August 2 game against the Sox—the last of the road trip. If somebody did not step forward that night and act heroically—allowing the team to return home in first place and with a vestige of dignity—I was convinced that the whole Orioles season might still go down the drain. Ninety defeats? Why not?

In retrospect, I don't know whether I still believe that Randy Milligan, with one swing, salvaged a whole team's season-of-a-lifetime. But from the moment Milligan's three-run homer tied the score, 6–6, in the eighth—erasing what had been a 6–0 deficit entering the seventh—I began to proceed from the assumption that everything would be all right. The Orioles' tale would have an appropriate ending of some kind. They would make it to the wire.

Pennant Race by Committee

Major league baseball is a game within a game within a game. It is psychology within technique within talent. Or you can call it personality within experience within ability. First, you learn that you can play the game. Then, you learn how to play the game. Finally, you learn something about yourself through the game.

Fact accumulates. Every detail seems to carry over to the next day or the next week, locked in somebody's mind—maybe your own. You don't escape your past very often. What you have done right, learned properly, observed correctly, tends to reinforce and protect the future. Whatever or whomever you have neglected or disdained "returns to haunt you"—a favorite baseball cliché.

Although they were a team of limited talent and experience, the Orioles survived a two-month pennant race with barely a hint of a haunt. After Milligan's home run settled their stomachs, the Orioles went 33–24—a solid pennant-contender pace. Their persistence, interdependence, and resiliency carried them through a distinguished performance in August and September. In sports, is habit just a synonym for character?

Above all, the Orioles took strength from the example they set for one another. They admired one another. So they removed egos from their clubhouse and invented baseball by committee. If their cleanup hitter and catcher (Tettleton) was disabled for a month, they simply picked up old Jamie Quirk, released by three teams in one year; the Orioles went 18–11 until Tettleton returned, as Quirk produced runs faster than Tettleton had.

The tire-patching and canoe-bailing projects became almost comical. When second baseman Bill Ripken was disabled, Tim Hulett (who'd been gone from the majors for two years) was summoned out of desperation. He came up five times with the bases loaded and got five hits. When Finley's wrist wouldn't heal, someone named Stan Jefferson was brought from Rochester. In 127 at-bats, he produced at a 20-homer, 100-RBI, 45-steal pace.

The consensus star of this off-Broadway production of *Les Misérables*, however, was Dave Johnson—Baltimore native, shrimpy, slope-shouldered, ten-year minor league veteran, off-season truck driver, proud owner of a mobile home, and one gutty little right-handed spitballer. Sorry, sinkerballer.

Until Johnson arrived, the Orioles thought Kevin Hickey was the ultimate in baseball humility. Hickey had been out of the majors for five years and, the previous season, had slept in his minor league team's clubhouse to save rent. As an Oriole, his job was easy: Face left-handed-hitting superstars in crucial situations. Light lifting. Wade Boggs, Don Mattingly, George Brett, and Harold Baines went 1 for 17 against the pudgy, balding Hickey, who seemed to be throwing his heart to the plate along with the ball.

Johnson quickly topped that. In his home debut, with thirty relatives and hundreds of friends in the stands, the Overlea High grad pitched a 6–1 complete-game win. Five days later, with the Orioles' rotation and bullpen both in tatters, Johnson did it again—another 6–1 win, another complete game.

American League Player of the Week: Dave Johnson.

Such deeds have repercussions. The next day, on August 14, the Orioles negotiated the most modest victory of their entire Meek Shall Inherit the A.L. East season. Robinson didn't have a single starting pitcher fit to put on the mound against Jack Morris of Detroit. So the manager named three starting pitchers—and prayed that each could survive three innings. No first-place team had ever resorted to anything so obviously desperate.

After nine innings, the score was 1–1. Brian Holton, Mark Thurmond, and Dave Schmidt had done their jobs. But would the Orioles ever score again?

In the tenth inning, the team got a glimpse of its future. A spring rookie is not the same as an August rookie. With 100 games under his belt, Craig Worthington was not the same hitter Morris had seen in Lakeland, Florida, in March. By now Worthington was thinking along with pitchers—hitting to the opposite field with men on base, guessing pitches, building a book on the league. Morris threw a perfect fastball a couple of inches off the outside corner. The only way Worthington, a pull hitter, could smack the ball with any authority was if (1) he was looking for that exact pitch and (2) he had decided to hit it to rightfield.

As the three-run, game-winning home run landed in the upper deck in the rightfield corner, Morris put his hands on his knees and looked at his feet as Worthington circled the bases.

Aarrrgggh!

There's always one game you want back. You know if you could just play it over again, you'd win. The only reason you lost was that you wanted the damn thing too much.

This was the one.

It was Fan Appreciation Day, as if the fans hadn't been rewarded enough already. For a month, the Orioles had regrouped every time they faced a true crisis, managing to win almost every time. Head to head, Baltimore had won games from Boston, Milwaukee, and Toronto when those teams could have moved into first place with a victory. And after September 1, when the Orioles finally fell out of first after ninety-eight straight days in front, they really gave their followers something to value.

Instead of resigning themselves, as most thought they would, the Orioles stayed in the race. While the Blue Jays put on a 26–9 rush, the Orioles maintained cruising speed at 22–14. For a month, from August 20 to September 20, the Orioles never won on a day the Jays lost. Though they never gained ground, they didn't despair. When the remnants of Hurricane Hugo blew three cheap Yankee home runs out of the park one night, the Orioles won, 10–2, the next evening. When Johnson became exhausted, Robinson gambled on a three-man rotation, and all three—Ballard (7–2, 2.64), Milacki (6–1, 2.50), and Harnisch (4–4, 3.57)—were in top form down the stretch.

Finally, on Fan Appreciation Day, the Orioles were poised to catch the Blue Jays with a week left in the season and a three-game head-to-head series due to end it in Toronto. The Orioles had their best, Ballard, set to start against one of the Yankees' worst—Chuck Cary, a career nobody worthy of an Orioles uniform. The left-handed Cary even said he'd become an Orioles fan.

But he beat them, 2–0, as a crowd of 51,173 held its breath, waiting for a home-team explosion that never came. Screwballs down and away, fastballs on the fists, showcase the breaking ball down and in, 10 strikeouts in seven innings against a lineup of nine right-handed batters—the best game of Cary's career. Where did this lifelong wild man find such control?

The stats say the Orioles played better against left-handed starters (35–25) than righties. But the stats lie. The Birds hit, slugged, and scored far better against right-handers. The won-lost numbers were just a fluke. In particular, southpaws who could spot the ball, first in, then away—even for just one day—drove the Orioles crazy. Ripken, Tettleton, and Milligan—the heart of the order—couldn't touch 'em.

This one game may have been more bitter for the Orioles than all the late pennant race nights of listening to the Blue Jays win extra-inning games—six in a row over the closing weeks. Once, Kevin Hickey became so mesmerized listening to a Toronto-Boston game on his car radio—with the Red Sox taking leads in the eleventh and thir-teenth innings—that, by the time the Blue Jays finally won the stupid game, he discovered that he'd driven entirely out of Maryland and into Pennsylvania.

That Cary defeat did not unravel the Orioles. They still won two out of three in Milwaukee to stay one game behind the Blue Jays and force that final weekend showdown in Toronto. But losing the season's final home game, when Memorial Stadium was full to the top row with throats anxious to sing hosannas, whittled the Orioles' margin of error down to almost nothing.

One Pitch Equals One Season

Like a good soldier leading his men over the top, Phil Bradley hit the first pitch of the first Toronto game into the second deck of the SkyDome bleachers. It was a monstrous, resounding 420-foot home run that created an instant atmosphere of high tension.

In that pressurized setting, the Orioles couldn't hit in the clutch, and the Blue Jays, a scatterbrained team for years, couldn't run around the bases without getting in each other's way. The score stayed 1–0 into the eighth inning, though the Blue Jays were giving such a clinic in bad fielding and running that two well-known former big leaguers kept the press box snickering with a sarcastic running commentary on Toronto's mental blunders.

With one out in the eighth inning, the Orioles called Olson. He had not allowed a run since July. Yes, two scoreless months. August ERA: 0.00. September ERA: 0.00. Twenty straight games.

With two out and a man on third, Olson got ahead in the count to Kelly Gruber, 1–2. One more strike and the inning would be over. Then, one more inning, and the pennant race would be tied. The pressure, if it wasn't already on the Jays, would certainly be there with a vengeance. Would the *Toronto Sun* spell CHOKE in mere 60-point type or go for the World War III 120-point kind? Waiting in the wings for the regular-season ender, the Orioles had Milacki, one of the game's hottest pitchers; Baltimore had won his last seven starts.

Jamie Quirk called for a curveball and set a low target. Either throw a perfect unhittable pitch or else waste one.

Olson got on top of the pitch a bit too much, snapping it short and wide of the plate, and fifteen-year veteran Quirk didn't get the best jump moving out to block the ball. Once, long ago, the Red Sox kept a season-long count of how many pitches in the dirt Carlton Fisk blocked with a runner on third base: 71 in a year. Exceptional defensive catchers (like Quirk) block so many balls in the dirt you barely notice one of the game's difficult plays.

"I should have blocked it. I think I should block everything. I'm a professional catcher. Olson's supposed to throw that curveball there," said Quirk. "I've blocked that same ball before."

But this time, the ball kicked up high and hard and Quirk had no chance. Wild pitch. Tie game.

A better team than the Orioles would have surmounted this disappointment. But a better team than the Orioles would not have been such an interesting team. When Olson shut out the Jays in the ninth (and then the tenth too), it did not save a victory. It merely prolonged the Orioles' agony as the Blue Jays' fabulously deep bullpen held Baltimore scoreless and waited for its own sluggers to greet whoever might eventually follow Olson.

Many fans think the race ended the next day as the Orioles were eliminated in another gallant one-run loss. That afternoon, Dave Johnson, an emergency starter for the injured Harnisch, made a one-day national hero of himself by taking a two-hitter and a 3–1 lead into the eighth inning. Few will forget his determination or his tears in the dugout as he watched the lead and the season disappear.

Earl Weaver's classic response to all the hypotheticals of baseball was to shrug and say, "Everything changes everything." But some of us stubbornly persist in believing that Olson's wild pitch changed everything. Is that really how close the Orioles came to going from worst to first—one pitch that was nobody's fault?

The Orioles won their last game of 1989, then returned home to a rain-soaked celebratory parade. In every way, they finished with organizational dignity and individual pride. Mark Williamson, who had the best year of his life but lost those two games in Toronto in relief, was congratulated by everybody up to team president Larry Lucchino after the elimination game. Quirk, the oldest player on the team, set an example of unselfishness by repeatedly taking blame for the wild pitch and, thus, removing the stigma from Olson, the franchise player. "I didn't go out and get it," Quirk would say, sipping his Labatt's beer as teammates shook their heads respectfully, knowing that Johnny Bench might not have stopped that one.

This Orioles season will almost be a laboratory experiment in baseball behavior. Many believe that the team will collapse, that 1989 was an utterly unrepeatable fluke. Perhaps. But remember, in baseball, good young players almost always get better. The last time the Orioles used nine key rookies in one year (1977), they became a powerhouse for the next six years and ended up in two World Series. Those Baby Birds, including Eddie Murray, Scott McGregor, Dennis Martinez, and Rich Dauer, were not nearly as deep a group and probably not as good as the '89 Orioles rookies. And this isn't even counting Ben McDonald, the top pick in the '89 draft.

A team can't end a season with a better opinion of itself than the Orioles did. But what now? This is a year of countless questions. As a team, will they take the next steps up the ladder of professional craftsmanship?

Will Ballard, Milacki, Tettleton, and Worthington be future All-Stars or just journeymen? Maybe Olson, as long as he's healthy, is a "can't miss." McDonald too. But these other guys could go either forward or back.

Moving down one level of potential, will Milligan, Devereaux, Harnisch, and perhaps Finley develop into front-line players? Or will they be role fillers, part-timers, " 'tweeners," and might-have-beens? And what about the Birds who are probably closest to our hearts because they're closest to our abilities? Will Everymen like Johnson, Hickey, Hulett, Jefferson, and even one-game wonders like Mickey Weston return to the world of Never Was? Please, we say, let some of them stick around for the rest of the ride back to the top.

April is the time for such harsh questions and reality-tested answers. Will the Orioles think that one thrilling year, one parade, make them stars? Is harmony a temporary state of grace? Or can it be recaptured? Years from now, will the Orioles and their fans think of 1989 as a distant sweet memory or a living touchstone?

Soon enough the picture will start to come into focus from that sea of dots, another season of baseball detail.

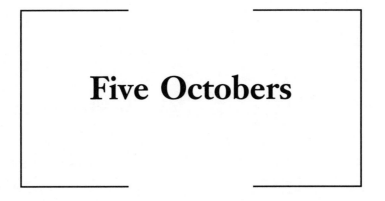

Five Octobers

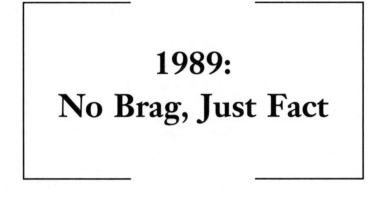

1989:
No Brag, Just Fact

PHOENIX, March 17, 1989—If you assembled several zebras, a few giraffes, and a yak, they wouldn't know how to act. They couldn't function as a herd, even if each was the best of his species. However, if you had nothing but yaks, they'd know just what to do. They'd be comfortable with themselves. Nobody here but us yaks.

Even though the Oakland Athletics lost the last World Series, and looked funny while doing it, they have reassembled this spring with as much bumptious, bragging, bodacious good cheer as if they'd never heard of that gaggle of Stunt Men from Los Angeles.

"We look mah-vel-ous," says Dave Henderson, imitating Billy Crystal. "You know, it's not how you play that counts. It's how you look. And we look mah-vel-ous." Henderson is partly kidding, but not entirely. The A's do look better than any other team in baseball—on the field and on paper, where they not only are without weakness but, in fact, have strengths everywhere.

The last team as good as Oakland (104 wins) to be beaten in a Series by a club as humble as the '88 Dodgers was the mighty Baltimore Orioles juggernaut of 1969, which fell, also in five games, to the Miracle Mets. How did those Orioles respond? With two more pennants in a row and a world title in '70.

"I'll go for that [comparison]," said A's manager Tony LaRussa as he slapped out fungoes to his Bash Brothers here. "We've got the makings of a helluva club. And nobody seems to be taking [success] for granted."

From the day that Henderson, with his Mr. Olympia–type body, and mammoth Dave Parker arrived last season, the A's found their style: They'd be big, cocky, hardworking, and show their love of the kill. This week, in a game televised back to the Bay area, the A's scored 14 runs—that's f-o-u-r-t-e-e-n runs—in the top of the last inning to humiliate the San Francisco Giants, 20–7. As 19 men came to bat, the A's mercilessly kept pouring on more punishment for the home folks to watch and digest.

"You won't believe what just happened to us," said one Giants coach when he phoned a Padres scout that night. "We go into the ninth leading the A's by a run—and lose by thirteen."

That's Oakland for you. Henderson, when asked what team these A's remind him of, smiled wolfishly and said, "The old Oakland Raiders." The guys with the skull and crossbones on their helmets.

The A's want to scare you, numb you, beat you in batting practice or during the introductions when you see Mark McGwire, Jose Canseco, Dave Stewart, Dennis Eckersley, Carney Lansford, Storm Davis, and Bob Welch in those skin-tight yellow, green, and white pajamas. If you're 6-foot-5, 210 pounds like reliever Eric Plunk, nobody even notices you on this team.

"I've never seen a team this big," said LaRussa. "And they're in better shape than they were last spring. . . . I became a believer in weight training back in 1966. One of our secrets is [strength coach] Dave McKay."

As if the A's needed more, they signed Moore—free agent Mike Moore, a dainty 6-foot-4, 205-pound right-hander who fanned 182 batters for the miserable Mariners last year. Where do you put him? Sophomore Todd Burns (8–2) is back for a full year, and such proven pitchers as Greg Cadaret, Rick Honeycutt, Curt Young, and Gene Nelson are already short of work. "How can our pitching get better [than last year]? Jeeez," said pitching coach Dave Duncan, looking perplexed. "If we go with ten pitchers, it's going to be tough" to make cuts.

At least on the outside, the A's make it a project never to admit anything gets under their skin. Especially the way '88 ended. "They don't talk about last year. They talk about what they're going to do this year," said Duncan.

"Once in a great while, during a long season, if we needed a little juice, a little boost, you could use that. You could say, 'We could screw up like we screwed up the World Series,' " said LaRussa. "But if you do that too often, it'll tap out. It's too negative to carry you. Day in and day out, you need better motivation than that.

"Last year, this team set a certain standard about how hard they played every day. That's what I want to see again, that consistent effort. The rest will take care of itself."

If the A's have any hints of a haunting lingering about their ability, they'd be the last team to show it. That's not their act. The perfect illustration is Canseco, who's had a world of bad publicity about missing a couple of off-season appointments, then being ticketed for traffic violations in his new Jaguar in both Florida and Arizona. Standing under the Phoenix palms, taking in everything with an eerie casualness, the sport's first 40-40-140 (home runs, stolen bases, RBI) man said that as his fame has grown, his problems have been "blown out of proportion."

"Nothing seems to bother Jose. Nothing," said LaRussa. "But I always try to remember with all my players, especially the young ones, they are not machines."

It's easy to yawn and set your calendar watch for October 3. Why not forget about Oakland, and the entire American League West, until playoff time? Then tune in to see if the '89 A's can use their deeply buried and well-camouflaged frustrations as well as those 1970 Orioles.

The Athletics look mah-vel-ous this spring and they flaunt it. They seem to have kept the courage of their boisterous convictions intact, while tucking away just a smidgen of motivational bile for any hard times that may arrive. Over the next year or two, baseball will almost certainly find out just how formidable a herd of bull elephants the Dodgers actually stampeded.

□ □ □

TORONTO, October 7, 1989—A great slugger must be intimidating. It should be part of his walk, his stance, and, perhaps, part of his talk. Even as sweet a man as Ernie Banks was surrounded by a lethal composure at the plate, a sense of coiled danger.

A great base stealer must be obnoxious. It should be part of his crouch, his fakes, his slides, and even his facial expression. Ty Cobb was not only obnoxious but vicious. When he was sixty years old, playing in an old-timers game, he told the catcher to back up so he wouldn't get hit by the bat, and then beat out a bunt. Maury Wills was an arrogant pest who taught the world how to steal with a five-run lead. Even Lou Brock, who spoke like a mathematician off the field, was imperious and defiant on the bases. Obnoxious in his way.

Rickey Henderson is the most obnoxious baseball player who ever lived.

The Oakland A's leadoff man and leftfielder has raised irritation, cockiness, and insubordinate defiance to a high and infuriating art form. In every city, except the city where he plays, he is despised. His every gesture is a preen, a reaffirmation that he loves himself more than you have ever dreamed of loving yourself. For that alone you yell:

"Get in the box and hit, you hotdog. Stop stalling. This isn't a movie of your life. (He's gonna kill us again.)

"Swing the bat like a man. Are you paying the umps to call balls? (What a great eye he's got.)

"Stick it in his ear. Step on his hand. (If he didn't move so fast.)

"Catch the ball with two hands, Rickey. You're gonna drop one. (Never.)"

Rickey likes to get his batting glove just right. Rickey likes to call time out. For anything. He'll be the first player to install a car phone on his bat so he can talk to his agent between pitches. A little half-hour chat with the first-base coach is always nice. If Rickey's pants get dirty from sliding, he sends them to a one-hour laundry while your pitcher waits.

It's all part of being Rickey—like spelling your name wrong. I'm different. I'm better. Stop me if you can. But, of course, you can't because you're so busy being mad at Rickey that you can't do the calm, sensible little things that are necessary to neutralize him.

Of course, if Rickey's hamstrings are bothering him or he has a sprain—the kind of injuries every base stealer has always gotten—he takes a few days off. Just as he should. But, as a result, sometimes Henderson's teammates, usually the touchy ones who aren't making millions, start thinking that Rickey is pretty obnoxious even if he plays for your team.

So even though he is the greatest leadoff man and the greatest base stealer who ever lived, sometimes Rickey gets traded. From Oakland to New York. From New York to Oakland. And maybe he'll go free agent this winter and leave Oakland if they don't love him, er, pay him enough.

Henderson is a double-edged sword. He ignites the offense of every team he plays for and steals the heart of many foes. But against the best teams, he can inspire the opposition too. In eleven seasons—and 871 stolen bases and 1,171 runs scored—Henderson has never played in a World Series and made it to only two League Championship Series. It's not his fault, certainly, but it might not entirely be a coincidence.

Certainly this year's American League playoffs have, so far, been nothing more or less than a demonstration of, and a discussion about, Rickey Henderson.

You can't play any better. And you can't make people any madder.

In three games he has reached base nine times, stolen seven bases and scored five runs. He also makes the odd sprinting catch in the leftfield corner. In Game 2 he stole four bases—the most ever in any World Series or playoff game in history. For reference, Pepper Martin, the Wild Horse of the Osage who ran wild for the St. Louis Cardinals Gas House Gang, was such a base-stealing threat in the 1931 World Series that Philadelphia A's catcher Mickey Cochrane checked himself into a hospital between games so that he could have complete rest and seclusion to prepare for the mental torture of facing Martin. In seven games in that Series, Martin had five steals. Henderson almost had that many in a day.

Only Lou Brock, in '67 and '68, ever stole seven times in one postseason series. It took him seven games both times. Think Henderson has a chance to break that record?

In the process, however, Henderson has angered the Toronto Blue Jays, a team some observers never believed could be moved to any emotion more violent than getting picked off second base. The Blue Jays are talented and they give a professional effort, but they aren't what you would call an intense team.

In Game 2, on one of his steals of second base, Henderson noticed out of the corner of his eye that catcher Ernie Whitt had not bothered to throw. Ah ha! A chance to be obnoxious! Rickey slowed to a tiptoe, inched toward the base, walked around the base, then finally touched it from the far side.

"He showed up our whole ball club. He's bush," said Whitt. "You don't see [Oakland's] Carney Lansford doing that. . . . He may inspire them, but he's doing everything to fire up our club too."

Other Blue Jays took the point further, noting that while Rickey is the Pièce de la Dog, two other A's—Dave Parker and Dave Henderson—are locked in mortal combat trying to outstyle the king. Parker, who once wore a Star of David because "my name is David and I'm a star," specializes in what Kelly Gruber called "the day-and-a-half home run trot" as well as the obscene dugout threat and the base-running finger wigwag. Dave Henderson? Watch him. He only styles when he's awake.

"I tell you what, if I was a pitcher, I'd have some guys decked. I mean [Rickey] Henderson, I mean Parker. And I don't care if they know it," said Gruber, the Jays third baseman. "It kind of makes me want to get vengeance. It burns me up inside."

All this delighted Rickey, who earlier this week said that if the A's made it to the Series he thought the key reason would be himself.

In Game 3 Friday night Rickey Henderson had a performance that could stand for his whole career. He walked, took an extra base on a fly, and scored in the first inning. He doubled, stole third base on Whitt, then scored in the third. And he robbed a Blue Jay of a double with a fine catch.

However, the players whose wrath he had aroused scored seven runs while he was manufacturing two. When he made a symbolic out, failing to advance a man from second to third with none out in the seventh with Toronto ahead, 4–3, it seemed to make his team sag and the Jays erupt. Bulletin: Rickey actually fails! In the bottom of the inning, Toronto scored three. Goodnight Rickey.

Has Henderson awoken a team that was ready to die? Or is he the cinch Most Valuable Player of these playoffs and the catalyst of a new world champion?

Stay tuned. Rickey always returns.

□   □   □

TORONTO, October 10, 1989—Baseball hasn't seen a team as good, as colorful, as exciting, as easy to like and as easy to dislike as the 1989 Oakland A's since the heyday of the 1977–1978 world champion New York Yankees.

Those Yankees, of Reggie Jackson and Thurman Munson, Sparky Lyle and Catfish Hunter, Ron Guidry and Graig Nettles, Chris Chambliss and Mickey Rivers, Billy Martin and George Steinbrenner, were tough as nails and ornery as dirt, mean as a bucketful of snakes and not too fond of each other. They coexisted to conquer. Nettles celebrated one flag clinching by knocking the Straw That Stirs the Drink on his rear end with a left hook at the victory party. Reggie asked for it by knocking a beer bottle out of Puff's hand.

Those were the days.

And they're back again.

Of course, these '80s A's haven't proven themselves like the '70s Yankees. They don't fight each other. They just feud with the other guys. And they haven't won three straight pennants or back-to-back Series. In fact, their historical significance to date is that they blew a Series to the weakest lineup in modern times. That is, unless you have a kinder description of their pratfall against the Stunt Men last year.

It's easy to forget, however, that it took a year for the Yankees to get their act together. They were swept in the '76 Series by a great Cincinnati team and that defeat, in its way, galled the cocky Yankees as much as the Athletics' loss last year burned their hides. The Yankees needed something extra to get over the talent and charisma gap.

So they got Reggie in '77.

He was extolled, vilified, booed, adored, and, finally, accepted on his own terms. He was the slugger, the leader, the lightning rod the Yankees needed. He took pressure off everybody else.

The A's needed something too. Jose Canseco and Mark McGwire are wonderful. But they're slump-prone free swingers who can sometimes be pitched to, or around, by top-quality staffs. The Bash Brothers strike out 250 times a year. Carney Lansford, Dave Parker, and Dave Henderson are a superb supporting cast. But, except Parker, they're all righties so you can play percentages against the A's and not always pay a price.

The A's needed Rickey Henderson. And they got him.

Lightning rod, leader, money player, egotist, Hall of Famer, scene stealer, monologist on himself—but too much fun not to like.

Sound familiar? He's Reggie, but with a perpetual playful teasing grin.

Rickey, whose first name may soon be as recognizable in baseball as Reggie or Orel, is a nightmare for right-handed pitchers, who can't hold him on base. Start a lefty and the rest of the A's mulch you. Henderson is also the ideal complement to a sluggers' lineup. He's a one-run rally, made out of nothing, all by himself. In close games against the best teams—the kind you meet in October—he lifts the burden of production from the long-ballers.

For Henderson in particular and the A's in general, the World Series will be a proving ground. If any group should sense how fleeting glory can be, the A's would be it. Just look at Rickey. One day ago, he'd had the greatest playoff in history—conceivably the best anybody would ever have. He batted .400, slugged 1.000, produced 11 runs, got on base 14 times, stole 8 bases, had 31 aggregate bases, and hit a double, a triple, and 2 homers.

In the twenty-four hours (and two San Francisco Giants games) since Oakland started celebrating, Will Clark actually might have surpassed Henderson. In his five playoff games, he hit .650, slugged 1.200, produced 14 runs, reached base 15 times, had 26 aggregate bases, and hit 3 doubles, a triple, and 2 homers. Talk about an amazing Take Your Pick.

As the A's enter their Bay Bridge Series, they will be larger-than-life overdogs. A role they'll love just as much as that other team a decade ago. In almost every way, the new A's are as delightful, as exasperating, and as certain to start a barroom debate as the old Yankees. For starters, they are just as defiantly heterogeneous. You can't lump or categorize this team any more than you could the Yankees. Lansford, McGwire, Dave Stewart, and Bob Welch are upright, old-school hardball, just like Chambliss, Hunter, Randolph, and Guidry. No frills, no flash, no controversy.

Dave Parker is just as quick to bench-jockey, to get into the thick of a beanball brawl, or to fire off a witty but barbed quote as Nettles once was.

The Yankees had their characters—Lou Piniella and Mickey Rivers, the racetrack twins, and Munson, who always was mad at somebody. And, of course, George and Billy.

In different ways the A's are inflammatory. That is, unless you think Canseco's adventures with guns and cars are bland. Dave and Rickey Henderson together require as much mustard as Reggie. Dennis Eckersley is the Rickey of pitchers, talking trash at hitters.

"It's fun having a personality and winning. We have some guys who like to hotdog, but what's wrong with that? It makes the game more fun for the fans," Lansford said after Sunday's fifth-game whipping of the angry Blue Jays. "We back things up."

The A's credo: No brag, just fact.

The A's don't just beat you, they rub it in, from Rickey's trot to Eckersley's pretending to six-gun hitters after he strikes them out. Then, if you complain, the A's mock you. "The Jays topped off all their crying and whining by accusing Eck of cheating," said Lansford. "You didn't hear us give excuses when we lost that one game."

The A's may never be more fun to watch than they are now, because they will probably never be more motivated. "There's so much heat generated by this club [in the dugout] during the game," said LaRussa proudly. "They just don't talk about it much before and after."

The fact that the A's maintain they can barely remember the '88 Series may prove how profoundly they are driven by it. Sometimes, someone, like McGwire on Sunday, breaks radio silence: "We're going to do everything we have to do to prove to people that we can win a World Series."

The more you wish you were like the A's, the more losing to them galls you. As the Blue Jays' George Bell put it: "A lot of people have told me that I'm a hotdog and controversial, but the A's have got the worst attitude I've ever seen in baseball. . . . I hope they enjoy the World Series. I hope they get their butts kicked."

Baseball needs the new A's just like it needed the old Yankees. Whether you love to watch them do the stomping or hope they get the boot, they're just too much of a kick to miss.

1990:
Hubris, the Sequel

CINCINNATI, October 17, 1990—Does Eric Davis, bad shoulder and all, look just a little like Kirk Gibson? Is Jose Rijo, the right-hander on the roll of a lifetime, beginning to bear a resemblance to Orel Hershiser?

Funny how one solid fact, like that Gibson homer of 1988 or Rijo's decisive victory over Dave Stewart Tuesday night, can obliterate millions of words of abstract speculation. A World Series that was of dubious interest before it began is now, thanks to this night of concrete work, one of high drama.

The Reds did not just beat the world champion Athletics, 7–0, in Game 1 of this 87th World Series. The Reds gave them a front-to-back thumping with all manner of symbolic trappings.

To upset the A's in a Series, you have to get them thinking. Prove to them that you're not intimidated. Show that you grasp their flaws. And show that you have worthy heroes too.

A lot of that went on here Tuesday night.

First and foremost, Stewart looked awful. He was wild—with four walks in four innings as 25 of his first 43 pitches were balls. Attempting to lay a 3–0 pitch down the pipe, Stewart bounced his fastball to the screen.

When the A's stopper did throw strikes, they traveled a long way. Eric Davis crushed a first-pitch fastball so thoroughly that he had time to stand and admire his 400-foot two-run homer over the centerfield wall. Billy Hatcher's RBI double was traveling about 150 mph when it zoomed over Carney Lansford's head.

After more than 1,100 innings in the past four seasons—far more than any other pitcher in the game because of his postseason work—is Stewart's mortality showing? And if the A's need him to come back twice on three days' rest, will he improve?

"He wasn't right," said A's manager Tony LaRussa. Asked if a six-day hiatus might have gotten Stewart out of sync, LaRussa said: "I've learned that explanations sound like excuses. Let's just say he was not quite right."

The A's entered this Series with a ten-game postseason winning streak. Half—five wins—belonged to Stewart. The A's success for the past two Octobers has, out of all normal baseball proportion, been Stewart's success. He's the heart of this team.

Ignore what Rickey Henderson and Jose Canseco say, even on their pay-to-listen 900 numbers. (Yes, Rickey has one too now—the Man of Steal Line.) They're the gifted, fun-loving children in the A's locker room who sometimes get out of hand and have to be reprimanded. Nobody on the A's takes their bravado seriously. The worst they can do is inspire the A's foes. Stewart is the A's adult. What he says and how he performs set the Oakland tone.

In the '88 Series, the A's lost both games Stewart started. Both times the Dodgers foe was . . . Tim Belcher. About as famous a name as Jose Rijo.

Like the Dodgers in '88, the Reds needed an emotional jump start to prove to themselves they belonged on the field with the A's. Davis provided it. Over the weekend Manager Lou Piniella suggested that Davis, because of his various injuries, bat leadoff and, essentially, give up trying to be a power-hitting cleanup man.

"I had a little meeting with Lou," said Davis. "It was pretty much to the point. I told him I didn't want to do it. I've been batting fourth most of my career and that's where I want to stay for this Series."

"We got our big guy going tonight," said Hatcher, whose walk, single, double, double night was not as vital to his team's confidence as Davis's homer, RBI single, and long fly out. "It took a load off his shoulders and ours. . . . Maybe Lou made him a little upset and that was just Eric telling Lou, 'Leave me at fourth.' "

While Davis looked good in every at-bat and almost made a tumbling catch to rob Henderson of a double, the A's comparable strongman—Canseco—still seemed pained by back and wrist injuries. When the Reds took an extra base on his arm, he stood in rightfield and shook his wrist conspicuously.

Davis wisely is playing the Caveman Kirk role to the hilt. Asked if his diving catch attempt hurt his shoulder, Davis said: "It hurts my shoulder when I'm just standing here. I don't think about how I feel when I'm between the white lines. My shoulder was still on my neck when I got up, so I knew I was all right."

The Reds, like the '88 Dodgers, also got a look at some of the A's mini-flaws. Mike Gallego, out of position at shortstop because of Walt Weiss's knee injury, made a ludicrously wild throw to the plate to help generate the Reds' fourth run. Willie Randolph, filling in at second base, failed to make a potential inning-ending double play. Chris Sabo followed instantly with a two-run hit.

The emergence of Rijo as a pitcher who relishes big games also gave this game extra impact. Twice he faced McGwire with a total of five men on base and twice Rijo got McGwire to end the innings meekly. Once, Rijo even fielded a ground ball through the middle behind his back—out of necessity.

"Rijo got what he deserved—seven shutout innings," said LaRussa generously.

As usual, Rijo had to have his postgame fun. Against the Pirates, he said "It's over" before it was over and, poking fun at himself, wore an "It's Over" T-shirt on Monday. After this game, he praised the A's but added, "Pittsburgh's lineup might be just a little tougher than Oakland's."

Statistically, Rijo is right. The Pirates hit right-handers better than the A's, who have eight righty hitters.

Rijo also had the incentive of knowing his father-in-law—Hall of Famer Juan Marichal—was in the stands. "He works for the A's," said Rijo, "so he can't say much to me. But just having him here watching me is so important to me. I want to look good when he's watching. I even play golf better when I play with him."

This victory puts the Reds in the picture. Especially because a seventh game here probably would pit Rijo and Stewart in a rematch. Rijo's ERA is a full run lower in Riverfront than on the road. Stewart, on the other hand, gives up twice as many runs on the road as he does in the huge Oakland Coliseum. Rijo may not match up to Stewart overall. But he might in this park.

So what have we got? Rijo proves he can stop the A's. The Reds prove they can beat Stewart and beat him soundly. The Nasty Boys get two innings of shutout work. Davis breaks out of his playoff slump. Canseco and McGwire both continue to hit as they did against Boston, which is not much at all. The Reds run on the A's outfield arms, as they said they would, and the A's makeshift infield messes up a little.

Is that enough for one night?

Next, we get the biggest mismatch in many a year. Bob Welch (27–6) against Danny Jackson (6–6). The joker in the deck, however, is that Welch has been a poor postseason pitcher in other years and Jackson has been superb. Jackson stopped the Pirates on one hit for six innings to clinch the NL pennant. Welch will, no doubt, recall that October 17 is the anniversary of the World Series Earthquake—a day when he was scheduled to pitch but instead went home to find his house destroyed.

On one hand, the A's are the A's are the A's. On the other, as Yogi Berra said, could this be déjà vu all over again?

□ □ □

CINCINNATI, October 18, 1990—Please, Doc, just let us wake up. We know these are only the aftereffects of the anesthetic. Soon, the surgery will be over. We'll all wake up and . . .

Ahhhhhh, you mean it's all real!!??

Yes, the Oakland A's have had better nightmares than this World Series.

If baseball's defending champions aren't spooked out of their wits, and maybe hallucinating some too, then it's 'cause they're totally unconscious after what has hit them in the first two games.

Is it really possible that Dennis Eckersley lost to the Cincinnati Reds, 5–4, in sudden death in the tenth inning? Wasn't that the score of the Kirk Gibson Game? When did Eck become Prometheus, suffering the same pain repeatedly?

Did the Reds actually win on a ground ball hit by Joe Oliver that nicked the outside edge of the foul line? And who started the rally off the greatest relief pitcher in the universe? Yes, Billy Bates: zero career hits as a Red.

After their legendary embarrassment in the 1988 Series, the proud, often downright vain A's thought those who learned from history would not be condemned to repeat it.

Soooorry. What we have in the works here is A's Agonistes.

Is Billy Hatcher, who has begun this Series with seven straight hits and nine consecutive times on base really Mickey Hatcher, the unknown Dodger who drove the A's crazy two Octobers ago?

Are Ron Oester and Glenn Braggs, whose pinch-hit RBI tied this game, really the Dodger Stunt Men in disguise? Will they pull off their simulated human-skin masks and reveal themselves to be Mike Davis and Rick Dempsey?

After Game 1 we knew that injured Eric Davis was really Kirk Gibson and Jose (0.00) Rijo was Orel Hershiser. But the events of Game 2 in Riverfront Stadium Wednesday night seem to carry the notion of baseball reincarnation to extremes. Can a game as fabulous as this Reds win really be nothing more than a reductio ad absurdum? What have these A's done to offend the gods to such a degree?

It's not just that the hugely favored A's—Jose Canseco flatly predicted a sweep—have lost. It's the way they have lost and the people who have been picked to bear the pain.

Dave Stewart, the Ace, lost Game 1. Eckersley, for three years almost perfect—except in his first Series save chance—lost this one.

Manager Tony LaRussa, the brains of the outfit, managed horribly in this one. It will take a week to dissect his dubious decisions, several of which did not blow up in his face. Most of all, why did he get Eckersley warm in the bullpen twice—in the eighth and ninth innings —and then not use him until the tenth? LaRussa may not have done that all year. When Eck gets up, Eck comes in. He doesn't heat, cool, heat, cool, then finally heat up, come in, and lose.

As for Canseco, he's got to be having second thoughts about this Joe Namath, Muhammad Ali braggadocio act. If he doesn't get the message—that baseball always comes back to bite you—after this game, then maybe he never will. Canseco drove in one run with a ground out and another with a home run.

Yet he had as horribly unflattering a game as a man could fear. He misjudged Barry Larkin's leadoff double in the first inning; that proved to be worth two Reds runs. He fell fielding another ball. He threw wildly to the plate in a crisis and was saved only because Hatcher was held at third. He let a routine liner fall in front of him.

Above all, however, Canseco made a huge mental error in the bottom of the eighth with the A's holding a 4–3 lead. In that situation, you guard the lines in the infield and play an exaggeratedly deep out-field to prevent any ball from getting up the gap or over your head.

Hatcher hit a high liner that never made it to the warning track on the fly. Yet the ball ticked off Canseco's glove and ended up a triple. When Braggs scored Hatcher with a ground out, the Dy-Nasty Boys were faced with a tie game and the prospect of seeing the whole Nasty Boys bullpen, if needed.

"If you're going to win, you have to catch that ball," said LaRussa, coldly and evenly. "Canseco did not get a very good jump. The question is why?"

LaRussa, asked if it hurt more to lose games with Stewart and Eck-ersley, answered: "No, it makes it better. When you take your best shot, if you lose, you have no complaints or regrets."

What have we here? A tone of philosophical resignation already? With the next three games back in the Oakland Coliseum?

The A's have to be forgiven for anything they say or think after this game. Ballplayers are superstitious as a group. And these two games would make an irrationalist of Isaac Newton.

"We didn't come here to be an opponent. We came here to win the World Series," said Reds manager Lou Piniella after this miraculous 11:57 P.M. finish. Lou loves the ponies. But he's never held a ticket on a long shot like the one to which he holds the reins right now.

As this Series returns to Oakland, much of underdog-loving Amer-ica will feel something akin to euphoria at this ghostly repeat of one of the greatest of all World Series. Nobody brings chicken soup to Goli-ath.

Still, if the A's—battered and bruised from the top of their lineup to the bottom—can resurrect their spirit in the face of these first two games, they will lay the groundwork for great deeds. How many times in the last two winters have the A's asked themselves, "If only we could go back and play the Dodgers again. If only we hadn't let our nerves get the better of us. If only we hadn't pressed when we got down."

Now the A's get to go back in time. It is October 1988 again—or as much a re-creation of that moment as any mind could imagine. They get to live their worst hour all over again. They can make it right. Or they can suffer a repeat of pain the likes of which few athletic teams have ever known.

□ □ □

OAKLAND, October 20, 1990—On the first pitch of the second inning on Friday night, big Mike Moore of the Oakland A's sent a message to smallish Chris Sabo of the Cincinnati Reds. Moore brushed him back, gave him a shave, stuck one in his ear, whichever phrase you like. On purpose? Who knows?

But the A's do send messages to their foes. They play intimidation baseball. And Sabo had finished Game 2 with three straight hits, including the one that set up Joe Oliver's winner.

Sabo didn't change expression, didn't glare. Gradually, he worked the count full, then drove one of Moore's pitches so far over the leftfield fence that Rickey Henderson couldn't even draw attention to himself by pretending to climb the fence.

Sabo jogged around the bases quickly, head down, shook hands at home plate, gave a perfunctory hand slap to the on-deck hitter and disappeared into the dugout with the Reds ahead, 1–0.

The next time Sabo and Moore met, the Reds led, 3–2, in the third inning and had a man on base. Sabo, who wears a crew cut and goggles so that he won't get dirt in his eyes when he dives head-first, made himself inconspicuous in the batter's box. A little man who lifts a lot of weights and has made himself a minor power hitter.

This time, Sabo's home run did not go quite so far into the bleachers. But his home run trot—or, rather, his brisk, businesslike sprint— was identical. No emotion. No words of welcome for Moore as he rounded third. No elbow bashing at home plate. The Reds led, 5–2. By the end of the inning it was 8–2.

The first batter of the next inning, Henderson, hit a home run into the same leftfield bleachers. He stood and watched his work. He bellied out so deep as he began his trot that it looked as if he might stop in the Reds dugout for a drink of water. As he neared second base, he went into his twinkle-toes dance. At home plate, he celebrated himself some more.

His team still trailed by five runs. His team was about to lose the third game of the World Series—its third straight defeat. His A's were headed toward joining the '54 Cleveland Indians as the biggest bunch of upset losers—losers in a sweep—in history.

But Rickey had to do his trot.

It's a question of style, isn't it? That's always been the problem with the Oakland A's. That's the reason they're not loved outside of this city as much as they deserve to be. And that's the reason why so many people took such delight in watching the Reds humiliate them again, 8–3, in the third game of a World Series that may end in four utterly amazing games.

When Mark McGwire and Jose Canseco bash their big forearms after a home run, that's essentially a question of taste, of style, isn't it? When Dennis Eckersley embarrasses a batter by fanning his imaginary pistol at him after he strikes him out, that's a matter of style. Perhaps too much style. When Canseco flexes his muscles to fans who taunt him or when Dave Henderson does his tippy-toe snatch catch in centerfield or when Dave Stewart goes into his Death Stare, it can seem just a little too much, especially from a team so talented, so rich, so physically big, and one which under manager Tony LaRussa comes so close to playing bully ball at times.

As individuals, the Oakland A's respect themselves and, usually, respect one another—although seismic clubhouse rumblings involving a half dozen players have been reported in the last forty-eight hours. However, it's a legitimate question to ask whether the A's, as a team, give proper respect to others.

In Game 3, the Reds paid back in spades the disrespect that they have felt at the hands of the A's. The way to embarrass the A's, expose their mortality, make them look like big, silly, tangle-footed Goliaths, is to run on their catchers and all of their weak-armed or fundamentally careless outfielders.

And run they did. Billy Hatcher, after his eighth hit of the Series, went first to third as first baseman McGwire booted a grounder. Paul O'Neill went first to third, drawing a wild overthrow of the cutoff man from centerfielder Dave Henderson that allowed Eric Davis to take second base in a cloud of dirt. Oliver legged out a double into the leftfield corner on Rickey Henderson, then challenged Dave Henderson on a single to center and scored. Barry Larkin hit a routine rope double off the 375-foot sign in left, but, just to show up the Hendersons, he stretched it into a pointless, but pointed, two-out triple.

All of this happened in one inning.

Granted, it was a seven-run inning. And it probably ended this World Series. Of the seventeen teams that have trailed the World Series three games to none, fourteen rolled over in Game 4; the other three won one game. Do these A's have more stomach for battle than the '54 Indians, who gave up the ghost after Willie Mays's catch on Vic Wertz and Dusty Rhodes's seven RBI in the first three games? Do the A's, divided as they are over Canseco's general behavior, have more gumption than the '66 Dodgers of Sandy Koufax and Don Drysdale, a team like the A's, with two super pitchers who combined for 49 wins? After being shut out by Wally Bunker and twenty-year-old Jim Palmer, those Dodgers called it quits in Game 4.

Before this evening was done, third baseman Sabo showed every aspect of what his Reds are about. He picked a Dave Henderson smash and made it look like an easy play. When Mike Gallego dropped a perfect bunt, Sabo swung out into foul territory, just like the textbook diagrams, so he could pick up the ball with his momentum headed toward first. Sabo has time to make the play with all deliberate speed and the appearance of perfect stylelessness.

Finally, leading off the seventh, in what might be his last chance to hit a third home run in one Series game—joining Babe Ruth, Reggie Jackson, and no one else—Sabo worked the count full once more.

The next pitch was over the plate but low, barely. A pitch that could, perhaps, be golfed for a home run. Or fouled, to get another pitch.

Sabo took it for ball four. He was the leadoff man. It was his job to get on base. When the next batter hit a routine double-play ball to second base, Sabo sped toward second, then slid to avoid the relay throw. With his team five runs ahead, with the Nasty Boys ready and on call to round up any stray A's prisoners, Sabo barreled toward second baseman Willie Randolph, bowed his shoulders, dropped his head, and tried to let the throw hit him in the batting helmet to break up the double play.

For Sabo to be both the hero and the symbol of this game had a perfect but troubling symmetry. You see, Sabo has, since adolescence, modeled himself and his game on one old-time player whom he's worshiped for twenty years and who was his first major league manager. To this day, Sabo will speak only good of the man he idolizes, the man who had faith in him and put him into the Reds lineup when nobody in the organization thought he'd be more than a mediocrity.

No one has to ask for whom Chris Sabo played the game of his life this night. He already has said it a thousand times.

Pete Rose.

□   □   □

OAKLAND, October 21, 1990—The most shocking World Series sweep since 1954 came to a gloriously dramatic and suitably incongruous conclusion Saturday night. The Cincinnati Reds beat the hugely favored world champion Oakland A's, 2–1, on an error by pitcher Dave Stewart that was as freakish and destiny-spiced as this entire Classic.

Perhaps this should be known as the Total Recall Series since it so eerily paralleled the A's comparably infamous five-game collapse at the hands of the Los Angeles Dodgers two years ago. When has a team so good conspired to inflict such suffering on itself while inspiring its irritated foes to such heights?

"You get what you earn. We got what we earned here," said A's manager Tony LaRussa, whose team has won the most games in baseball each of the last three seasons, yet has only one world title of which to boast.

Just five days ago, the A's came to this stage trying to prove they were as good as any team since the 1927 Yankees. Jose Canseco, the highest-paid man in the game, even called his team the greatest ever and repeatedly predicted a Series sweep over the Reds to match the A's sweep of the Boston Red Sox in the playoffs.

Now the A's place seems clearly, but painfully, defined. Their progression mirrors the 1969–70–71 Orioles—called the Best Damn Team in Baseball—who were upset twice in three years with one world title in between. Those O's begat the Miracle Mets and lost a seven-game Series to Pittsburgh.

The A's embarrassment, however, far surpasses the Orioles' and may be greater than that of any team in modern times. Why? Because the contrast between their dominance before the Series and their meek, almost numb submission during it is so stark and difficult to explain.

A week ago, who would have believed that Jose Rijo would outpitch Stewart twice; Dennis Eckersley would be beaten in extra innings; the A's would twice take one-run leads into the eighth inning, then blow them without LaRussa ever bringing in the Eck; Canseco would end the Series 1 for 12, to go with his 1 for 19 performance in 1988; and Canseco would be benched in this game.

What odds could you have gotten on the Reds outscoring the A's 22–8, outhitting them .317 to .207, and crushing their bones in two blowouts. Even granting the greatness of the Nasty Boy bullpen, who thought the ERA of the Reds' five-man crew would be 0.00 for thirteen innings? Who'd have thought Chris Sabo would have as many RBI as Mark McGwire, Dave Henderson, Carney Lansford, Willie McGee, Rickey Henderson, and Canseco combined? Hell, Sabo and unknown Billy Hatcher had 31 total bases; the whole A's, who got just two hits in Game 4, had only 41 total bases all Series.

Nothing in this wonderfully shocking Series made conventional baseball sense, so, naturally, Stewart's decisive misplay was grotesquely unique and, almost, unbelievable.

The A's led, 1–0, in the eighth inning when the Reds put men on first and second with nobody out. Paul O'Neill laid down an adequate but routine sacrifice bunt toward Stewart. O'Neill, who would have been out by five yards anyway, pulled a muscle as he ran to first and almost came to a stop.

But Stewart's unnecessarily hurried throw to Willie Randolph, the second baseman who was covering first base, pulled Randolph off the bag—by perhaps one inch. As Randolph staggered into foul territory after catching the ball with a lunge, O'Neill hobbled the last 20 feet to first base. Stewart could have rolled the ball to first in time.

The A's can argue all winter that Randolph's toe brushed the bag. But they will still see the image of Stewart, one of the game's most loved and respected men, cracking in a crisis.

When Glenn Braggs grounded into a force play—which would have been a double play if Randolph had made a relay worthy of his Bronx Zoo days—one run scored to tie the game. When Hal Morris hit a high, long sacrifice fly to right, the Reds had a lead to hand to Rijo and Randy Myers, who got the last two outs.

If Stewart had made his easy bunt play, Morris's game-winning fly would simply have ended the inning. This was a Reds victory by unearned run. But not, in any sense, an unearned victory.

The Reds, who won 91 games this season compared with the A's 103, put so much pressure on Oakland's injured and suddenly suspect defense that the eighth-inning fold should not have been a surprise. Before this Series, pundits saw statistics. Only three times in history ('06, '54, and '74) had the Series been won by teams with at least a dozen fewer regular-season wins than their foes. Only twice have defending champions been swept, the Dodgers by the Orioles in '66, the

Athletics by the Braves in '14. Once the games began, everyone saw how the Reds' speed and base stealing, their hit-and-runs and bunts, their pursuit of the extra base, and their mighty bullpen both unnerved and unmanned the A's.

The Reds' whole winning rally was A's ugly. After Barry Larkin's leadoff single, Herm Winningham failed in two sacrifice attempts, then took it on himself to lay down a bunt on an 0–2 pitch. Catcher Jamie Quirk, normally a third-stringer but playing on a hunch by LaRussa, made a molasses-paced play as Winningham beat out the bunt.

"We got beat on a couple of bunts we didn't play, a ground ball, and a fly ball," said LaRussa, shaking his head. The Reds didn't score 2 runs as much as the A's gave them six outs.

This final, fourth game also completed the parallels to the '88 Series with such exactness that it was almost frightening. Then, the Dodgers lost one player after another to injury—four front-line men in all. Yet they played more tenaciously the more their manpower was depleted.

This evening, Billy Hatcher, batting .750 for the Series, was hit on the wrist by an 0–2 Stewart fastball that some will think was a deliberate brushback. No sooner had he left the game than superstar Eric Davis injured his kidney while diving for a Willie McGee double to left. Davis would have been lost for the Series, though the A's did not know it until after the game. "I was running out of outfielders," said Reds manager Lou Piniella. "I thought I was going to have to activate myself."

So, what happened? Braggs replaced Davis and ended up driving in the tying run. Winningham replaced Hatcher and ended up scoring the winning run.

Naturally, the A's final out came on a meek popup—which landed right in the celebrating Nasty Boys bullpen.

In defeat, LaRussa said, "I feel like we lost." He did not say the Reds did not deserve to win. Only that he never believed that his A's fate had left their own hands. That, like much else in these last few days, reflected the A's inability to believe in their proud hearts that any team could compete with them for high stakes. That is also how they talked and played in 1988.

In victory, Sabo took the podium and spoke for the Reds, a team that led the National League West wire to wire, then did the same in the Series. The Reds have never felt they got their due from the public or the A's.

"In the '90s, we will be the best team in baseball," predicted Sabo. Don't they ever learn?

October 22, 1990—How and why? That's what everybody in baseball wants to understand after one of the most exciting and surprising of World Series.

In technical terms, how could the Cincinnati Reds not only beat but demoralize and sweep a defending world champion Oakland A's team that clearly had more talent, more experience, even more motivation?

And why are the A's so prone to such embarrassment? No team has ever been so shockingly upset twice in the Series—let alone twice within three seasons. What's wrong with these A's?

Let's look back at several crucial junctures.

Eric the Red's Home Run

First inning of the first game on the first pitch he saw, the Reds' supposedly injured and half-speed star Eric Davis hit a 400-foot two-run homer off four-time 20-game winner Dave Stewart. The pitch was a mistake—a fastball down the middle—soon to be an A's trademark. Good stuff, poor location. The Reds' response was a clutch capitalization on that mistake. A pattern was set.

Memories of Kirk Gibson's home run off Dennis Eckersley in Game 1 of '88 were evoked. New data can trigger old emotions. The A's were put in touch with a past they thought they'd killed.

Leadoff Leaders

Barry Larkin and Billy Hatcher, the Reds' first two hitters, drove the A's crazy the whole Series. Of the Reds' 22 runs, 18 came in innings led off by Larkin. In every case, Larkin or Hatcher or both got on base and scored. The Reds were lucky to have the batting order roll over so fortuitously so many times. But an underdog needs luck as well as heroism.

Big Mac Flops—Again

In the first five innings of the Series, Mark McGwire was right back in his Classic Coma. Two on, ground out. Bases loaded, pop up. In three Series, McGwire has 2 RBI. By Game 4, A's manager Tony LaRussa paid McGwire a kind of ultimate insult—batting him seventh behind Jamie Quirk. Why not just hire a plane with a trailer sign: My First Baseman Is Killing My Team?

Jose Rijo reported back to the Reds' bench that he'd hung two sliders to McGwire and survived both. With Jose Canseco visibly injured and the A's stripped of their designated hitter in road games, the Reds began to suspect that the heart of the A's batting order might be mush.

Super Sabo Savors Spotlight

His first at-bat with runners on, Chris Sabo singled home two runs. While the A's went 3 for 27 with men in scoring position, Sabo produced in every game. In Game 2, he had three hits, including the single that set up Joe Oliver's winner. In Game 3, he answered a knockdown pitch with back-to-back homers. In Game 4, his three rocket hits off Stewart showed that the A's ace was vincible.

A's Get F's for Defense

The Oakland defense always has been overrated. The A's just don't make many errors. With shortstop Walt Weiss injured, centerfielder Dave Henderson recovering from knee surgery, and Canseco's throwing hand hurt, the A's were pathetic afield. In Game 2, four Reds runs were total gifts. Catcher Ron Hassey muffed a perfect throw home that should have nailed Slo-Joe (Oliver) by yards. Canseco misplayed two flies into a double and a triple that netted three runs. His new theme song: "I Can't Touch This."

Both LaRussa and Stewart ripped Canseco after Game 2, igniting long-dormant A's clubhouse problems. Tony and Dave said Jose was asleep with the season on the line. Jose said he'd appreciate not being a scapegoat. Tony had a half-hour closed-door meeting with Jose. Jose went to dinner with Reggie Jackson. Everybody rolled his eyes. Even

Jackson said, "I didn't cause problems at this time of year. I was a pain in the butt earlier in the season."

Where is Dave Parker when you need a clubhouse enforcer? The A's always knew, sooner or later, they'd need Big Dave to quell a cell-block riot, just as the '77 Reds desperately missed Tony Perez after they traded him. In '88 Canseco popped off about beating the Dodgers in five games. The Dodgers won in five. In '89 Parker promised to clean, stuff, and mount Jose if he spoke above a whisper. The A's swept. Now Dave's gone, Jose predicted a sweep. General manager Sandy Alderson makes a lot of good moves, but saving money on Parker may have cost him a world title.

Tony, Stop Thinking

If the A's had picked an usher at random to manage them in this Series, they'd have been better. The usher would have brought in Eckersley to start the eighth inning of Game 2 with a 4–3 lead. The usher would have brought in Eckersley to start the eighth inning of Game 4 with a 1–0 lead. And this Series would be two-all.

LaRussa could write a book on why he did what he did. But the bottom line is that every manager in the Hall of Fame would have brought in the Eck. Twice Tony didn't and twice the A's lost. This time, the goat's horns start at the top.

The A's manager also failed to snap his team to attention fast enough. They viewed their Game 1 defeat as a sort of gentle wake-up call, when they should have known that any Series deficit is a crisis. They viewed their Game 2 loss as a fairly serious matter meriting their attention, when in fact they should have circled the wagons, invoked every cliché, and called Game 3 a battle for their lives. After their Game 3 loss, who cared what the A's thought? They were DOA and didn't even know it.

The Runnin' Reds' Big Inning

Cincinnati's seven-run third inning in Game 3 showed everything the Reds could do and everything the A's could not stop. In one humiliating, ego-deflating inning, the Reds took, or were given, 10 extra bases. A steal. A wild pitch. A two-base boot. A missed cutoff man. A single stretched into a double. A double stretched into a triple.

And a couple of other guys going first to third. Mike Moore looked like a Ferris wheel operator.

"I said before in September if we didn't win the whole thing, we choked," said Eckersley. "So we choked. Now that it's over, I'm relieved because it was killing us. It was killing me. I felt responsible and I feel embarrassed. Nobody wants to feel like that."

Of the Reds, Eckersley said: "It's a bomb in the first inning of Game 1 and it was domination in every game. They crushed us twice and they beat us at our own game twice."

Some other A's were gracious too. The most insightful Oakland player was Dave Henderson, who saw the signs but couldn't slap his teammates' faces as hard as Parker would have. After Game 2, he said, "We're well on our way to making sure that we are a team that will not be remembered."

Unfortunately, even in defeat, the dominant tone of the A's was that of the disbelieving, excuse-seeking blowhard. Rickey Henderson said that, in 100 games with the Reds, the A's would win "70 or 75." Snap to, Rickey. The A's couldn't beat anybody but the Yankees that badly. Stewart was least generous of all, harping on how the Reds wouldn't even have been in the Series if they'd played in the A's division. Then Stewart "guaranteed" that the A's would be back in the Series next year.

Oh, stuff a sock in it.

For their gumption, the Reds will go down as one of several miracle teams in recent years. This has been the age of upsets. We've seen: The aging '81 Dodgers who won in six games. The injured '85 Royals who trailed, 3–1, in both the playoffs and World Series. The '87 Twins who became champs despite an 85-win pedigree. The overmatched '88 Dodgers whose victory may still, in retrospect, be the most remarkable because of their seven-game playoff war with the Mets and their many injuries.

As for the A's, they have etched a place in history for themselves too. In a week, they've gone from being a contender for Greatest Team of the Last Twenty-Five Years to being a favorite in a new category:

Biggest World Series Flops—Ever.

1991:
Cinderella, Cinderella

MINNEAPOLIS, October 9, 1991—"Instructions for the use of Chain Saw Ear Plugs: (1) With clean hands, roll plug into a small cylinder. (2) Place hand over head, pull on upper part of ear to straighten ear canal, and gently insert plug. (3) Hold plug in ear until it fully expands."

There, that's better. In fact, it's wonderful. It's almost like you're not even in the Metrodome, except that your whole body vibrates.

Now, if only somebody will please distribute these babies to the entire Blue Jays team before they are blown back over the Canadian border with their ears shriveled into their skulls and their poise permanently shattered.

Until events prove otherwise (oh, please, prove otherwise), the assumption here is that the Minnesota Twins won't lose any postseason series in which they have the home field—aka the Thunderdome—advantage.

The Twins' 5–4 win over Toronto Tuesday night to open this American League Championship Series was a perfect example of how a crowd can administer a standing eight-count punch to a visitor before it knows the fight has even started. As 120-decibel waves of noise washed over them, the Jays found themselves behind, 5–0, after three innings. They spent the rest of the night in pursuit of an honorable defeat.

Perhaps only ink-stained wretches who spend their lives in ridiculously loud places (nobly sacrificing their hearing for the public good) can truly grasp and properly detest the Metrodome. Maybe you need to have been in the legendary loud joints to know that none of them is remotely like this.

Hometown passion is wonderful. But this is too much. Here, because baseball is being played indoors where it never belonged, the crowd frequently is the game. Anybody who doesn't root for the Jays to overcome this bass-drum ballpark and beat the Twins at least once here doesn't have baseball's interests at heart because the Thunderdome's growing mystique is bad for baseball.

At the '87 playoffs and Series, headaches, nausea, and a kind of dizzy disorientation became a part of the fun of watching the ol' ballgame from the stands. Imagine what it feels like on the field with the crowd aimed at you.

Let's make one thing clear: The noise conditions here are not equal for both teams. The reason that this jet-landing level of noise does not bother the Twins is that the crowd explodes only when it will rattle the visitors. These nice midwesterners have Dome booming down to a science. When their boys need quiet to think, you can hear the air conditioners hum. When the bad guys need some peace, the world's largest high school gym feels as if it's about to rip itself apart.

To add injury to insult, a local radio station gave away thousands of toy whistles to fans. Before the game, the Twins PA system announced that "Whistles and other artificial noisemakers are not permitted. . . . Fans will be ejected."

So, of course, everybody blew their shrill whistles just for practice.

The Twins themselves think nothing of letting their PA system explode with drumbeats and distracting music during at bats. The PA, naturally, is used only to bother the visitors. How can the commissioner allow this to continue?

Thanks to the *Elias Analyst*, we already know that, year in and year out, the Twins have the biggest home-field edge in baseball; they play about 16 percent better at home than on the road. (This year it was "only" 9 percent.) In '87, the Twins were 56–25 at home, 29–52 on the road, and won the Series by winning all four games played here while losing all three in St. Louis.

The Jays' Cito Gaston, like all AL managers, knows he just has to live with the Metrodome for eternity, so he said afterward, "No, it doesn't bother us. I think only the National League teams complain about that."

Twins manager Tom Kelly, however, told the total truth. The

Thunderdome, as a unique and troubling phenomenon, exists only in October. "It's not like this in the regular season," said Kelly. "On the weekends, we sometimes get 37,000 or even 44,000. But you can't compare that to tonight [with 54,766]. It doesn't get nowhere near this loud."

One of baseball's most basic appeals has always been that it has little home-field advantage. Baseball teams win about 54 percent of home games compared with 58 percent in the NFL, 60 percent in the NHL, and 64 percent in the NBA. It's no accident that the indoor sports illustrate the enclosed-noise factor.

Baseball has also fallen into a postseason schedule format in which teams from the AL West have the chance to get the home edge in both the ALCS and Series in odd-numbered years, such as this year, while teams from the NL West have the same home-and-home chance in even-numbered years.

No AL or NL East winner can ever have this edge under the current deal. Since the last four world champions (three of them underdogs) have had this home-and-home edge in October, it's clear that baseball has a double whammy. Which, you can bet, it will try to solve by putting its head in the sand and saying, "Gee, those Twins sure look good, don't they?"

This opening contest became lopsided quickly and was in ugly accord with memories of 1987. Toronto had beaten the Twins in 8 of 12 games this season. But none was played before a capacity crowd with white homer hankies, whistles, and a full postseason head of steam. Give the Twins crowds credit. They know the impact they have and they do a magnificent job of distorting the game.

The first two Twins hit singles and the joint came unglued. Chili Davis flared a two-out, full-count, opposite-field, handle-hit single to left to score two runs and it seemed like this game, and maybe this whole series, came to an end. Man, you don't want to play comeback against the Twins in this place. It's like being trapped in a garbage can while gorillas beat it with tree limbs.

The Twins scored two more runs in the second inning as poor knuckleballer Tom Candiotti, who has spent most of his career in the peace and solitude of Cleveland's cavernous, silent Mistake by the Lake, looked like he couldn't get his fingernails to stop quivering. The Twins hit line drives off his shins, stole bases, and slapped singles to all fields on the lovely concrete turf. By the third inning, Candiotti was a wreck, allowing a walk, a steal, and the last of the eight hits and five runs he permitted.

So this is what America's pastoral summer game has become—a sport played in a large, loud tin drum.

Starting with Game 2, for the sake of being a good sport, this column will resume the pretense that what is being played here is honest, fair baseball and that anybody can win.

Go Twins.

□ □ □

ATLANTA, October 24, 1991—The 1991 World Series is one long-standing tribute to people named Lemke and Knoblauch, Willis and Mercker, Ortiz and Olson, Belliard and Leius, Treadway and New-man, Guthrie and Clancy, Blauser and Pagliarulo. And a lot more Bushes, Larkins, Leaches, and Greggs too.

In baseball, there is a fairly simple expression that's used routinely in talent evaluations: "He can't play." That doesn't mean you don't have some skills. It doesn't mean you aren't a hard worker and a heady contributor. It just means that, all in all, you can't play the whole game of baseball. You're a temporary measure until someone who "can play" is found.

About thirty of the fifty men in this World Series just "can't play." They hold on to their jobs by the narrowest margins and are always one bad season, or perhaps one bad month, from anonymity.

This is their Series and that's great. Let's not allow it to happen again, mind you. But once is hot stuff. Usually, teams get to the World Series by jet. Most of these guys came by bus—years and years of bush league buses.

Look at the Braves. Rafael Belliard is 5-feet-6, has a .226 career batting average, and hits a home run once every 150 games. Mark Lemke has an even lower average than Belliard: .225. His manager calls him "the original dirt player." Together, they're the least elite double-play combo in Series history.

Jim Clancy, at thirty-four, was in Tucson last year. Now his 5.71 ERA this year earns him the chance to win Game 3. He did it by retiring one batter—a pitcher—who hit a rocket right at an outfielder.

Just eighteen months ago, Greg Olson thought he had retired after eight years as a .247-hitting bush league catcher. A wave of injuries forced the Braves to un-retire him. Now he's a hero.

Jeff Treadway can hit, but he can't field or run. Mark Wohlers, Mike Stanton, Armando Reynoso, Keith Mitchell, Francisco Cabrera, and Brian Hunter are all rookies or so close to it as to make the distinction moot.

Even the better Braves aren't that good. John Smoltz's career record is 42–42. Tom Glavine's is 53–52. Terry Pendleton hit .230 in 1990 and may hit .230 in 1992. In between, he won the batting championship. Go figure.

Because they improved by only 24 wins over last season, rather than 29 like the Braves, the Twins like to pretend that they didn't really go from worst to first. Manager Tom Kelly always nags, saying, "Last to first. We were never worst." Yeah, but the Twins were lousy.

This is the team that has found a place on its World Series roster for Jarvis Ardel Brown, Adalberto Ortiz, Paul Sorrento, Al Newman, and Carl Willis.

Kelly has long since replaced Earl Weaver as the game's best user of his entire roster. He's found valuable roles for Randy Bush, Gene Larkin, Terry Leach, Scott Leius, Mike Pagliarulo, and portly portsider David West. The reason Kelly could use twenty-three players in Game 3—a record, of course—was that he plays these guys all the time.

He trusts them. (Because he has no choice.) So they begin to trust themselves. And play above themselves.

Anyone who watched the '89 Baltimore Orioles—the team that originally test-piloted this worst-to-first idea—knows how inspirational such teams are to their fans and to themselves. You fall for clubs like these far more easily than the recent A's.

Game 3 illustrated both the high tension and the low slapstick that is entwined in this Everyman Series. The reason the affair took 244 minutes, 42 players, and 12 innings was that these teams couldn't get unstuck from each other.

No sooner would the Braves get a lead because Scott Erickson was pitching batting practice than Pendleton knocked out his own star pitcher with an error. On came the Braves' "stopper"—Alejandro Pena—to face the equally well traveled Chili Davis, who took him deep to blow away Steve Avery's win.

The Twins might have won in the eighth or twelfth if their stars—Kirby Puckett and Kent Hrbek—hadn't struck out with men on third and only one out. In this Series, the stars feel double pressure because, if they don't do it, who will?

As this Series unfolds, don't ask yourself why Kelly and Bobby Cox are willing to use seven pitchers in a game or pinch-hit for almost anybody.

It's because, with some exceptions, these guys aren't terribly gifted. They are trying incredibly hard and performing better than they ever have or ever will.

Naturally, in the bottom of the ninth in Game 4, the Braves sent up Jerry Willard, an eleven-season minor leaguer who never even held a starting job in the bushes, to pinch-hit for Cabrera. Whom did he drive home with the winning run in a 3–2 game but the little legendary Lemke, who had tripled.

To some of us, rooting for two teams full of "original dirt players" is more interesting than watching some recent World Series, filled with fellows such as Rickey Henderson who, after setting a career stolen base record, summarized his view by saying, "I'm the greatest."

"There are a lot of guys on both these teams who are castoffs," said Twins catcher Brian Harper who in 1987, after ten years in pro ball, could not get any team to sign him. "But we're playing well. These teams really respect each other. And we're having a lot of fun."

So much fun that these teams have now become the first in Series history to play back-to-back sudden-death games.

□ □ □

ATLANTA, October 25, 1991—Someday, these last three magical balmy southern nights in the World Series will probably be remembered as Mark One, Mark Two, and Mark Three. Or perhaps Lonnie One, Lonnie Two, and Lonnie Three.

And someday, Mark Lemke and Lonnie Smith will probably be known simply as Triple Lemke and Series Smith.

Monikers like those would be so much more worthy of their deeds than mere mortal names. Already they sound like something you'd order from a bartender on Peachtree Street. Gimme a Triple Lemke.

After all, Frank Baker didn't really hit that many home runs. But he had a couple of big ones in the 1911 World Series, so for most of a century he's been Home Run Baker.

For three straight nights, Smith and Lemke have driven stakes into the hearts of the Minnesota Twins. Smith has done it with a crucial solo home run in each of these games. For perspective, Reggie Jackson was the last man to homer in three straight World Series games. If any man has ever been a Series charm, it's Smith. He's already the first player to reach the Series with four different teams. He could soon become the only man to start every Series game for four different world champions. Whether it takes injuries (in Kansas City in '85) or misfortune (such as Otis Nixon's cocaine problem last month), the Series finds Smith or he finds the Series.

Lemke has done the Twins damage in so many ways so many times that you have to look back to Dusty Rhodes in 1954 to find a player of so little renown who has done so much. His little man's legend long ago surpassed belief.

First, Lemke singled home the winning run in the twelfth inning on Tuesday. That came just minutes after he'd made a hideous error on an easy play—which looked almost certain to lose the game.

Then on Wednesday he tripled and scored the winning run in the bottom of the ninth with a wonderful slide. Thanks to Lemke, Atlanta had not only witnessed its first World Series games but seen the first back-to-back sudden-death games in history as well.

Finally, Thursday evening, in a ludicrous 14–5 drubbing of the Twins, Lemke had two more triples—that makes three within four at-bats. On a night when the Braves had a Series-record 34 total bases—three homers, three triples, two doubles, and nine singles—Lemke had the most total bases of all (six).

In all, Lemke produced five runs with his bat in Game 5 and saved two runs with a superb snag of a hot short-hop smash when the game was still close. Beside the tiny second baseman's work, the five RBI of David Justice seem like small potatoes.

"They kicked us around pretty good," said Twins manager Tom Kelly. "I lost track." He could be forgiven. Most of the night, his outfielders were picking up a small white object that had rolled to rest on the warning track.

The Braves should win this Series after all these doings. They've earned the honor and deserve to be the modern Miracle Braves. Now, will the dumb Thunderdome allow the Braves their hour? Or will Minnesota abscond with its second tainted title in five years?

In Series history, only one team has ever lost all three games on the road yet still become the sport's champion. Yes, the Twins in '87, thanks to their freak ballpark that spooked the St. Louis Cardinals.

Now the Braves have every imaginable form of momentum—both the psychobabble and the real strategic kind—on their side. Twice they won games of enormous nerve in spirit-crushing fashion. Now they've shown the Twins' pitching to be entirely mortal.

The Twins arrived here in the land of chops and chants with a simple and manageable task. Win one game out of three, then go home with the Series all but clinched. They couldn't do the job.

Two of the Twins' best pitchers—Scott Erickson and Kevin Tapani—were met with a hail of line drives. Their outfielders have consistently failed to make tough catches. Tom Kelly has been locked in a suicide pact with Bobby Cox, with Kelly so far doing his team more damage.

As if that weren't enough, the Braves' two best pitchers—both effective here—are ready for the Dome. Steve Avery and John Smoltz. With Poison and Marmaduke, plus Lonnie and Lemke, how can you lose?

Don't ask. The Thunderdome has far too many answers.

If any two players can stand up to the Dome's pressures, it should be Smith and Lemke. Cox has dubbed Smith "the bravest player I've ever seen" and Lemke "the original dirt player."

Smith stands on top of the plate and dares pitchers to hit him. He runs face-first into walls. What he did to Brian Harper at the plate in Game 4 was pure Lonnie. Smith is also the only major league player with a cocaine problem who ever turned himself in, and cleaned up his act, before anybody found him out. When his career seemed over four years ago and he was back in class AAA, he fought his way back with hard work. In this Series, he began with five rocket outs. Sliding catches, diving stops, atom balls—he got it all. So he just started hitting the ball over the wall.

Lemke is even more beloved than Smith among his teammates, who view him—not any offended Native American—as the team's true mascot. He is brave in the generic, not racial, sense. Before this Series, he had three career triples. Now he has three Series triples. Asked after Game 4 if he'd ever had a single, double, and triple in one game before, Lemke said he wasn't sure he'd ever had three hits. Did he think his triple might be out of the park? "I never think it's out when I hit it," said the 167-pounder now hitting .438. He already may have locked up the MVP trophy, even if the Braves lose.

"I spent a lot of time in the minors—I spent a lot of time all the way down in A ball," Lemke said. "But I said, 'This is what I want to do.' Nothing was going to get in my way."

In the season of worst-to-first, the sagas of Smith and Lemke surpass anything the Twins, noble as they may be, can offer. It's time for America to send its psychic energy toward Minneapolis. The Thunderdome must be silenced. Justice must be served.

□ □ □

MINNEAPOLIS, October 28, 1991—If you're scoring, the play that probably decided the 1991 World Series goes Knoblauch-to-Gagne-to-Nobody, the greatest double play never made.

Lonnie Smith still wonders where the ball is. He hasn't seen it yet. He's still watching Chuck Knoblauch and Greg Gagne turn a phantom double play—a mime, a joke, a sucker play, a moment of genius—just as Johnny Pesky is still holding the ball in Boston.

Smith will stand there forever, just past second base, alone and confused. They still haven't found a place to put the second-base coach. It's the eighth inning of a scoreless Game 7 of the World Series. Lord, what a time to take your eye off the ball.

Out of a crowd of 55,118 in the Metrodome, every single one knew NL batting champion Terry Pendleton had hit a drive in the gap of left centerfield for a ringing double with no Twin near the ball.

But they weren't running on the play as Smith was. They weren't the first half of the hit-and-run. And they didn't forget to peek at the batter, halfway to second, the way every high school kid is taught. Five strides into your break, sneak a glance. That's about when the ball gets to the plate. You might see something. Smith never looked back.

For the moment, only Smith knows for sure whether he got lost entirely on his own or whether Knoblauch and Gagne deserve the accolades that the Twin Cities are already heaping on them.

After the Twins won, 1–0, in ten innings, Smith wasn't talking. Whatever the cause, the one certain thing is that the run that Smith did not score cost the Braves the world title.

It's remotely conceivable—despite all appearances to the contrary—that Smith never saw the ball because he never looked for it. A very strange oversight on a hit-and-run.

It's far more likely—and baseball lore will almost certainly record it this way no matter what Smith says—that he was duped by the Twins.

Replays show that he watched second baseman Knoblauch drop to one knee as if he'd stopped a hot smash, then fake a hard shovel pass to shortstop Gagne, who caught on to the deke in time to race toward second base.

Smith was only fooled, distracted, for a second. But it was enough. The crack of the bat had been swallowed in Metrodome noise. He hadn't heard it and he couldn't see it.

"He lost the ball," said Pendleton. We can debate why for decades.

As the ball bounced off the wall, Smith finally broke for third. But it was too late. On a play on which he could, and normally would, have scored by 10 yards, he had to stop at third.

Sure, there were no outs and the Braves still should have scored. But the Thunderdome was full of demons pointing at him and saying, "Lonnie stopped. He'll never score now."

And he didn't.

As if to make the misery of the Braves complete, this game went into extra innings, doubling the ominous significance of Smith's base-running gaffe. If Smith had scored, the Braves could have won, 1–0, in regulation, with John Smoltz and Mike Stanton sharing the heroic shutout.

Gene Larkin eventually got the game-winning hit in this master-work of tension that ended the only Series ever to have four extra-inning games.

In the only seventh game of a Series ever to stay scoreless so long, you'd think that getting the winning hit would be good enough for immortality.

But Larkin merely got a hit. Lots of people get hits to break ties in the seventh Series game. Bill Mazeroski in 1960. Joe Morgan in 1975. It happens every twenty years or so, like clockwork.

However, a play like Knoblauch and Gagne pulled—especially Knoblauch, the twenty-three-year-old rookie who gets the most credit —that happens only once.

Perhaps to his discredit, Braves manager Bobby Cox refused to give credit to the Twins for their play.

"There was no decoy at all," Cox insisted, despite both eyesight and replays that showed the Twins infielders' fraudulent acts and Smith looking at them. "Why he stopped I don't know."

Thanks, Bobby. Why not just shoot the poor guy? Smith gets fooled by a great play, a classic piece of skullduggery from the John

McGraw era that has conned many a good player, and you say it's all a big mystery. Like Smith just had brain lock. Like it's all his fault.

Lonnie Smith isn't Bonehead Smith. He's not Fred Merkle. He didn't have a mental lapse. Or, if he did, only a tiny one. He just got fooled by heady ball.

A few days ago, Knoblauch, who probably will be the consensus AL Rookie of the Year, said, "I may be young, but I don't feel like a rookie. I've played a lot of baseball."

It showed. Knoblauch lives by the little things. Like the unheralded sacrifice bunt that he laid down in the tenth inning after Dan Gladden's broken-bat, turf-hop, bloop double to left center. That got Gladden to third. Two intentional walks were mandated and Larkin summoned.

He stepped in the batter's box at 11 P.M., Minneapolis time and exactly midnight in Georgia. It was the eleventh hour for the Twins and the witching hour for the Braves.

At one minute after the hour, on the first pitch from Alejandro Peña, Larkin hit what would usually be a routine fly. But not on this night.

Black Jack Morris, clutch pitcher supreme, raced from the dugout first, as befits a man who has just pitched an 11-hit, guts-and-glory shutout to win the Series for his hometown. He showed Gladden where the plate was—protected it, almost—so Gladden could find it.

No trick could hide it.

□ □ □

MINNEAPOLIS, October 29, 1991—And the answer is: '06, '12, '24, '34, '46, '56, '60, '75, '86, and '91.

The question, of course: What was the best World Series of each decade?

They are, in order: Hitless Wonders Upset 116-Win Cubs. Snodgrass's Muff. Walter Johnson and the Pebble. The Gas House Gang Amidst the Garbage. Slaughter Sprints, Pesky Holds the Ball. Larsen's Perfect Game. Mazeroski's Homer. Red Machine Tops Fisk Homer. Buckner's Error. Cinderella Extra-Inning Series.

All ten of those Series went seven games. All involved teams of historic interest. Four were decided on the last pitch ('12, '24, '60, and '91). Two others were decided in the winning team's last at bat ('46 and '75). In yet another ('86) the winning team was down to its last strike in the sixth game.

The Top Five, please: 1924, 1946, 1960, 1975, and 1991.

And the winner?

No, you won't get that here. It's unfair enough to pick five. Fans of the '27 Yankees, '69 Mets, and '88 Dodgers are already mad that their Series were downgraded because they weren't close.

What's certain is that the Series we have just finished—or would "survived" be a better word?—is way up there.

The Twins-vs.-Braves Worst-to-First Anti-Classic was too tense, too full of slapstick managing, too chocked with dramatic and controversial plays to take a backseat to any Series. At the least, it was the best bad Series in history.

This war between the tomahawk choppers and the hankie wavers didn't surpass '60 or '75. The number of marquee stars and the quality of play in those Series were obviously better than the gritty underdog grapplings of all the Lemkes and Larkins who couldn't get untangled from one another this October.

What we've just seen was the closest, most drama-filled, but surely not best-played or best-managed Classic of all time. If we want a more exciting Series, chances are we'll have to wait until the next century.

What will last, what will burn into our baseball memories, rather than dissipate like smoke, from the last nine days? Kirby Puckett in Game 6 and Jack Morris in Game 7, first of all. No player ever had a better total game than Puckett on Saturday. No pitcher ever rose higher on a seventh-game stage than Morris. Someday, they may be the only two players from this Series in the Hall of Fame. (Or will David Justice and Steve Avery end up in Cooperstown while Puckett and Morris fall short?)

Most of the big hits in this Series were provided by Greg Gagne and Scott Leius (the man with Kent Hrbek's missing vowel), by Mark Lemke and Jerry Willard (the AAA kids), by old Lonnie Smith and splintered Gene Larkin. However, in the game that swung this Series of glorious castoffs, Puckett dominated everyone. The Braves should've won Saturday by five runs. Because of Puckett, and hard luck, they lost by one in eleven innings.

"I'd love to smile, but I can't. I'm so tired," said Puckett after a single, triple, homer, sacrifice fly, stolen base, and back-to-the-wall catch. "My emotions, man. I don't know where they are."

Other pitchers have won the Series with shutouts. Ralph Terry even did it 1–0 ('62) while Sandy Koufax ('65) and Johnny Podres ('55) won 2–0 in Game 7. But nobody ever won 1–0 in overtime. In fact, the only previous pitcher to go more than nine innings in a deciding Series game was Christy Mathewson ('12), and Smoky Joe Wood beat him in relief.

Perhaps Morris's work was summed up best by manager Tom Kelly's account of their talk after the ninth inning.

"That's enough," said Kelly.

"I'm fine. Save Aggy [i.e., Rick Aguilera]," said Morris, a St. Paul native who said he wanted to pitch a game that his young sons, eight and ten, could remember him by.

"Jesus Christ, Jack, that's enough."

"T.K., I'm fine. I'm fine. If I wasn't fine, I'd tell you."

"Jack, you've already done so much for us."

"I'm fine. Ask [Coach Dick] Such."

"He's fine, T.K."

"He's fine. He's fine. Okay, what the hell, it's just a game."

Don't you just love this stuff? If they cast the Morris role in a movie, they'd need Tom Selleck with character lines, a red mustache, and a bad temper.

"I'm a lousy loser," said Morris last week, grinning evilly. "But I've learned to accept it."

Morris wasn't kidding when he said after Game 6, "This reminds me of the words of the late, great Marvin Gaye. 'Let's Get It On.'" So, before Game 7, the Thunderdome's Darth Vader PA system played Gaye's song. Morris ate it all up. "I live for the noise. I live for the pressure. . . . In my weird little way, I even loved it in here when I was a visiting player."

You see, Jack Morris wants to get up close and personal with you. He tried to throw the ball through plate-crowding Lonnie Smith five times in this Series.

It's going to be some Hot Stove League this winter. We've got Games 3–4–5 to chew over—the Triple Lemke visit to Atlanta. We can replay Justice's slide to win Game 3 and Lemke's slide to win Game 4. We can wonder how Kelly could run out of players and pinch-hit Aguilera in the twelfth.

We can also ponder what Cox's morbid fascination is with Charlie Leibrandt. Cox started him, not Tom Glavine, in Game 1, then kicked him out of the rotation only to bring him back Saturday as an eleventh-inning reliever. Leibrandt's fourth pitch was Puckett's homer.

Leibrandt hasn't spoken since and some assume it's because he fears he might say, "Cox better watch his back."

Cox's rationale was that Leibrandt had fanned Puckett twice in Game 1. Yes, but Puckett was baseball's leading hitter against left-handers in '91 (.406) and in his previous at-bat against Leibrandt, back in his AL days, Puckett had hit a home run. If you're going to play a hunch with the Series at stake, at least have all the data.

Finally, after we've chewed over the justice or injustice of the Metrodome, after we've screamed to high heaven that baseball should give postseason home-field advantage to the team with the better regular-season record, we can try the almost impossible. We can try to get inside Lonnie Smith's head.

Pick up the ball. Pick up the coach. As far as base running goes, those are the first two rules. In the one play from this Series that will probably be mentioned as often as Pesky Held the Ball and debated as much as Babe Ruth's Called Shot, Smith never lifted his head to see where Terry Pendleton's double had gone in the eighth inning of a scoreless Game 7. Then, when Smith got confused rounding second base—where is that darn baseball?—he never looked for third-base coach Jimy Williams.

Was Smith faked out by the phantom double play enacted by rookie Chuck Knoblauch and Greg Gagne? Was he confused by leftfielder Dan Gladden, who, 10 yards from making a catch, stuck up his glove in a deke? Or was he just paralyzed with all of it—the noise, the tension, the bad homer-hankie background, the exhaustion of the Braves' 176 games, and the sight of Twins everywhere he looked, Twins pretending to catch baseballs?

So, Skates stopped. For once, he fell down while standing up. The run that would have won the World Series for the Braves—the run that might have made them the most famous underdog Series champions in history—stopped at third base with him. And died there.

Only the questions live on.

1992:
The Keepers
of the Blame

INTRODUCING:
THE BLESSED BRAVES

ATLANTA, October 15, 1992—When a former president of the United States jumps the box-seat railing, dodges police horses, and breaks the law so he can run onto the field to hug and kiss the players, you know it was a pretty good country ballgame.

Actually, when the hometown Atlanta Braves score three runs in the bottom of the ninth inning of the seventh game of the playoffs for a 3–2 victory over the Pittsburgh Pirates to win the National League pennant, it's not really a ballgame. It's a piece of mythology dropped into our communal life like some ultimate innocent confection. No, it hasn't been done like this—three runs in the bottom of the ninth to pull out the pennant—since Bobby Thomson's Shot Heard Round the World in 1951. So we can talk about it forever and feel warm and silly every time. We can spend the rest of our lives saying, "Don't leave until the last out. Remember Francisco Cabrera."

Yes, the name is Francisco Cabrera. You never heard of him. Now, everybody who loves the Atlanta Braves, everybody who loves baseball, loves Francisco Cabrera. Whoever he is. From now on, whenever the bases are loaded with two outs and your team is a run down, you'll pay attention, because if Francisco Cabrera can rifle one into leftfield to win it all, then anybody can.

"It's ironic," said Pirates manager Jim Leyland, "that the guy they added on the 31st of August is the guy who beat us."

At 11:52 P.M. on Wednesday night, Jimmy Carter—of the peanut-farming Georgia Carters—wanted to kiss this Señor Cabrera. However, it's unseemly for an ex-president to crawl to the bottom of a pile of twenty big-league players, heaped up along the first-base line, just to say, "Hello, Francisco. Wanted to tell ya that's one helluva way to win the pennant for us, son. They'll probably be talking about you round here after they've forgotten me."

Almost nobody had ever heard of Cabrera until last night, unless you follow the Richmond Braves. He came to bat just ten times for the Braves this season. With the National League season down to its final out, he was all the Braves had left. The bench was empty. It was either Cabrera or activate the batboy. With the Pirates still ahead, 2–1, and pulling fresh miracles out of their pockets each inning, Cabrera—pinch-hitting for tiny Rafael Belliard—was the last chance.

He was all the Braves needed.

Now he'll be remembered as long as they play softball in Plains.

Where David Justice, Terry Pendleton, Jeff Blauser, and Ron Gant had failed—sometimes agonizingly, sometimes by a hair's breadth—Cabrera succeeded. On a 2–1 pitch from Stan Belinda—poor sidearming Stan Belinda who never hurt nobody but will now live forever next to Ralph Branca and Donnie Moore—Cabrera hit a clean bullet of a single in the hole to leftfield.

David Justice trotted home to tie the game. But what about Sid Bream, the slowest Brave, the human moving van, the guy with the knee braces, what about him? You going to send him home from second or hold him at third?

Send him, for the Lord's sake. It's only Barry Bonds in leftfield. The best leftfielder in the league—the fastest at charging the ball and the man with the strongest arm. But, go on, send Sid Bream. Lend him a dolly.

And here Sid came, running faster than he ever had in his life and slower than you could imagine your Uncle Ralph on Sunday afternoon. Where was Barry? Playing on the warning track? Well, almost. Bonds played a conspicuously deep leftfield the entire inning. But he came charging, scooping, and, finally, unleashing as strong a heave as you'll see to the plate.

If it had been on line, Sid Bream would have been back out at first base with a glove in the tenth inning and they'd be measuring third-base coach Jimy Williams for a coffin in a shallow grave in the morning. If the throw had only been a little off line—a pretty good throw—you can bet umpire Randy Marsh would have called him out on general principles. If you're Sid Bream, you've got to score clean to get any calls.

But Bonds's throw was at least two paces up the first-base line. Spanky LaValliere did all a catcher can do. Which means Bream was safe by 6 inches.

Nobody ever gets to make any wisecracks about Carter and softball again. The man he sought out in the postgame melee—and it was a world-class mess—was third-base coach Williams. Carter gave him a long The-Buck-Stops-Here hug.

In baseball, you wait and wait, crushing peanuts, ordering another beer, filling out your scorecard, all in anticipation of the split second that will decide everything. You wait for the moment of lightning.

Sometimes only one game is at stake. But sometimes a whole season can be boiled down to one stunned gasp of action. Sometimes the difference between a double play and a three-run double is so small, and happens so fast, that you feel a chill of delight at the raw, powerful capriciousness of the whole thing. Yes, like a bolt of lightning that strikes where it will and no man knows why.

This game will be remembered and analyzed for baseball generations because it had three such moments. If Cabrera had popped up, as the previous batter—Brian Hunter—had done, then everybody in Pittsburgh would have spent the week saying novenas of thanks for the scalding liner by Jeff Blauser of the Braves with the bases loaded and nobody out in the sixth inning that found the glove of Pirates third baseman Jeff King.

When the ball left Blauser's bat, headed toward the leftfield corner, it seemed—if the mind had time to compute such things—that a 2–0 Pittsburgh lead was about to become a 3–2 Atlanta lead. At the least, the game would be tied with a none-out bonfire of a rally at full rage with the Braves' best hitters, Terry Pendleton and David Justice, coming to the plate.

Instead, King took a step, caught the ball waist high as easily as if he were playing catch before the game, and let his momentum carry him casually to third base, where he doubled an immobile Mark Lemke off the bag by 15 feet.

If ever a team had a right to think it was jinxed, it was the Braves. They should have seen their fate written on the outfield walls—first team in NL history to blow a three-games-to-one lead in the playoffs. You better believe that Braves manager Bobby Cox understood the eerie, queasy feeling. The same thing had happened when he was manager of the ill-fated '85 Blue Jays, the team that gave birth to the Blow Jays.

Now he'll meet their Toronto descendants in the World Series.

The Braves were given one last amazing chance to lose their faith and their heart in the ninth. The Pirates left in struggling starter Doug Drabek, who'd already worked out of three jams, because they have never trusted anybody in their short-relief bullpen. Belinda is the best of a seriously suspect lot. After Pendleton opened the ninth with a double into the rightfield corner—fair by two feet, and two feet from Alex Cole's glove—the Braves got their break. A huge one. A pennant-deciding one, as it proved. The best of all the Pirates' excellent glove men, second baseman Jose Lind, had a hard, but routine, worm-burner trickle off his glove for an error. An error that made the game's final two decisive runs unearned.

Drabek walked Bream on four pitches; the Bucs had no choice. Drabek was obviously cooked. In came Belinda. Up stepped Gant, who had hit a grand-slam home run—the first of his career—in Game 2. This time, he proved another of those lightning moments of truth. He crushed a deep line drive to left—directly at the sign commemo-rating Hank Aaron's 715th home run. Bonds went back, back, and, right at the wall, reached high for the catch. Two feet higher and it's off the wall and the merry-go-round starts spinning. Instead, only one run scored.

First Blauser, then Gant. How many nuclear bombs could the Bucs duck? When Hunter popped up for the second out, leaving the bases still loaded, it looked as if the baseball gods had made an incontrovert-ible decision. For the sin of profligacy, the squandering Braves were going to be penalized at the cost of a pennant.

Perhaps redemption really is at hand, alive in every moment as the Plains preachers say. His name is Francisco Cabrera of the Dominican Republic. Bats right-handed. Career average, .257. Position, catcher. Last man activated for the playoffs, on August 31.

He is baseball's perverse idea of fate. And he may be remembered down here in Georgia longer than quite a few presidents.

□ □ □

ATLANTA, October 16, 1992—For ten minutes after home plate umpire Randy Marsh signaled "safe," it felt as if the midnight Georgia sky would split with the thunder of 51,975 voices.

As Atlanta–Fulton County Stadium trembled from the volume, as two huge piles of Atlanta Braves formed, one on top of Sid Bream at home plate and another around Francisco Cabrera near first base, you wondered if people had ever celebrated a sports victory with such totally unrestrained, untainted delight. Why on earth would this crowd, this celebration for a 3–2 come-from-behind win in the ninth inning of the seventh National League playoff game, seem to reach a level that was wilder than so many other World Series or Super Bowls or Final Fours?

Maybe, in part, it's because the Braves are a young team. On Wednesday night, they also were a terribly frightened team, just a gang of big kids scared silly that they would be remembered as a bunch of red-white-and-blue-clad bums who blew the pennant after leading three games to one. That's why David Justice and a dozen other millionaires ran all around the infield aimlessly, waving their arms over their heads begging the crowd to make it louder—louder than any crowd had ever been.

Ten minutes is a long time. Time for the goose bumps to come and go, then come again as midnight passed and the booming just kept rolling around the park.

Such moments have to pass, however, though much of Atlanta wanted to hold its high until dawn.

Surely, Cabrera's two-run, two-out, pennant-winning single on Wednesday night cannot have been all that special. In good old ancient baseball, we can always be sure of one thing—everything's happened before, right? Why so much fuss?

To get this Game 7 in perspective, let's set up our dispassionate criteria for Enormous and Unique Clutch Hits. Once the hysteria abates, where does Cabrera's moment rate?

First, the hit has to win the pennant or World Series.

Second, our hero's team has to be down to its last out.

Third, the hit has to turn defeat into victory. Breaking a tie does not compare.

Finally, to be fair, let's say the hit does not have to be a sudden-death blow; it can come in either the top or the bottom of the final inning.

So, how many times had this been done before since 1868?

Answer: Never.

Gulp.

Everybody's going to scream, "Bobby Thomson."

Thomson's Shot Heard Round the World in 1951 came with one out in the bottom of the ninth. If he'd struck out, Willie Mays would have batted.

History buffs are going to point out that the '51 Giants were not the only team that ever came from behind to win in the last inning of the decisive final game of a playoff, League Championship Series, or World Series. It happened one other time. The 1972 Cincinnati Reds scored twice in the bottom of the ninth to beat Pittsburgh, 4–3, in the fifth game of the NLCS.

That game, however, had no hero, only a goat. The Pirates' Bob Moose wild-pitched home the winning run with two outs.

That's it.

Oh, baseball has had a zillion other great moments. But none where the drama was twisted so tight and the stakes were quite so high. Bill Mazeroski ended the '60 Series and Chris Chambliss the '76 ALCS with sudden-death home runs. But their teams entered their last at-bats in nice comfy ties. They couldn't lose. When Cabrera stepped up, the Pirates still led, 2–1.

Cabrera was the one with a gun to his head. If he'd known how unique his situation was, maybe he'd have been tied in a knot. But he didn't know. He'll spend the rest of his life being reminded.

"They say that two-out hits are golden," said Pirates manager Jim Leyland, who should be awarded a special commemorative World Series ring. "Cabrera had a golden hit."

Nobody would want to diminish Dave Henderson's game-tying home run when the Red Sox were down to their last out in the '86 ALCS. But it was only the fifth game of seven and it only sent the game into extra innings. Same deal with Kirk Gibson's down-to-the-last-strike homer off Dennis Eckersley in the '88 World Series. Fabulous theater. But it was Game 1.

Cookie Lavagetto's game-winning hit off Floyd Bevens in the '47 World Series broke up a no-hitter. But it didn't come in a decisive game. Even the game's most famous misplays—like Bill Buckner's error in the '86 Series or Pesky Held the Ball in the '46 Series—did not come in the last inning of the last game.

Wednesday night's seventh game was not the best game I've ever seen, much less the best game anybody's ever seen. But the bottom of the ninth is probably going to be my personal favorite half inning.

Each batter raised lovely baseball issues. With Pittsburgh leading, 2–0, leadoff man Terry Pendleton doubled into the rightfield corner. Cecil Espy barely missed it. Should Leyland have pinch-hit for Alex Cole in the seventh, then pinch-run for Lloyd McClendon in the top of the ninth? Those are his top rightfielders. With a lead, don't you stress defense? Cole might have caught Pendleton's drive.

Next, Justice hit a hard grounder just to the right of Jose Lind, who, earlier in the day, had been presented with the Gold Glove. Justice's ball clanked off Lind's mitt as if it were gold, not leather. "Lind catches that ball ten out of ten," said Leyland. Lind's misplay will be semiforgotten, but it probably hurt the Pirates as much as Buckner's hurt the Bosox.

Any other contender would have pulled Drabek after Lind's error. But the Pirates are too poor or too cheap to buy or trade for a decent closer. Everything in Stan Belinda's career, especially his 3.50 ERA, bespeaks an adequate setup man, not an ace. Nothing but his fastball is worth mentioning, and it's not great. Ironically, the Braves picked up just the sort of veteran discount reliever that the Pirates overlooked —Jeff Reardon, who saved Game 4 and won Game 7. The Pirates could have had him. Anybody could have had him.

Fearing Belinda, Leyland left Drabek in to face Sid Bream. The four-pitch walk felt inevitable. And fatal. It was Bream who scored the winning run.

Finally Belinda had to be summoned—one, two, or maybe even three batters later than most good teams would have waved to the bullpen.

Belinda tried. He threw strikes to Ron Gant. And almost had a heart attack. Gant hit a sacrifice fly. Some sac fly. If the trajectory had been a smidgen higher, Gant would have had a grand slam fifteen rows deep.

Belinda started nibbling. With the crowd booming and the memory of Gant still fresh, what would you do? Damon Berryhill was patient and walked. Pinch hitter Brian Hunter was not, chasing the first two pitches. He popped up.

Except for Lind's error, that would have ended the game.

But Belinda still had to face Cabrera. They'd met only once before in the majors, when Cabrera, a dead fastball hitter who can't touch a curve, hit a home run. Wednesday night, after two balls, Belinda had no choice. He had to throw his mediocre fastball over the plate to a fastball hitter who knew it was coming. Cabrera smoked the first one into the leftfield corner, but foul. The next fastball—not too bad a pitch, on the outside corner but waist high—was drilled six feet to the right of shortstop Jay Bell into left.

Although Cabrera's hit will make this game a writer's favorite, Bream's trip to home plate will make the video generation grateful. Bream has had five knee operations and runs as if he's still under general anesthesia. Bonds, in left, charges balls faster and throws to the plate stronger than any leftfielder in the league. But he doesn't always throw exactly straight.

My favorite baseball photo in many years is the shot of Bream's left foot touching the plate just as the diving Mike LaValliere tags his trailing right foot. The play looks like a dead tie. On live stop-action replays, you can see that Bream is clearly safe—by about three inches.

The 5-foot-8 LaValliere didn't need TV to tell him the awful truth.

"If I were six feet tall," Spanky said, "he'd be out."

INTRODUCING:
THE CURSED BLOW JAYS

September 28, 1990—At the medieval Battle of Agincourt, the English army—hungry and far from home—was outnumbered five to one. The French had the home field, more horses, more armor, the high ground, and a heck of a party the night before the fight.

Some say the English had the newly invented long bow on their side and a nasty trick of driving wooden stakes in front of their ranks to spear the French horses as their knights charged.

Still, that doesn't quite seem enough to account for the final score. History texts differ slightly on the stats, but all tell the same story. In one day, more than 10,000 of the 60,000 French soldiers were killed. Barely 1,000 of the 12,000 Englishmen died. The English also took 10,000 prisoners.

Confronted with these facts, William Shakespeare speculated that a pep talk by the courageous young English king might have been a factor. So he wrote the all-time pregame speech as the centerpiece of *Henry V.*

Perhaps before the Toronto Blue Jays get to Fenway Park on Friday night, Boston manager Joe Morgan could do worse than take his Red Sox to the movies to see the new hit version of *Henry V.* Watching it is like drinking a cup of adrenaline. By the time Harry finishes giving his men a few final words, you're ready to punch the nearest usher.

These days, the Red Sox are grousing that Roger Clemens may not be able to pitch in this three-game series. They say they're tired and undermanned and depressed after blowing a 6½-game lead this month. To hear the Sox talk, you'd think the season had 100 games to go and that they were 20 games behind; the Red Sox have just 5 games to play and are tied with Toronto for first.

The Red Sox might well think of the '85 Royals, the '87 Twins, the '88 Dodgers. The better team doesn't always win. There's such a thing as banding together and rising to the occasion.

("If we are mark'd to die, we are enow to do our country loss; and if to live, the fewer men, the greater share of honour. . . . I pray thee wish not one man more. . . . He which hath no stomach to this fight, let him depart; his passport shall be made, and crowns for convoy put into his purse. We would not die in that man's company that fears his fellowship to die with us.")

All month, the Red Sox have been whining about how New Englanders won't let them forget all the team's collapses in other years. Wouldn't a good general remind his troops that the greater the obstacles to be overcome, the more permanent the glory? What the Sox really have at this point is a romantic chance—a free opportunity to make history. Many Bosox teams have choked before. But what if one then rose from the dead?

("This day is call'd the feast of Crispian. He that outlives this day, and comes safe home, will stand a-tiptoe when this day is name'd. He that shall live this day, and see old age. . . . then will he strip his sleeve and show his scars and say, 'These wounds I had on Crispin's day.'

("Then shall our names, familiar in his mouth as household words . . . be in their flowing cups freshly remember'd. This story shall the good man teach his son; And Crispin Crispian shall ne'er go by, from this day to the ending of the world, but we in it shall be remembered; We few, he happy few, we band of brothers.")

Only the underdog gets to use this speech. That's why every manager and every coach in every sport wants the role—and will bad-mouth his team on the graves of his ancestors if that's what's needed to avoid being the (shudder) "favorite." The Blue Jays don't get to pull out the "band of brothers" stuff this weekend. It just doesn't work when everybody thinks of you as the French, bragging in their tents.

Of course, if the Blue Jays meet the Oakland A's next weekend in the AL playoffs, then it will be Cito Gaston's turn to buy twenty-four movie tickets.

("For he to-day that sheds his blood with me shall be my brother. Be he ne'er so vile, this day shall gentle his condition; and gentlemen in England now abed shall think themselves accursed they were not here, and hold their manhoods cheap whiles any speaks that fought with us upon Saint Crispin's day. . . . All things are ready, if our minds be so.")

Whether they know it or not, coaches often use King Henry's commonsense warrior wisdom. Guess what Harry's first order was after the victory at Agincourt? "Be it death . . . to boast of this, or take that praise from God which is his only."

Isn't that what Joe Gibbs said after the Redskins beat Phoenix, 31–0, on opening day? Hey, you never know when you might have to fight the French, or the Cardinals, again.

Old Joe Morgan, the manager who took so many years to ascend to the Red Sox managerial throne, does not strike many as an eloquent man. Yet he may be headed down the right track, intuitively. This week he said, "We're a streaky club and so are they. Let's see what the final streak will be. We've got Toronto for three games. What more do you want? If worse comes to worse, you look at the big dogs in front of you and beat them, that's all."

The Red Sox have beaten Toronto's big dogs in eight of ten games this year. And the Blue Jays are infamous for their poor fundamentals, lack of team cohesion, and bad pressure performances.

Still, if Clemens's shoulder stays stiff, a Morgan movie matinee might not be a bad idea.

□ □ □

BALTIMORE, October 4, 1990—At 10:39 P.M. Wednesday evening at Memorial Stadium, the Toronto Blue Jays gathered on the lip of their dugout to watch their public execution.

Tom Brunansky pulled the switch, 400 miles away in the rightfield corner of Fenway Park.

Usually, reception on enormous stadium TV screens is not terribly sharp. But you could practically see the stitches on the ball as it left Ozzie Guillen's bat like a shot as two White Sox runners sped round the bases, hoping to tie the game.

As the camera sought Brunansky, the Blue Jays walked up the dugout steps as a group. They knew their game with the Orioles was tied, 2–2, heading to the bottom of the ninth. They knew that Boston led, 3–1. And they knew they trailed Boston by one game on the last day of the regular season.

But they did not know that the Red Sox game, and their season, had ended three minutes before. Their fate was past-posted.

Like fish to bait, the Blue Jays stood on tiptoe as Brunansky went into his head-first dive across the gravel track. They stood, uncomprehending, as Brunansky, the ball, and their season disappeared from view into the corner. Were all those White Sox scoring? Were both games now tied? Were the Jays still breathing, still dreaming of a one-game playoff on Thursday in Toronto?

As Brunansky fought his way back into view, elbowing fans and leaping, the Blue Jays asked themselves what everyone else asked. What took Bruno so long back in that corner? Was he signing scorecards? Dusting off his cap? Or picking up a ball that he'd dropped but was now pretending that he'd caught?

Even as Brunansky leaped and screamed, even as the Red Sox celebrated their escape from calumny, the Jays kept their perch, refusing to believe. But, when the first-base umpire fought his way through the erupting crowd and reached into Brunansky's glove to pull out the ball, the Blue Jays finally knew the truth the videotape had recorded.

They'd squandered another season.

Once again, the better team—them—had found a way not to win the crown.

In an instant, the Toronto dugout lip was empty. Five minutes later, Jays relief pitcher Tom Henke laid a fastball down the center of the plate and Mickey Tettleton cut the gallows rope and let the corpse fall free. Tettleton's home run brought the Orioles from their dugout in a celebration that lasted for a quarter hour.

Everybody loves to beat the Blue Jays. The way the Torontonians are such insults to the niceties of the sport that it's almost a civic duty among big-league ballplayers to punish them.

The Jays walked off the field like silent strangers, ashamed of their 86 victories and runner-up money. The Blue Jays, now in their eighth straight season of largely unrewarded excellence, see the sand in the hourglass slipping to the bottom with each season. Won't they ever bring a World Series to Canada, much less a world title? How much must they suffer?

Last night Jays ace Dave Stieb grouched, stomped, gave the choke sign at a teammate, threw his glove, threw his hat, fired the resin bag in the air, and blamed his teammates for misplaying the line drives that he allowed. Will the Blue Jays continue to be victims of their own past with angry grumps such as Stieb and George Bell playing the roles of Keepers of the Blame?

God is in the details, the old saying goes. But, in the case of the Blue Jays, so is the devil. How can a team so undeniably good have accomplished so little over a period so long? Yes, it's in the details. Both of their play and their key personalities.

How do they do it?

The first batter of the game, Mookie Wilson, swung at a 3–0 pitch and flied out. Bell was thrown out trying to stretch a single (at least he was trying). Luis Sojo, trying to sacrifice, bunted into a force that cost Toronto a run. Tony Fernandez struck out on a fastball down the pipe with the bases loaded and one out. On consecutive plays, the aging Wilson misplayed high liners into a double and a triple. The first should have been caught. The second might have been.

Finally, Cito Gaston, managing sentimentally, let Stieb talk him into leaving him in the game with two on and none out in the eighth. Stieb almost hit Bill Ripken with one pitch and then came inside again so Ripken could take one for the Red Sox and load the bases. That led to the tying run.

In all, a typical Blue Jays defeat.

"It's amazing that Stieb has never won twenty games. Nobody has better stuff," said Orioles coach Elrod Hendricks. "His problem is that he never points the finger at himself. It's always somebody else's fault."

Stieb, who is a royal pain in the earlobe to teammates, was in rare form both pitching and showing up Wilson after his two misplays. Stieb glared at Wilson at least ten times in the course of his sin-filled inning; once Stieb reached the dugout, he threw everything that wasn't nailed down as fans watched his tantrum. The Mookster is supposed to be the Jays' try-hard, overachieving sparkplug. Could Stieb resent Wilson's image?

"We'll go home and hold our heads up," said Gaston. "We battled pretty hard."

Pretty?

"We had the talent here," said Henke, not bound to the company line. "If we had played the way we're capable, we could have run away with it."

□ □ □

TORONTO, October 9, 1992—As the ball rolled toward the Toronto Blue Jays dugout, with Oakland A's runners spinning around the bases, an amazing thing happened. The whole Blue Jays team—you know, the dumb guys—knew Rule 7.05(h).

"Let it go," they screamed at their catcher, Pat Borders, as he slid toward the dugout, his hands inches from the trickling ball.

"Don't touch it," they yelled, just as Borders reached to grab it.

What? Deliberately let a ball roll down your dugout steps? With Willie Wilson rounding third base and heading for home in the fifth inning of a 0–0 game? With Mike Bordick right behind him, already heading for third base?

Come on, man, you've got to pick up that ball. You've got to take your shot at Wilson or Bordick. You can't just quit and let 'em run all day.

But you can quit. In this one instance, you can and you better. And the whole stupid Blow Jays dugout, led by manager Cito Gaston, knew it.

"I think all of us were hollering at him," said Gaston.

"That was the key play . . . the reprieve," said winning pitcher David Cone.

Only time will tell if, in that split second, the Blue Jays came of age and came together. Thanks to that play more than any other, they beat the A's, 3–1, to even the American League playoffs at a game apiece. The Blue Jays are proud of Kelly Gruber for his two-run homer and they're happy about Cone's strong victorious pitching. But what really has them crowing is their distinctive un–Blue Jays display of brains on that crucial play.

What the Jays knew, even though most in the crowd of 51,114 were totally in the dark, is that when a ball goes into the dugout, every runner is awarded "one base" and the ball is dead.

Wilson began the play at second, Bordick at first. They'd run on a double steal as Cone threw a pitch in the dirt that bounced off Borders and, eventually, rolled into the dugout. Even though Wilson scored easily and Bordick reached third base at a trot, they each had to go back a base. Logical? Maybe not. But that's the rule—a semi-obscure one. And the Jays knew it.

Wilson, screaming and protesting, was ordered out of the A's dugout and back to third. Bordick was returned to second. Neither scored as Cone fanned Walt Weiss and Rickey Henderson to end the inning.

That was the break the Jays needed. Three batters later, they had a 2–0 lead on a walk and Gruber's homer. They never looked back. Make no mistake, Toronto needed this game desperately. Teams have lost the first two games of a seven-game series in their home park and come back to triumph. The '86 Mets did it in the World Series. But it's a rarity. When you blow the first two at home, you're supposed to be stone dead.

When the Jays play smart and the A's also play dumb in a game of enormous importance, you know the baseball world is standing on its head. Anything might happen next. The World Series might even leave the United States.

As soon as the Jays found their savvy, the A's seemed to lose their heads. His team down two runs, Ruben Sierra was thrown out stealing in the sixth with the heart of the order due up. A rally was defused. Worse, in the eighth, with Oakland down, 3–0, Weiss tried to go from second to third on a fly to left. That's a good gamble only if you're safe by 10 feet. If you're out, it's a horrid mental mistake. Candy Maldonado threw Weiss out.

It's hard to overestimate how important it is to the Jays to establish their credibility as an intense, alert team in this reformed era of Jack Morris, Joe Carter, and Dave Winfield. For a decade, the Jays have, a hundred times over, earned their bitterly deserved reputation as a team with cotton batting between their ears. Sometimes they seemed to be whistling a happy tune or absent-mindedly counting the crowd when the pennant was on the line. For years, they've provided a baseball clinic for youngsters from coast to coast. You could take children to watch the Jays play a big game and say, "See, kids. That's the way not to play."

You sure didn't expect a whole dugout to know Rule 7.05(h).

In fact, the umpires didn't appear to know the rule immediately. It's not an appeal play. Why did Gaston even have to race on the field to argue and, as he diplomatically said, "remind them of the rule"?

This game was vital for the Jays because, all summer long, they've played on cruise control. They won just enough, never straining themselves too much, keeping the upstart Baltimore Orioles and, in the final days, the Milwaukee Brewers comfortably at bay. The Jays never faced a truly crucial series.

When the Jays didn't wrap up their division as swiftly as they might, management traded young prospects for Cone, the sport's strikeout leader. You see, baseball is usually pretty lux for the Jays. They play in a building as big as a city. They draw four million fans, no two of whom have ever booed at the same time. They never get a bad hop on their AstroTurf. If it gets an itty-bitty bit chilly, they close the roof. Their life is either balmy or climate-controlled.

So, in Game 2, it was fair to wonder if the Jays were capable of a real sense of urgency. After the A's stunning Game 1 win, when Harold Baines broke up a 3–3 tie with a ninth-inning homer off Mr. Morris, not one Blue Jay talked about Game 2 being a Must Game or called a team meeting or acted as if SkyDome were falling.

"We're all right," said Winfield. "Really, everything's all right."

Really?

The A's offer such a contrast. They truly understand urgency. They are about to be blown to bits and they know it. They have so many free agents, all worthy of big contracts, that A's management, with its middling budget, freely acknowledges that the team will probably lose a couple of its present stars.

"You hate to say it—the last go-around or last hurrah—but we know this team will be substantially different next year. That has put everyone in a bad mood," said Ron Darling, the A's Game 3 starter. "We really, really want to win this thing. I think everyone is trying to own up to their responsibility to concentrate. There aren't too many smiles that come with that thinking. Whatever you call it—the eye of the tiger—whatever cliché you want, this team has it more than any I've been on."

The A's are intense every night. Will the Jays match them, or merely rise to the occasion when they are as desperate as they were in Game 2? Was Borders's play, and his teammates' help, an omen? Or was it just a temporary reprieve for a team that loves to ride on cruise control? We'll find out. Because the A's are in a bad mood and they're going back home too.

THE TURNING POINT

ATLANTA, October 19, 1992—As the old goat walked off the mound in the ninth inning, dragging one of the most crushing ninth-inning home runs in World Series history behind him, Jeff Reardon hitched his pants.

It's not a pretty body and never has been, not in any of its 357 saves, the most in the annals of his game. After thirty-seven years, sixteen of them throwing a baseball as a pro, the short and rather dumpy Reardon physique needs a well-fitting uniform and a hitched belt just to look presentable to other major leaguers.

Reardon never wanted to preserve his enormous and well-earned dignity more. He knew they'd show the pictures of him walking off that mound forever.

Look at him, old Jeff Reardon, washed-up Jeff Reardon, trying for one last hurrah, trying to give the Atlanta Braves—the near-great team without a trustworthy bullpen—its first world title.

Zoom in close. Look at his black, deep eyes and the black beard—so fierce for so long. This is the man who gave up Ed Sprague's pinch-hit home run—the one that turned a 4–3 Atlanta lead into a 5–4 Toronto victory in the last inning. This is the man who, maybe, reversed the direction of a World Series by putting a fastball right where the Blue Jays wanted it. Down the middle. Knee high. The Braves' scouting report on Sprague said: "Low fastball hitter." Why not just put it on a tee, Jeff? Now, instead of being down two games to none, the Jays are even and alive and going home.

For Reardon, it was the longest imaginable walk to the loneliest possible seat on the Braves bench. One of the toughest and most respected overachievers of his generation had just blown the biggest save of his life.

Veteran pitchers don't need to follow the flight of home runs, and Reardon barely took a peek. He knew that awful, numbing 400-foot first-pitch blast was going over the leftfield wall—right into the heart of a hundred Blue Jays fans waving Toronto placards.

Ed Sprague? Nice guy. One of the hundreds of nice guys who've come and gone while Reardon has survived. At the end, they all climb up on the stage with you, don't they, then nudge you toward the edge until they can push you off.

As he walked, Reardon seemed to get visibly smaller even as Sprague, suddenly a very big man in Toronto, seemed to get larger. One minute, Reardon was a giant, an all-timer, even a marginal Hall of Famer. The next, he was looking up—way up—at this broad-shouldered, young, twenty-five-year-old backup catcher who put one in the bleachers. One minute, he's the guy whose wife won a gold medal in synchronized swimming at the Barcelona Olympics. The next, he's Mr. Edward Sprague, Esq., instant legend and semi-heir to Kirk Gibson.

For seven weeks, since the Braves got Reardon from the Red Sox for a pair of used sanitary hose, the Braves have told themselves that this baseball grand old man, hobbling on his last legs, would be enough to fake them through. Surely, after all he had done, after all the courage and toughness he'd shown from New York to Montreal to Minnesota to Boston, baseball wouldn't let the world collapse on this particular pair of shoulders.

Come on, this is the same Reardon who, two years ago, came back from disc surgery against the orders of every doctor to pitch the Red Sox into the '90 playoffs. Can't be done, they said. Your season is over. But they didn't know Reardon from Dalton, Massachusetts, raised in a hard mill town. Boston general manager Lou Gorman called Reardon "the guttiest player I've known."

Before that, it was Reardon who helped the Expos to their only postseason appearance and the Twins to their first world championship.

Sure, Reardon didn't throw hard anymore. Sure, he'd had to add an odd-looking four-finger change-up just to bluff and bluster his way along. But hadn't he saved a game in the playoffs? Hadn't he backed into a victory in the legendary Game 7? Didn't Francisco Cabrera bat for him? Wasn't that a sign? Baseball doesn't go in for fairy-tale signs. This reality-testing business is tough stuff.

More than a half hour after Terry Pendleton popped up to end the game with two men on base—that is to say, after Tom Henke got just the sort of save for the Jays that Reardon could not muster—the Braves' victim emerged to talk about his disaster.

Of course, as he has been in 811 other games, Reardon was stoic. "What can I say? I threw the wrong pitch. But you can't second-guess yourself," he said. "It was no cheapie. He hit it good. When I give one up, I really give one up."

For the Braves, this was a stunning blow to the solar plexus. They have tried to focus on Reardon's late-season Atlanta stats—a 1.15 ERA, a 3–0 record, and three saves in fourteen games. They have tried not to hear all the horror stories from Boston where Reardon saved 27 games but squandered so many—usually for Roger Clemens, it seemed—that his final two-league numbers for the year were fairly harrowing: 30 saves, 10 blown saves.

That's not good enough. Not to close out World Series games.

For more than a month, ever since Reardon arrived just hours before the trading deadline on August 31, he has been a spooky figure in the Braves clubhouse. He was going to be the salvation, the final romantic last-minute piece of the puzzle.

Or he was going to be another failed piece of southern romanticism, another huge, heartbreaking, totally unfair, but utterly real disappointment.

Yes, as he walked off the mound, Jeff Reardon hitched his pants. He'll be ready tomorrow if the phone rings, as he's always been. He'll be ready to atone, to give it his best shot, to strike out Kelly Gruber with two men on to kill a rally—just as he did to end the eighth inning Sunday night.

But you wonder, all things considered and hardball being what it is, whether the phone will ever ring for Jeff Reardon again.

NIGHTMARE'S END

ATLANTA, October 25, 1992—Every ghost, every demon, every hound from hell that ever stalked the imaginations and evil dreams of the haunted Toronto Blue Jays circled round that supposedly jinxed team Saturday night. Mere baseball players should not have to endure what the Blue Jays suffered round midnight.

But then, if the Blue Jays' nightmares had not been so horrible, so close to being unbelievably cruel, their dream of a victory, their world title after so long and so much endured, could not have been so glorious.

There's never been a final score—Toronto 4, Atlanta 3 in eleven innings—that told so little. There's seldom, if ever, been a game—

even a Game 6 of a Series—that contained so much. It took more than four hours but felt like it took four days.

Blue Jays fans, never again to be denigrated as followers of a team called the Blow Jays, are going to rhapsodize about Dave Winfield's World Series–winning two-run double in the eleventh inning off Charlie Leibrandt until the last, long, into-the-cold Arctic winter.

But they're not really going to focus on Winfield as much as you'd guess. Sure, it was fabulously, stupendously great to see the old man, just turned forty-one, atone for so much October embarrassment. Mr. May, indeed. Take that, George Steinbrenner, exiled nemesis.

Still, Winfield's double, enormous as it was, was only one percent of this game's drama.

This night was about the entire Jays team standing up to its own history—its history raised to an incalculable baseball power—and winning.

You have to know what they endured to know what they won.

Like the Boston Red Sox six years ago, the Jays came within one strike of their world championship, only to have it torn away. And, like the Red Sox, like Bill Buckner, the barely thinkable happened.

Otis Nixon was down in the count 0–2 against Tom Henke. Nixon did the only thing left available to him. With his Atlanta Braves trailing, 2–1, with men on first and second base and two outs, he slapped at the ball. Defensively. Just to stay alive. Just to make something— anything—happen.

The result was a ground ball. A lousy, choppy two-hopper to the left side. Guided by Satan, the ball found a hole.

The Jays still had a chance to win their title right then and there. The man trying to score from second base was not-so-swift Jeff Blauser. And here he came, waved home by Jimy Williams, just the way the third-base coach waved home a milk truck named Sid Bream on Francisco Cabrera's season-saving, pennant-winning hit ten days ago.

The Jays had the man for the job all ready—leftfielder Candy Maldonado. Wasn't he the Jay who'd hit a home run, way back in the fourth inning off Steve Avery to give Toronto that 2–1 lead that five different pitchers had milked into the ninth? And wasn't it Maldonado who had just saved the game—saved it just two minutes before?

Cabrera had fouled off three 2–2 pitches, then crushed a wicked line drive to leftfield. Maldonado stood stock still—frozen by the ball screaming at him. It's the toughest play an outfielder faces. The murderously hit ball, straight at him. At the last instant, Maldonado realized that all the Blow Jay demons had conspired against him. The ball was going over his head. Two runs would score. The Braves would force a seventh game. And you know what happened to the Red Sox in '86.

Maldonado leaped and snagged the ball in the web of his glove.

After that catch, how could Maldonado not throw Blauser out at the plate. Oh, you forgot about Blauser coming to the plate? Well, he's dead, my friend. A good throw, a standard-issue played-all-my-life-in-rightfield-'cause-I-pack-a-gun peg to the plate and that world championship trophy would be in Canada.

Maldonado hit the backstop on the fly.

So the Blue Jays were dead. The lead blown. All their past sins suddenly running up before their eyes, accusing, reminding, mocking.

That's what makes this game so wonderful, so much the game that the Blue Jays deserved. They didn't die. They pulled that ground-ball stake out of their own hearts.

Henke, who'd thrown roughly a thousand pitches in the inning, got Ron Gant to fly out to end the ninth.

Maybe the old Jays would have sat on their behinds as that inning ended. Who knows? The New Jays burst from their dugout to congratulate Henke.

Way to go, Tom. You just let the world title get away. But you didn't blow the game.

You think that's it, right? You think the Jays just scored a couple of runs in the eleventh. Simple.

Are you kidding? The bottom of the eleventh was the bottom of the ninth all over again. Blauser singled to open the inning off Jimmy Key, and Damon Berryhill hit a perfect double-play grounder right at the shortstop.

It hit a rock. The damn thing bounced straight up over Alfredo Griffin. First and third. Mayhem in Fulton County. A sacrifice bunt put runners on second and third. A ground out scored one and moved pinch runner John Smoltz—the tying run—to third base.

Of course, Otis Nixon came to bat.

So what's the best and craziest ending you could cook up?

That's right. The suicide squeeze bunt. The ultimate choke play. "Jays Blow Suicide Squeeze, Prepare to Finish the Job in Game 7." But they didn't. Not this time.

Nixon, the speedburner, laid it down, halfway toward first base.

Mike Timlin raced off the mound and plucked at the ball. No, he didn't bobble it, though hundreds have. He didn't rush, though thousands have. And he didn't throw it into the runner's back, as countless pitchers have. He went as fast as was humanly possible—while still being under control.

Nixon was out by a fraction of a step.

The Blue Jays had stopped a suicide attempt. Now, they don't have to consider commiting one themselves—not now, not ever.

□ □ □

ATLANTA, October 26, 1992—Cito Gaston was asked what he was doing when Dave Winfield hit his double over third base to win the World Series for the Blue Jays in the early after-midnight hours of Sunday morning.

The Toronto manager explained, in all seriousness, that his dugout task was to "concentrate on the rightfield line," while coach Gene Tenace was in charge of "concentrating on the leftfield line."

That's right. After all the normal strategic considerations had been exhausted, the Blue Jays' brain trust resorted to "thinking positive thoughts."

Over the past two Octobers, almost every World Series game has been so close, so unbearably tense, and so prone to being decided by the most capricious or malicious Breaks of the Game, that teams have returned to the rites of tribal society for psychological refuge.

One team tries to magnetize the foul lines with its willpower. The other? In the bottom of the last inning, the Atlanta Braves dugout was full of lunatics. Grown men had their hats on backward with the brims up. Others had hats pulled low and rubbed their heads wildly, as though shampooing.

Before the sixth and final Series game, Gaston was asked why his Jays were winning. Their superior bullpen? His decision to start Jimmy Key, not Jack Morris, in Game 4? The collapse of noble old Jeff Reardon?

"We're getting the breaks," Gaston said. "That's it."

Game 1 was won, 3–1, by Damon Berryhill's three-run homer off Morris. But look what happened on the previous batter. Ron Gant barely beat out a double-play ground ball that would have ended the inning. Inches.

Game 2 provided one pitch for the ages—that meatball down the pipe by Reardon that Ed Sprague gratefully swatted over the fence, turning a probable 4–3 loss into one of the all-time comeback wins.

Once again, look at the previous hitter. Replays indicate that Reardon struck out Derek Bell with a 2–2 slider.

"Reardon struck Bell out twice," said Braves manager Bobby Cox bitterly.

Mike Reilly, one of the game's good umps and nice people, had a night as bad as Reardon's. Blowing the Bell strikeout was the last episode. If Bell is out, Reardon probably wouldn't have been so concerned about starting off Sprague with a strike.

Game 3 was also a one-play game: Devon White's triple-play catch. It ranks with Dwight Evans's double-play catch in Game 6 in 1975 as perhaps the best since Willie Mays's play in 1954. (For the record, even the umpire now admits it was a triple play.) The break here, and White will tell you so, is that the ball somehow stayed in his glove. When player, ball, and fence meet at full speed, the ball doesn't usually stay in the glove. If it drops out, the Braves win.

Game 4 still has the players buzzing. Why on earth was Toronto first baseman John Olerud guarding the line with the Jays ahead, 2–1, in the eighth and men on second and third with two out and a right-handed hitter at bat? You shade the line in the late innings if an extra-base hit will lead to the go-ahead or tying run. You sure don't guard the line when the tying run is on third and the winning run is on second. Then you play to prevent the game-losing single.

"I don't know why he was over there," said Braves first baseman Sid Bream.

"We don't play that way in our league," said Tom Glavine.

Sour grapes? Absolutely. But if Olerud had been shading the hole, as most players would have been, Jeff Blauser's sharp grounder would have been a two-run double down the line. Instead, third out.

The Braves got the break in Game 5. Nobody knows why Gaston, who had an excellent overall Series, let Morris pitch to Lonnie Smith with the bases full. If he brings in any of his forty-seven grade-A relievers, the Braves stop scoring. The Jays then shell laboring John Smoltz and Toronto has its Friday parade as originally scheduled.

When it comes to breaks, however, when it comes to the kind of inside baseball stuff that nut cases can't stop rechewing for weeks, then Game 6 was like a six-layer chocolate cake with ice cream. Everybody knows about Candy Maldonado's last-second leaping catch of

Francisco Cabrera's liner in the ninth. Candy took a step in, instead of a step back. If the ball is six inches higher, everybody scores, Braves win. Everybody knows that Winfield's game-winning hit was barely fair—from the kind of lunging, flicking swing on which the result is largely accidental.

But this game had a couple of hidden breaks that are just delicious. When Otis Nixon tied the game, 2–2, in the ninth when the Braves were one strike away from extinction, everybody was too busy going nuts when Blauser slid across home plate to see the real ending of the play. Lonnie Smith may have blown another World Series for the Braves. He froze—again—when he probably should have scored the winning run—again.

On Nixon's hit, Maldonado in leftfield made one of the most comic, awful throws in Series history. It hit the top of the backstop on the fly. When the ball passed over catcher Pat Borders's head, Blauser was a step or so from the plate and Smith was a step or so from third.

Borders had to turn, run to the backstop, stop, pluck at the ball, miss it once, then pick it up, and cock his arm to throw to the plate.

To Borders's amazement, Smith had rounded third, slammed on the brakes, stopped, started home again, stopped, started home again, then frozen once more before going back to third. If he'd just kept running—and the whole play was in front of him—he'd have scored standing up to win the game.

The final Series-winning break was a beauty too. Winfield's double came on a full-count two-out pitch. As a result, both Devon White on second and Roberto Alomar on first were running on the pitch. If they hadn't been going, if Winfield had hit the 2–2 pitch, Alomar would never have scored what proved to be the decisive run in a 4–3 game.

Even with both Jays flying, the Braves had one last prayer. If Winfield's ball had hit the right side of the bullpen mound, it would have ricocheted toward leftfielder Ron Gant, who might well have had a shot at holding Alomar. But it went over the left side of the mound. Gant had to play a hot, crazy carom off the wall. He missed it and the last shot at Alomar was gone.

No wonder so many people were still talking Sunday about how superb this Series, and especially the last game, had been. Cabrera's line out in the ninth, Nixon's last-strike RBI hit, and Nixon's failed drag bunt to end the Series were as thrilling as baseball gets. Winfield's Double is going to be the catch phrase for this game as surely as

Fisk's Homer, Buckner's Error and Puckett's Homer bring to mind the equally fabulous sixth games of 1975, 1986, and 1991.

Should Cox have brought in Reardon to face Joe Carter and Winfield in the eleventh? How can you leave in a left-handed starter with a bad Series history to face two right-handed 100-RBI men when you have the all-time save leader warmed up in the bullpen? And the reliever is right-handed to boot. Talk about a vote of no confidence. Note: Winfield is 1 for 13 in his career off Reardon. But, then, maybe that was some other, younger Jeff Reardon.

Gaston made exactly the same risky, game-saving move in the bottom of the eleventh that Cox had shied away from when the game was lost in the top half. Gaston had Jimmy Key on the mound with the tying run at third and Nixon up. He called for Mike Timlin, who has excellent stuff but one save all season. Talk about a gutsy move.

Gaston trusted his bullpen in a bullpen situation, even his last man. Cox didn't trust his in a bullpen situation, even his "best" man.

Those two decisions—those last two breaks—were the final ones in a riveting Series that ranks with any ever played. But then how can we be expected to make such distinctions anymore? We're numb from the fun. For the eighth year in a row, everybody walked out of the World Series feeling like we'd been hit by an earthquake. Once, we were. The other times it was just baseball, showing its stuff.

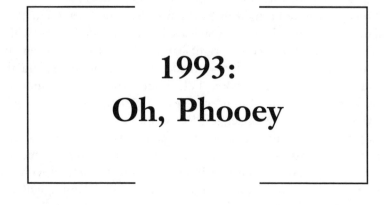

1993:
Oh, Phooey

ATLANTA, October 4, 1993—The Atlanta Braves couldn't wait for the San Francisco Giants to expire. They had to come out of their clubhouse and onto the field—champagne bottles in hand—to share the final moments of baseball's last, great pennant race with their fans.

The Giants, playing in Los Angeles, were down to their last three outs of the season. No, they weren't just down. They were losing, 12–1, buried under an avalanche of Dodgers home runs. They weren't coming back. Not this time. Not even the Giants. So it was time for the Braves and their fans, watching it all on TV, to gloat. Yes, after six months of agony—after being 10 games behind the Giants, then 4 games ahead, and, finally, dead even on the last day of the season—it was time to have the last laugh: 104 wins to 103.

The Braves stood in centerfield, staring up at images of the Giants on the centerfield video board. What could they do, what gesture could they make, to stick it to the Giants one last time for all the aggravation they'd caused?

In an instant, the Braves found the solution. As their tormentors went down one-two-three in the ninth inning, the Braves did the Chop, aiming every sarcastic salute right up at the Giants on the screen.

Maybe it was bush. Maybe the Braves, who'd been sitting in their clubhouse for more than three hours following their own 5–3 victory over the Colorado Rockies, just let loose with great relief. And maybe the Giants won't forget it, either—at least not for two or three generations. But the Braves couldn't help themselves. In a way, their questionable taste was a perverse testimony to the Giants' fabulous, dogged season. Battered, underdog San Francisco had gotten under the skins of the mighty overdog Braves so badly, and for so long, that they just had to act out.

"I couldn't be prouder. We came from way back," said Braves manager Bobby Cox, whose team played incredible .750 ball (51–17) after Fred McGriff arrived in trade.

"After the six-month ordeal that we had catching them, it's hard to believe that they came back and caught us," said coach Leo Mazzone, shaking his head.

But that's what the Giants did. After losing eight in a row in early September to disgrace themselves in some eyes, they found a final wind—certainly not a second wind, perhaps more like a tenth, considering the injuries they overcame—and sped to the finish like avengers, winning 14 of 16 before their final defeat.

Make no mistake, the Braves were a worried juggernaut on this final day. If Mike Piazza, who hit two home runs for the Dodgers, wants to enter the Atlanta mayoral race, which is now in progress, he only has to pick his party. He can probably win on either ticket. Even Dodgers manager Tommy Lasorda, the man who kept pitching to Barry Bonds on Friday night until the great Giant had seven RBI, could probably still get elected.

"I don't think anybody in here wants to go to San Francisco [for a one-game playoff on Monday]. I know I don't," said David Justice on Saturday night.

Even after Sunday's victory, while they awaited the West Coast result, the Braves refused to talk about a Monday playoff, as if denying its possibility would make it go away. And why wouldn't they be in denial? The Giants had the hottest pitcher in the league—21-game winner Billy Swift—waiting for them. He'd won his last four starts with a 0.56 ERA. And whom did the Braves have ready? Their coldest pitcher—John Smoltz—who'd allowed five runs in less than seven innings in each of his past three starts.

Of course, such stats and talk about "momentum" mean little. In 1978, baseball saw much the same scenario. The Boston Red Sox blew a 14½-game lead, then fell three games behind the Yankees before rallying to force a playoff in Fenway Park. The Red Sox seemed fated to win. But Bucky Dent's home run proved stronger than any omen.

"I grew up a Red Sox fan" in New England, said the Braves' Tom

Glavine, who won his 22nd game in the clincher. "I lived through '78. It wasn't fun. I hated Bucky Dent until I met him this year."

Confident as the Braves are, they're just as glad it ended this way. In fact, this whole town seemed on the verge of having a nervous breakdown at the thought of coming so far and then coming up short.

Why else would thousands of people sit in a ballpark for three hours and watch a TV screen 600 feet away? Were all their TV sets at home broken? Did somebody close every bar in town?

Maybe the Braves fans just needed to band together and convince each other that the bogeyman wasn't going to get them again—not like the other times. Not like what the Twins did to them in the awful Thunderdome in the '91 World Series. Not like the miseries that befell old Jeff Reardon last October in the Series, when the best plans were all undone for want of a dependable reliever.

All in all, this ending was perfect. An Atlanta victory seemed proper. Since the day McGriff arrived, the Braves have been the best team in baseball by a clear margin. If they'd had the Crime Dog for the first 94 games, they might have challenged every single-season record on the books. This stadium caught fire the night he arrived and the team followed suit. Firemen put out the blaze but even the heroic Giants couldn't extinguish the Braves. Any postseason without them would have seemed hollow.

The Giants, for their part, ended with their dignity utterly intact. If they'd had to soldier on deeper into the playoffs, how long could their overworked pitching staff have held itself together? Would they even have been able to represent themselves well had they reached the Series?

We should savor this day while its flavor still lasts. In baseball's brave new world with wild cards, we will never again see a final-day race decided between teams with 104 and 103 wins. One of them will be the wild card for sure. The six-month war of attrition—the summer-long war that leaves both teams with total, bone-deep respect for the other—will be diluted.

"Someday it's going to be a hell of a lot of fun to sit back and talk about this," said Glavine. "The way we came back after we were so far behind speaks well for us. But the way they wouldn't quit after we got ahead tells you plenty about them. You've gotta tip your hat to both teams."

Actually, a full bow would be more in order.

□ □ □

ATLANTA, October 12, 1993—The faces of the Atlanta Braves are a study worthy of an oil painter. How would you capture the rich play of emotions that compete in their expressions in the wake of their second brutal one-run defeat within twenty-four hours?

They were surprised at 12:17 Monday morning when they lost, 2–1, to the Philadelphia Phillies in Game 4 of the National League playoffs. What a loony, fluky game that was. The Phils got a game-winning hit from a pitcher, a couple of unearned runs, and a divine providence blown call from an ump to steal that victory. But the Braves were truly stunned when they lost Monday afternoon, 4–3, on a tenth-inning homer by Lenny Dykstra in Game 5.

In less than a day, the Braves had gone from heirs to the world title to a team on the brink of elimination. The Braves thought they might be popping champagne by now, not crying in their beer. It's hard to digest your life when it comes so fast and in such big chunks. Why, just eight days earlier the Braves were completing one of the greatest come-from-behind pennant chases in history, roaring to the wire 51–17. Isn't that enough? Does it have to get so hard all over again?

Braves manager Bobby Cox looks morally annoyed, as though he is on the wrong end of an injustice in progress. This shouldn't be happening to his mighty Braves with their back-to-back pennants and their 104 regular-season wins and their half dozen headed-to-the-Hall-of-Fame superstars. Don't the fat, hairy, slovenly Phillies, with their flawed defensive fundamentals and their undermanned pitching staff, understand that they are interfering with a handsome, clean-cut, and expensive team's appointment with its destiny? Can't the Phils stop dribbling tobacco juice down their chins long enough to figure out that the Braves drubbed them, 14–3 and 9–4, in Games 2 and 3? Don't the Phils understand "last call"? How often do you have to throw these guys out of the bar?

Leo Mazzone, the brainy coach whose Fab Four pitchers haven't done anything wrong yet, looks like he might stop rocking back and forth in the dugout and start exploding if somebody says the wrong word to him. What's wrong with the Braves offense that has scored 5.7 runs a game since the day Fred McGriff arrived? How can you get shut down by a 92–103 career pitcher like Danny Jackson in Game 4, then come right back and make Curt Schilling look like Roger Clemens for the second time in a week?

Tommy Glavine's mouth is a pinched line of paranoid intensity as he says: "What is there to say? We have to go to Philadelphia and win two games." Jeff Blauser adds, "It's nice to have Cy and Cy going." Meaning Greg Maddux (20–10) and Glavine (22–6), who've won the past two NL Cy Young Awards and who are on tap for Games 6 and, the Braves hope, 7. The Braves want you to know that the last time these two matchups rolled around—Maddux against Tommy Greene and Glavine against Terry Mulholland—they were Braves laughers.

But logic doesn't seem to apply to the Phils or this series. For one thing, the Phils don't play baseball right. They are an aesthetic abomination. Take Mitch Williams, for example. He's pitched three times and been horrible each time. He's blown two saves. He's walked the world. He's made one error and would have lost Game 4 with a wild throw if his third baseman hadn't saved him. Yet he's got two wins and a save. Wild Thing did it again in Game 5. He comes in to protect a 3–0 lead for Schilling. What does he do? Gives up three hits. Blows the lead. And watches in horror as a Mark Lemke liner, which would have won the game for the Braves, curves foul by a foot or two. This is the closer that gets you to the Series?

The Phillies love all this paradox. They play anti-baseball and revel in it. They break every rule. Assuming, of course, they know the rules in the first place. Fred McGriff missed a two-run homer by 6 inches in the first inning of Game 5. The ball ricocheted off the top of the rightfield wall at about 100 miles an hour. What did Wes Chamberlain do? Played it barehanded. That's how you butcher plays. But Chamberlain snagged the ball and gunned toward the infield, and an amazed Blauser was thrown out at the plate by 10 feet.

How do you beat a team that, in its opponents' eyes, is already doing everything necessary to beat itself? In the Braves' three-run ninth on Monday, Schilling walked the leadoff batter—a cardinal sin. Kim Batiste, the defensive specialist from hell, snagged a perfect double-play grounder, then threw the ball backward over his shoulder like someone tossing salt for luck. In the same inning, Dykstra kicked a ball in centerfield. Rookie shortstop Kevin Stocker entirely missed a chopper up the middle by pinch hitter Francisco Cabrera, turning a possible game-ending double play into a game-tying RBI single.

Any normal baseball team rolls over and dies after such embarrassments. But you can't embarrass the Phillies. And just when you think they'll quit, they spit in your eye. Especially that obnoxious Dykstra. He took a borderline 2–2 pitch from Mark Wohlers and stood at the plate, cocky as could be, as if to say to ump Jerry Crawford, "I led this league in walks and runs this season. This kid on the mound ain't nobody. That means it's 'ball three,' not 'strike three.'"

The Braves whined like offended purists.

"The 2–2 pitch to Dykstra in the last inning was pretty darn important. We thought it was strike three," said Cox, as though that would somehow erase the memory of the 400-foot, game-winning blast that Dykstra hit off the Royal Oak Charcoal sign on the next pitch. "We didn't get the call."

"Aw, that pitch," said Dykstra. "It was way outside."

Yes, it's great to be a Phillie right now. Just think how much it must get into the Braves' craws that the same umpire (Crawford) who shafted them in Game 4 with an incorrect out call was the same one who did not call Dykstra out on the pitch before the homer.

Poooor Braves. Pooooor babies.

Maybe they ought to get a clutch hit instead of griping about the umps. Maybe Ron Gant shouldn't go back to the wall, then act like his feet are in cement as the ball almost hits him in the head for a three-base error that leads to a run. Maybe the talent-rich Braves, for crying out loud, should have traded Ryan Klesko, Chipper Jones, Javy Lopez, Tony Tarasco, or another of their mega-prospects for a real closer instead of the collection of almost-but-not-quite-good-enough guys they have in their bullpen now. Once again, that bullpen that GM John Schuerholz won't improve killed the Braves. Greg McMichael gave up a solo homer to Darren Daulton in the ninth before Wohlers gave up the Dykstra 2-iron in the tenth.

Two days ago when the Braves led this series and all was right with their world, Glavine said, "We have to win the World Series this year."

Maybe they better find a way to beat the Philthy Phillies phirst.

PHILADELPHIA, October 14, 1993—The Philadelphia Phillies needed ninety-seven years to win their first world title. Now it's taken them a decade just to get back in the Series. So, for more than one hundred years, you could say the Phils were baseball's unluckiest team.

How were the Atlanta Braves to know that destiny would make it all up to the Phillies—a century of Pholds and Phlops—in one eight-day span. Make no mistake, these are the Phated Phils who are going to the World Series. If a scrawny utility man like Mickey Morandini has to smack a liner off the leg of Greg Maddux—hobbling the best of all the Braves' fabulous starting pitchers and ultimately sending him down to a 6–3 loss—then 'twill come to pass.

If the defending world champion Toronto Blue Jays are smart, they won't worry about setting up a starting rotation by Saturday. They'll hire an exorcist. As the baffled, befuddled Braves now know, the Phils can flat put a curse on you.

This lovably grubby team, which would look right at home hanging off the sides of a garbage truck, beat the Braves in Game 6 of this playoff for one reason more than any other—they got the kind of breaks that are borderline unbelievable, just as they had gotten them in their first three victories.

This should not be construed as any derogation of the Phillies. True, they are an acquired taste. As Pete Incaviglia said during the team champagne bath, "We're not America's Team. We're America's Most Wanted Team." Still, it is hard not to fall for this team. This is a club that could get both flags upside down at the World Series.

"We are a bunch of outcasts," said winning pitcher Tommy Greene. "We'll fight you in the mud and the rain. We're a gritty, dirty team. That's who we are."

The Phils deserve their glory. They're ornery and never quit, which is vital, because they make the kind of mistakes that cause other teams to die. They hit a ton. And their pitchers will work till their arms fall off. (That's just a figure of speech now. Next July we'll see if it's also prophecy.)

However, in addition to all their Gas House Gang virtues and their charming personal eccentricities, the Phils have also been—in these playoffs—one of the luckiest teams.

"They beat us in a short series. Give them credit," said the Braves' Terry Pendleton. Then he shook his head. Finally, he actually had to laugh. "But, man, I've never seen anything like that."

This time it was Morandini's liner that had Maddux limping and hopping on the mound all night, falling behind hitters, making a throwing error, and generally looking like a sad, gutty parody of the pitcher who has more wins in the last six seasons than anybody in the game. "That was a courageous effort on his part," said Phils manager Jim Fregosi. "But it bothered him. It did not look like he could push off."

Greene, who got crushed in the 14–3 Game 2, was pretty good this time, allowing just three runs in the first seven innings. But how often does that beat a healthy Maddux? The NL ERA champion hasn't allowed more than two earned runs in his last 14 straight starts and 18 of 19. Maddux beats everybody. But the team he has always owned the most has been the Phils.

Who doubts that the Phils would have made or received whatever benedictions they needed? Perhaps teams that get to the playoffs as worst-to-first darlings operate under a special dispensation. The Braves should remember the feeling. These Phils are the team that Wild Thing can't sink, the team that thinks Kim Batiste is a defensive replacement. The Phils' first two runs in this game came on a double that hit the rightfield chalk stripe.

Of course, the ump who called it fair was Jerry Crawford. Anytime he wants the key to the city, or perhaps a few square blocks of downtown real estate, it can probably be arranged. He's very popular here.

The Braves did all they could to help—help the Phils, that is. They kicked a grounder, walked a pitcher, and issued an intentional walk— all leading to Phillies runs. Symbolically, the man who knocked Maddux out with a two-run sixth-inning triple—and sent the Vet crowd of 62,502 to mock chopping and rapping, "Whoot, there it is"—was Morandini.

Maddux was the perfect ironic emblem of the Braves' unexpected downfall. Wasn't he the free agent the Braves bought to make absolutely sure they couldn't possibly avoid winning the World Series this year after back-to-back heartbreaks? Yet from the instant Morandini lamed Maddux, it was just a matter of time until the Phils—the highest-scoring team in the NL since 1962—would break through against a control artist suddenly gone wild, a slick fielder making errors. Even then, all the higher authorities had to come to the Phils' aid. Maddux walked Greene. A fluky turf chopper found its way through the infield. Another Phil walked to load the bases. And, with two outs, Darren Daulton hit the chalk with a ground-rule double.

Several key players started this playoff in slumps. But Daulton and Dave Hollins, who hit a two-run 422-foot homer off Maddux, worked their way out with long batting practice sessions in the afternoon before night games. The Phils faced their problems. Daulton at one point said, "You only have to write about it. I have to live with it." The comparable in-a-funk Braves—the wound-too-tight Ron Gant and David Justice—simply got worse and worse as the Braves lost three straight games for the first time since early August.

"We gotta get this thing done," said Pendleton of the title that just won't come. "We darn sure need it. My time is running out. Pretty soon it's going to be, 'What happened to Terry Pendleton?' " That pressure haunts all the Braves.

Now those who want to hug a Phillie can make all the jokes they want about how this is the team that can turn the tide of a playoff series by winning a game 2–1 on the strength of 15 strikeouts, 15 stranded runners, and a game-winning hit by a pitcher with a .077 career average.

The last laugh is sweet. Whatever happens in the Series, the Phils will have it. "People are always saying, 'How did these guys get here?' " said Lenny Dykstra. "We hear it." Now they have the answer.

The Phils are the team that enjoys the game, plays for fun, ignores pressure, and cares only if it pleases itself. In fact, in recent days, the Phils' Wes Chamberlain has even come up with what has been hailed as the perfect team motto: "Nothing is ever as easy as it looks. Take as long as you need. And if anything can go wrong, it will."

Just like the Phillies, it's wonderful and makes absolutely no sense.

□ □ □

TORONTO, October 17, 1993—In September 1990, Curt Schilling was horsing around in the Baltimore Orioles bullpen, not paying much attention, as might be expected of a twenty-three-year-old rookie with a Billy Idol haircut on a team 100 games out of first place.

When Schilling was called into the game, he got to the mound, took the ball, and, without giving it a second thought, said, "Who's up?"

That was the end of Schilling as an Oriole. The "Who's Up?" story spread through the organization until it became synonymous with his name. Million-dollar arm. Ten-cent head. The Orioles judged the book by its haircut. They didn't find out that Schilling actually read books. When the Glenn Davis debacle was being finalized, the Orioles

gave the Astros their choice of a middle-inning reliever as a throw-in
—Mark Williamson—or Schilling.

Saturday night, Curt Schilling, fresh from being named the Most
Valuable Player in the National League playoffs, started the first game
of the World Series for the Philadelphia Phillies. All around America,
past and present Big Thinkers for the Red Sox, Orioles, and Astros
held their heads and hoped nobody remembered. How could we ever
have given up on him? Not just traded. Given up.

Perhaps they shouldn't feel so bad. In baseball, just about everybody
gives up on just about everybody. Every player has nine lives. Almost
nobody makes it, or at least makes it big, where he started. You have to
change uniforms, change positions, change coaches, learn new skills,
or maybe just grow up.

Schilling is a perfect example. Ask him why he's won 30 games in
the past two years and he points at the bald spot on the head of
pitching coach Johnny Podres. "That's the guy. That's the reason.
. . . The day I got here, he told me he was going to scrap two of my
pitches and go with two pitches alone. It allowed me to focus on my
fastball and slider. . . . If you can throw two pitches for strikes, the
game's not that tough." That's not what the Orioles usually say.

It's usually something comparably simple. Another pitcher in the
Davis trade, Pete Harnisch, immediately made the All-Star team the
next season by, basically, abandoning the mechanics that pitching
coach Al Jackson had taught him and going back to his college
method.

In the Super Bowl or the NBA finals, you seldom see such things: a
starting quarterback or point guard who's been cast off by even one
team, much less three. How tacky. Traded for another star, occasionally. Tossed away, almost never. In baseball, it's absolutely commonplace.

The Phillies have ten pitchers in this Series. All of them started—
and failed—someplace else.

Tommy Greene was a minor league legend in the Atlanta organization. He'd strike out a man an inning but go 7–17 or 9–12 for the
Richmond Braves. Did the Braves write him off? They traded him for
Pat Vatcher, whoever that is. So who knocked the Braves out of the
playoffs? Tommy Greene.

The Blue Jays' opening night pitcher was Juan Guzman, who's 45–
11 so far in his career; the Dodgers watched him walk people or get
waxed for three years in the low minors, then traded him for Mike

Sharperson. The Blue Jays had seen a flaw in his mechanics. Guzman says they corrected it in no time. His ERA dropped from 4.75 to 2.36 in his first year in the Jays organization.

Talent in pro football and basketball is often measurable. If a 230-pound man can run a 4.45 40-yard dash, or a 6-foot-8 player with a soft jump shot has a 38-inch vertical leap, then it's your job to find a position for him.

But what do you do with John Kruk?

Baseball players don't come in officially approved shapes and sizes. In his first four full years in the minors, Kruk hit .311, .341, .326, and .351. But the Padres wouldn't bring him up. Maybe 5-feet-10, 220 pounds just wouldn't have looked right on their roster. When he finally got to the Show, Kruk still hit .300 but couldn't get a full-time job. The man's a born hitter but he was platooned, then traded for Chris James.

In his first World Series game Saturday night, he singled to the opposite field to drive in a run in the first inning, then pulled a single to right to drive in a run in the third inning. See, baseball's a simple game. At least for the naturals. And they don't always look like the naturals.

Perhaps we can reassure ourselves by saying that in this, as in many things, baseball is more lifelike than our other games. Maybe we can remake ourselves along the way or restart our projects. After all, the Mets thought Lenny Dykstra was a hard case and the Angels said Devon White had a bad attitude. Tony Fernandez and Roberto Alomar got traded for each other. Now they turn double plays together. Pete Incaviglia is a folk hero in Philadelphia right now, yet it's his fourth team in four years.

Unlike any other sport, baseball even casts off some of its very best players—repeatedly. The Chicago Cubs traded Joe Carter to Cleveland, where he drove in 100 runs three times—and got traded. The Indians saw a low batting average (.243) and figured the RBI total was an illusion. In San Diego, Carter drove in 100 runs. But that low average (.232) bothered the Padres. So he's driven in 100 runs three more times for the Jays and will make the Hall of Fame someday—with four uniforms and that horrible .261 career average.

Baseball even has a bizarre form of reverse rejection reserved for stars. It's called free agency. Last winter, the Brewers told Paul Molitor that, while they appreciated those 2,281 hits and 1,275 runs he'd scored for them—not to mention the money he'd put in the team's pockets for fifteen years—they just couldn't afford to re-sign him. So he went to the Jays and had his first 100-RBI season at age thirty-seven.

The Philadelphia Phillies brag that they are outcasts and misfits, unwanted by other teams and rejected by the system. But, really, that's the way the large majority of major leaguers feel about themselves. They've had to reroot, retool, and remake themselves—sometimes more than once. Only the strongest survive. And about thirty of them are carrying this World Series on their backs.

☐ ☐ ☐

PHILADELPHIA, October 21, 1993—Baseball started having its little October tournament in 1903, so it took the game a while to get it right. But on Wednesday night, after a century of practice, the sport finally produced its most deliciously delightful World Series game. Not its best game, mind you, nor its most dramatic, nor the one between the best teams. Nonetheless, this marathon of mirth and miracle was the most ridiculously foolish and fun-filled fantasy game the Series has seen.

Be sure not to replace those alliterative *f*'s with *ph*'s, because this was the night when the Philadelphia Phillies lost the mother of all heartbreakers, 15–14, to the Toronto Blue Jays in Game 4.

Game 4-ever, that is.

"This just might go down as one of the all-time games in World Series annals. It was unbelievable," said Phils manager Jim Fregosi. He was almost smiling as he said it. This game—in which the Jays scored six runs in the eighth inning to erase a 14–9 deficit—was that big a kick. Even to lose. Even when it puts the Phils behind three games to one.

In a four-hour, fourteen-minute game that had everything in triplicate, one long, melodramatic scene in the eighth inning will be remembered longest. On the mound in the Phils' red stripes is No. 99. Around him are tens of thousands of people with towels over their heads or hands over their faces, peaking between their fingers. Yes, Wild Thing finally went and did it this time. Oh, Mitch Williams really tore it good.

Called in with the Phils ahead, 14–10, with one out in the eighth inning, the Phils' wild, hairy cardiac-inducing reliever had a simple job: get five outs before four runs could score. Sure, there were men on second and third when he arrived. But he had enough rope.

To hang himself and, probably, his teammates too, as it proved. At 11:59 P.M. on the Veterans Stadium clock, the Wild Thing Mystique finally and utterly shattered. And, perhaps, 110 years of the Phillies' buzzard luck reasserted itself.

First, Tony Fernandez singled home his fifth run of the game. Then, Pat Borders, the number eight hitter, was walked in typically cavalier Mitch style. Mitch, this is the guy you can't walk. But he did.

With two outs, Rickey Henderson singled home two more runs to make the score an incredible 14–13. The Phils' amazing centerfielder, Lenny Dykstra, who had already scored four runs and driven in four with a walk, double, and two home runs, froze for a disastrous split second of indecision and never tried for the kind of nails-on-his-face, way-to-go-dude diving catch that is his trademark.

Dykstra let Henderson's ball drop.

Devon White finished the job with a two-run triple that will be recalled—probably for ninety more years—until somebody comes from miles behind to win, 16–15. The quiet, gentle White—the Least Wild Man—stroked his third hit of the night up the rightfield gap, perfectly placed between the Phils' ventricle and auricle.

In the short view, this game turned a tight, even Series in the Jays' favor. In the longer view, however, this game has a larger stature. This was a night that showed how marvelous a game can be when there are no time limits, no artificial infringement on the warfare except the need to get 27 outs—even if it takes days. This night was more fun than the Phillie Phanatic, more kicks than riding around in a fuzzy suit and sticking your two-foot tongue out at anybody you want. This is the way, once a lifetime, baseball in the World Series should be played.

How's that, you say?

Like a Sunday afternoon picnic softball game where every ball is hit so hard that, between innings, you have to check whether the stuffing is coming out. Where the score is 12–7—in the fifth inning. Where one starting pitcher gives up six runs in two innings. And "outpitches" the other bum who gives up seven runs in 2⅓ innings.

Yes, all those things happened in the mysterious, misty, mythological canyon of Veterans Stadium where the most offensive World Series in more than a generation has turned into a riveting, comical saga with more knockdowns than a bad *Rocky* remake. The Series record for most runs in a game (22) was broken—by a touchdown.

All night, the pitchers couldn't walk and throw a change-up at the same time. The home plate umpire helped. He was Charlie Williams, of whom Whitey Herzog once said, "It's a good thing he only has two guesses."

For those who've forgotten how hard baseball is to play and how much pressure the Series can lay on your shoulders, the Jays' Todd Stottlemyre and the Phils' Tommy "Jethro" Greene gave tens of millions of people a reminder.

With time and perspective, no doubt, we will all feel compassion for their Homer and Jethro Show. No doubt neither pitcher will ever forget this night.

One or both of their careers could easily be traumatized by the misfortunes—absolutely self-inflicted—that they endured. But right now, why bother with such excess niceties?

It's hard to pitch two innings, allow six runs, walk four men in the same inning, and practically knock yourself unconscious making a bonehead baserunning mistake. But Stottlemyre did it. His ludicrous face-first dive into third base—where he got thrown out trying to go first to third with two out—almost knocked him silly and left his chin a big bleeding blotch.

A week ago, the mayor of Philadelphia said that watching Stottlemyre made him want to "grab a bat and hit." Stottlemyre said he'd "throw three behind his head," then "paint the outside corner" on the mayor.

Not this night. Stottlemyre would have walked him.

Compared with Greene, Stottlemyre had control. You almost never see a man throw more balls than strikes in a game. Greene did it. And walked only two. Whenever he threw a strike, some Blue Jay tried to maim an outfielder.

Anyone who performs in public runs the risk of making a fool of himself. Anyone who stands in the spotlight knows the fear of "going up" like the actor who can't remember his lines or the singer whose voice cracks. And anyone who's ever been an athlete, even a bad one, knows the fear that, on some evil day, your skills will fail you and, time after time, the game will find you and expose you to ridicule. You dream about it, almost to exorcise it.

This evening, two entire pitching staffs fell apart. Everybody visited the mound to try to calm these guys down except their mothers. Wild Thing was just dessert.

Most of us have never seen a Series like this, where scores like 8–5, 6–4, and 10–3 are just a preamble to the real fireworks. Believe it or not, we get to hope that this show of shows isn't over yet. Starting in Game 5, these two slugging outfits get to see the other guys' rotation for the second time. It's a baseball axiom that when you see the same pitcher twice within a week, you hit him better the second time. Oh, goody.

Juan Guzman of the Jays and Curt Schilling of the Phils have incredible pressure on them on Thursday night. If they get knocked out, who's left? We might not have to wait ninety more years for that 16–15 game.

PHILADELPHIA, October 22, 1993—Whenever a team has trailed the World Series three games to one and has ultimately come back to win, the catalyst has almost always been a heroic, and often shocking, pitching performance on behalf of the demoralized underdog. This kind of individual courage—in defiance of the entire flow of events—happens about once a decade. When it does, it's deeply stirring in its stiff-spined, solitary dignity.

The Philadelphia Phillies needed Curt Schilling as desperately on Thursday night in Game 5 as the '85 Royals, '79 Pirates, '68 Tigers, and '58 Yankees needed Danny Jackson, Bert Blyleven, Mickey Lolich, and Bob Turley.

All those men were grand, but, if the Phillies rise from the crypt, they will take a backseat to Schilling, who stuffed a five-hit shutout down the protesting craws of the Toronto Blue Jays in Game 5 here on Thursday night. This season, in 172 regular and postseason games, the Jays had been shut out only once—by Fernando Valenzuela. Now, make that two.

The final three innings were excruciating drama for this crowd of 62,706, which knew that Schilling, who threw 149 pitches, wasn't coming out until it was won or lost. The Phils feared their own bullpen more than Schilling's fatigue. "I was running out of gas by the seventh," said Schilling. "Darren Daulton came to the mound and said, 'We may have to use some mirrors.'"

In the eighth, with men at the corners, none out, and the top of the order up, Schilling and the Phillies truly looked cooked. Then a strange and wonderful thing happened. "For the first time in my life, I looked at the bullpen," said Schilling. "When I saw nobody was up, it got me pumped. I knew we'd end our season or we'd go to Toronto [for Game 6] based on what I did."

With deteriorating stuff, with no help in sight, with the gaudiest lineup in baseball facing him, and with his own catcher's faith in him dwindling, this is what Schilling did: He hit spots. Time after time after time. Shaving the corners, changing speeds. And the famous monsters row of Rickey Henderson, Devon White, Roberto Alomar, Joe Carter, John Olerud, and Paul Molitor went out—six in a row—without a single solidly hit ball.

His jaw bulging with chew, the Phils oracle John Kruk shrugged and said, "The schedule dictated we had to play. So we had to show up. . . . Nothing is easy for us. We're just a difficult bunch."

Nothing was easy for Schilling, that's for sure. All he had for solace were two early runs off Jays ace Juan Guzman—both a result of dubious Blue Jays strategy.

In the first, the Jays played the infield back and gave up a run with a man on third and one out. Kruk hit a grounder directly to second base that wouldn't have scored anybody with the infield in. In the second, with a man at second and two outs, the Jays bungled, throwing a fastball strike down the pipe to Kevin Stocker with the pitcher on deck.

In the National League, where they play real baseball, teams understand words like "pitch around this guy." Stocker doubled home the second run. Schilling made that margin feel like 14.

Nobody would have guessed before this game that one man, cast off by three previous teams, could stand against the world champions and prevail. Make no mistake, Schilling was as alone as a pitcher can be. The Phillies might as well have come to Veterans Stadium in twenty-five hearses for all the chance that most fans gave them. No team in Series history had ever taken a more lethal-looking dagger to the heart than the Phils in their 15–14 loss in Game 4. After the Jays' wrecking ball of a six-run eighth inning, the headlines here moaned, "Vet Cemetery" and "Nightmare on Broad Street."

As Schilling watched Mitch Williams turn a 14–10 lead into a defeat, he kept a towel over his head, afraid to look—just like any passionate Phils devotee. At 11:59 P.M., when White's triple drove home the final two runs, the Mitching Hour had struck and to reasonable Phils hope seemed gone. Except in the large heart of the NL playoff's Most Valuable Player.

After that defeat, Schilling fell silent, his eyes filling. "I don't have anything to say." That stands to reason. Schilling's the pitcher who has written on the underside of his cap, "No talk. Just get it done." Schilling doesn't need to talk to motivate himself. Throughout this postseason he's left an empty seat beside his mother in honor of his late father.

For generations, the expression "You're in there for nine" had meaning. The staff was tired. You had to finish, no matter what a beating you might have to take. That phrase is an antique now. But Schilling revived it. Phils manager Jim Fregosi was asked if he would leave Schilling on the mound "until his arm falls off."

"Most likely," said Fregosi.

Hard as it is to believe, Schilling couldn't wait to face the Jays' mighty aggregation, whose first eight hitters in Game 5 had an amazing career postseason batting average of .323 in 869 at-bats. Schilling's a student of military history. He must love Thermopylae. After getting bashed for seven runs in his Game 1 defeat, Schilling took full blame and also sought out his old friend Carter.

"He said he'd studied films of us and had about eight ways to get each of us out, but he didn't use any of them," said Carter. "That's what happens sometimes. You put too much pressure on yourself."

Tens of millions of people saw the Best of Schilling this time. "He overanalyzed his first start," said Fregosi. This time, Schilling worked his fastball in and out to lefties and up and down to righties and got a couple of big outs with backdoor sliders to lefties. Three double plays helped too.

His final jam was his most thrilling. In the eighth, with men at the corners, he looked down the barrel of the Jays lineup. The immortal Henderson grounded to the mound. White fanned. And Alomar hit the weakest of grounders to second. That was, in its own way, a kind of knife in the Jays' hearts. Their ninth inning was a flaccid one-two-three, nine-pitch anticlimax.

Had the Jays juggernaut been demythologized? In Game 6 and, if necessary, 7, the Phils have left-handers scheduled. And the Jays are only 23–27 against lefties. Still, Danny Jackson and Terry Mulholland probably don't have a night like Schilling's in them. Few men do, even in a lifetime. And, if they don't, sooner or later the Wild Thing will be back.

It's a long road for the Phillies. But the first step was enormous. And 100 percent of it was taken by one man.

"I don't want to go to Toronto if we're not going to win," said Schilling. Then he added, perhaps to give his teammates a bit of his heart, "I can go an inning or two on Sunday."

Schilling, the former closer, ready to finish a seventh game? If the Phillies hear that, they may kidnap the Wild Thing.

TORONTO, October 24, 1993—Oh, not to be Mitch Williams, now that winter's here.

For the rest of us, it's still autumn. But winter came early for Wild Thing. And it may stay a long time. We can all count our blessings as long as we don't wear No. 99 for the Philadelphia Phillies on our backs.

You wonder, are the numbers burned into his skin as though Joe Carter's home run bat had been a branding iron? And what can we do to tell him it's just a game when the end of this World Series felt like something far more sinister?

Carter's three-run homer off Williams with one out in the ninth inning of the sixth and final game of this Series for an 8–6 Toronto victory was indeed a sudden-death blow. In Philadelphia, where they've booed Santa Claus, booed the Easter Bunny, and even booed the toddler sons of Phillies' players during parent-child games, what special ring of hell will be reserved for No. 99?

Or will Philadelphia prove itself to be truly baseball's City of Brotherly Love and welcome home its shaggy prodigal son?

Baseball has had a century of champions, including eighteen teams that have performed the feat back to back. The Toronto Blue Jays will find their rightful place in that distinguished hierarchy. Appropriately, the last such team was the New York Yankees of 1977–78—another team that played with an imperial sense of entitlement that carried it through the roughest waters.

However, does baseball have eighteen goats to match Williams? (Roger Peckinpaugh is off the hook.) When the bullpen phone rang with the Phils leading, 6–5, when Williams saw the top of the gaudiest lineup in baseball awaiting him to begin the ninth, did he want to plead nolo contendere?

For three weeks, Williams has been a relief pitching wreck repeating itself, each time worse than the previous time. Twice in the playoffs he blew one-run leads to the Braves, only to have his teammates save him with extra-inning comebacks. Then, in Game 4 of this Series, he was the architect of perhaps the worst heartbreak loss in Series history. He entered with a 14–10 lead and two men on base. He left with Toronto a 15–14 winner.

In Philadelphia, they will tell you that this Series was, indeed, decided in six games and that, with any normal semblance of a championship relief closer, the Phillies won. But that won't change the scores of Games 4 and 6.

Perhaps only those in the Phillies and Blue Jays clubhouses know how much Carter's home run—or, rather, Williams's horrible ninth—changed this Series. When the Jays left the bases loaded in the eighth against Larry Andersen, it looked as if the classy Torontonians had been left with tobacco juice, scraggly hair, and ambergris all over their pretty blue and white uniforms.

If nothing else, the magnificently obnoxious Phillies have proved that they are positively baseball's least gracious guests. Until the very instant when Carter swung at a 2–2 slider, down and in, and curled it over the leftfield fence, it seemed almost certain that the Kruksters had dribbled and drooled all over the Jays' parade.

Who dreamed that revenge for 15–14 could come so swiftly and perfectly? Few thought that the Philthy Phils could regroup after their historically heartbreaking loss in Game 4 at the Mitching Hour. How do you rebut a team that's come from five runs behind to beat you with a six-run eighth in your own park? Simple. Come from four runs behind with a five-run seventh in their own park. And do it when they're already cashing their Series checks.

That's what the Phils did on Saturday night. Until Wild Thing arrived, folks were fitting Lenny Dykstra for that MVP award. His three-run homer off Dave Stewart cut a 5–1 Toronto lead to 5–4. The Phillies sent ten men to bat and walked away with a 6–5 lead.

Until Williams's four-pitch walk to Rickey Henderson, his one-out single to Series MVP Paul Molitor, and Carter's blast, it looked like enough. Say one thing for Phils manager Jim Fregosi, he's got more faith than the pope. The current population of the United States is

252,686,000. Only Fregosi would have brought in Wild Thing to protect a one-run lead in the ninth.

But then he trusted all his relievers. Even David West—the man with the 63.00 ERA in three Series games. From now until the end of baseball time, it may not be quite so easy for managers to hide behind "I danced with the one that brung me." Even if it's Mitch?

This ninetieth World Series wasn't decided by strategy or matchups or, perhaps, even by talent, although the Jays have tons of that. If a team ever won with presence, with an aura of utter confidence, it was these '93 Jays. It stayed with them even in the ninth when many fine teams would have wilted—yes, even against Wild Thing. These Jays look right at home next to the '77–78 Yankees of Reggie Jackson, Thurman Munson, Graig Nettles, Ron Guidry, Catfish Hunter, and Goose Gossage. Some of them were past their primes, just as Stewart, Molitor, and Henderson, and perhaps even Carter, are now. But all of them were sure that nobody but them deserved to be world champions.

Maybe nothing beats a sense of entitlement. Who knows where it's born? Do parents give it to their children? Can it be taught? Is it, perhaps, contagious? If you watched the Jays rallying against the poor shaggy-haired Thing—a man who'd accidentally made himself look like a caricature of defeat—you'd have thought that confidence was a germ, passed man to man.

One lawyer makes a brilliant summation and sweeps the jury up in his words and gestures, convincing twelve out of twelve of his case. Another, perhaps as well prepared, isn't as convincing, as mesmerizing. Actors, singers, preachers, politicians, and many more walk the same wire. Some people think the stage belongs to them, and the highest prize as well.

Where do the Blue Jays, who won 95 games, get off acting so positive that they're clearly better than the Philadelphia Phillies, who won 97, then denied the mighty Atlanta Braves their third straight pennant?

Perhaps the man who understands a sense of entitlement—who has it and who doesn't—is Pat Gillick, the general manager who's stitched together these back-to-back champions with the thread of Labatt's gold. For years, he was called Stand Pat and his team was known as the Blow Jays. Born an expansion team, the Blue Jays tried to win with their own farm products or low-budget trades. Season after season,

Dave Stieb and George Bell, Willie Upshaw and Lloyd Moseby came up just short.

Finally, Gillick gave up. The expansion tag, the loser label, had to be torn off the Jays' backs. So he signed or traded for players who felt they were entitled to be champions. He built his deals around personalities. He learned that Carter loved pressure and that Roberto Alomar, son of a major leaguer, thought he was destined for the Hall of Fame. First he got Dave Winfield for a year, then replaced him with Molitor. Talk about studying breeding lines. When Jack Morris got old after one 21-win year, he signed Stewart—not because he was still great but because he was still Stewart. For this year's stretch drive, he got Rickey Henderson.

What chance did Wild Thing have? There they were—all of them —the entitled ones, the gifted Jays, arrayed against him. Henderson, Molitor, Carter. And if Carter's ball had gone foul, Alomar was on deck.

Philadelphia, be silent. Mourn a while, but don't boo. Don't ask too much.

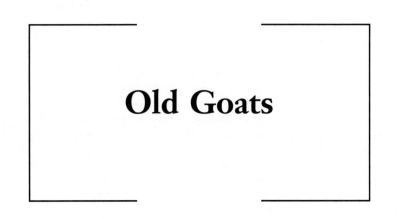

Old Goats

Mike Schmidt

May 1989—The best all-around baseball player of the last fifteen years, and the greatest third baseman of all time, retired suddenly Monday, unable to live with a level of performance that satisfied everybody but him. Mike Schmidt's career died of natural causes; he could not play like himself anymore, so he quit.

Schmidt was still listed among the National League's RBI leaders in the latest issue of *The Sporting News*; he was on a pace for nearly 100. But his pride wouldn't let him kid himself. More errors than home runs? Barely hitting his weight? No, that was not Schmidt. So he walked away from more than a million dollars in salary and bonuses.

Schmidt's place in history is so secure as to be almost uncontested. Aside from Babe Ruth, perhaps no player would be such an instant consensus pick for baseball's all-time team. (Even Johnny Bench might have more competition at catcher.) Schmidt won the NL home run title eight times—the league record. He won the third-base Gold Glove ten times—the league record. And he hit 30 home runs thirteen times—matching Ruth and within two of Hank Aaron. His career stats, the 548 home runs and 1,595 RBI, were as lean, devoid of late-career padding, as his body was trim to the end at age thirty-nine.

"I could ask the Phillies to keep me on to add to my statistics, but my love for the game won't let me do that," a tearful Schmidt said at his retirement. Teams still wanted him. As a DH in a cozy American League park, taking his rest and ducking tough pitchers, Schmidt could probably have become the fourth man to hit 600 homers. If he'd cared about it.

Most great players these days torture their teams, their fans, and themselves, playing for years past their prime, for the checks and the cheers. Instead, Schmidt left memories—of the player who finally dragged the Philadelphia Phillies to five division titles, two pennants, and their only world title.

No third baseman ever matched his offensive knockout power, not even Eddie Mathews. Only a few in a century, like Brooks Robinson, were better glove men. Nobody ever did both so well.

As for the claim that he was the best everyday player of the last fifteen years, that is a kind of farewell bouquet. Go back further and you'd have to include Bench, Pete Rose, or Reggie Jackson. If you discussed only the '80s, the issue might also be murky. But fifteen years fits Schmidt perfectly. Only Jim Rice, who hit 160 fewer home runs, and George Brett, who had 300 fewer RBI, approached him in that time frame. Over fourteen seasons, from 1974 through '87, Schmidt averaged 37 homers, 104 RBI, 99 runs, and 98 walks.

In the '70s and '80s, baseball's greatest era for third basemen, Schmidt was the prototype—except that nobody honestly thought the species could be expected to produce another specimen like him. Brett, Wade Boggs, Buddy Bell, Graig Nettles, Bill Madlock, Gary Gaetti, Darrell Evans, Paul Molitor, and Carney Lansford were among the All-Star third basemen during his time. All of them combined drove in 100 runs a total of nine times. So did Schmidt.

To be remembered for numbers would infuriate Schmidt, a stylist in all things. To him, batting practice was a personal display of fireworks; with his long swing arc, he looked like a man hitting golf balls at a driving range as white blurs streaked into the upper deck of Veterans Stadium. To him, a meek dribbler up the third-base line was a chance to make the grandstand judges give him a 10.0 for executing a sprint-and-scoop into a full somersault.

At bat, Schmidt was a 6-foot-2-inch scorpion with his bat held high, waving slightly like a huge menacing stinger. He did not simply hit home runs. He hit conversation pieces. The roof of the Astrodome was not safe from him, nor were the avenues outside Wrigley Field. He was a danger to traffic as well as pitchers. If the Liberty Bell hadn't already been cracked, you might've suspected him. When he hit four homers in one game, it was met with a shrug of inevitability.

In the field, Schmidt was a 203-pound cat, always leaping, pawing, diving, or pouncing. Some feline image attached itself to him in almost every profile. Maybe it was his manelike hair. More likely, it was his proprietary presence at third base, where he always seemed to be pacing in an invisible cage, making sure no inch of his domain was out of his control. A line drive in the hole or a smash over the bag might as well have been an antelope and he a creature of the veld. He fielded ground balls as though they were his prey.

Off the field, Schmidt began as a marvelously complex blend of extrovert and introvert, prima donna and team man, thinker and brooder. Always streaky and given to entire weeks which could be summed up by the letter K, Schmidt could be a prisoner of his mediocre batting average (.267). Even with three MVP awards and a World Series MVP behind him, he lived a slump as though he had never been in one before and might never get out of this one. Though he had as superb a physique as anyone in the sport and possessed every imaginable raw skill, from fine flowing foot speed to a quick powerful arm, the game often tasked him as it might a journeyman.

Yet, once his silence was punctured, Schmidt loved to talk and analyze, laugh at himself, and find a colorful phrase for his feelings. Those who thought him self-absorbed, especially early in his career, were perhaps put off by his vivid scowl. His face in a funk seemed to hold entire soliloquies of suffering. When he was young and struck out as much as 180 times in a year, it was said that he "thought too much." When old, and hitting .290, he was called "wise."

"I'm the same," he'd say, amused.

Schmidt could sulk or swagger but, with the years, he took to being a role model with uncommon grace. Wealth and fame seemed to soothe him. What the public finally saw was a man at ease with his wife, children, and a quiet Christianity. He pitched milk, helped charities, and built electric trains.

Above all, Schmidt was marked by his pride. Cursed with unlimited potential, he lived to fulfill it.

In some players, who epitomize doggedness or the gift for compromise, longevity is inspiring. Tommy John, for instance, never cut a dashing figure; so we hope he staggers all the way to 300 ugly victories. So what if the Yankees cut him? Some desperate outfit may yet bring him back again.

Schmidt, however, was not meant to comb gray hairs. From him, we only expected the sublime. He looked like some huge, graceful shortstop misplaced at third base. When he came to bat, the No. 20

on his back might have stood for the number of rows he intended to hit the ball into the bleachers.

For many fans, Schmidt's departure was a shock that left a sense of loss. Didn't we half-expect him to hit 35 more home runs this year as though the trick were done without effort? Once in a while, however, the man himself knows best. On Memorial Day, Schmidt connected again. He did what so many great athletes have failed to do; he left us wanting more.

Dennis Eckersley

May 1989—The old Dennis Eckersley is dead and nobody is going to kill the new one. Not even Kirk Gibson.

Once, Eckersley was a charming hard-luck wastrel, a cocky playboy with a desperado mustache. His facade of cool hipster lingo was so impenetrable that the Eck spoke his own private language. "Showed him the cheese, then punched him out with the yakker," he'd say of his pitching effort. Then, Eckersley was every scared kid in a black motorcycle jacket with a chip on his shoulder and pain bottled up inside him. Lots of people liked the old Eck's act. That wasn't the problem. It was Eckersley who didn't like the Eck.

One broken marriage, two career-threatening injuries, three trades, and a dozen mildly disappointing baseball seasons later, Eckersley changed his life. It took a lot of slaps in the face, but Eckersley finally said, "Thanks, I needed that." He remarried, cut back the nightlife, worked himself into top shape, and, generally, wised up to himself.

By luck, Eckersley also discovered—just in time—that he was born to be a great reliever, not a good starting pitcher.

That's the reason Gibson's World Series home run for the Dodgers doesn't haunt his sleep. It's the reason Eckersley can say, "I have more drive this year than last. I want to prove it was not a fluke."

And that's why Eckersley already has 10 saves, a win, and a 0.00 ERA for the 1989 Oakland Athletics: the same stratospheric pace as in '88 when he saved 45, won 4, and had a 2.35 ERA. Then, he broke

Dan Quisenberry's major league record for wins-plus-saves-minus-losses (48). He had one of those seasons that can never be duplicated.

Except that he's duplicating it.

"This is a second chance for me. Not too many people get a second chance. I am just so happy about what has happened to me that I don't want to stop," he says. "I've been so lucky, how could I be [upset about Gibson's homer]? You wouldn't be very appreciative if you acted that way, would you?

"It's hard for me to comprehend it," Eckersley says of a career in which he pitched a no-hitter at twenty-two, won 20 games at twenty-three, but appeared washed up at age thirty-two when he was traded to Oakland just two years ago. "I don't want to look back. . . . [I'm here] by the grace of God."

The old Eck a decade ago had a wall around his emotions. "A cocky facade," he says. "You do a lot of crazy things out of fear [of failure]." Now he tries to look his experience as squarely in the face as he can. "I'm more sincere now. But that's because I'm all here."

That clearheadedness extends to looking unblinkingly at his horrible historic moment. Many say he threw Gibson a good pitch in that ninth inning of Game 1—a backdoor slider on the outside corner on a full count. Eckersley does not buy it. No alibis, please.

"I shouldn't have thrown him a strike," he says. "But think how hard it would have been to take if it had happened to me ten years ago. . . . What if I'd been a bum [rather than a star]? Or if it had happened in a bad season?"

Like all his teammates, Eckersley is determined to return to the World Series. For a second chance. The A's are so intent that they have baseball's best record despite severe injuries. Perfection has been needed and it has been provided—by Dave Stewart (6–0) and Eckersley. Stewart probably will return to mortal size. Eckersley, however, is becoming a larger-than-life figure.

"Eckersley is not infallible," says his manager, Tony LaRussa, "but he has a hell of a chance."

Eckersley has begun to think his personality and his whole career were merely preparation for the bullpen. Pitching ten years in tiny Fenway Park and Wrigley Field taught him life on the edge. He lived in mortal fear of walks: "I don't even like to go three and two." Great control for a starter goes hand in hand with gopher balls. You can't give life-and-death intensity to every pitch. As a reliever, you can.

Now Eckersley comes in fresh, throws every pitch fiercely—and hits the corners of the plate with everything.

"He challenges hitters," LaRussa says, "but he's always on the edges."

In two seasons of relief, Eckersley has an almost surrealistic ratio of 197 strikeouts to 29 walks. "He has the best control I've ever seen in a relief pitcher of all three of his pitches [fastball, slider, and curve]," says Stewart. "He's got real stuff with great control. . . . When Eckersley comes in, the game is pretty much over."

Eckersley is the first to point out that the A's are a closer's dream. No other team has four quality setup men in the bullpen. "Goose Gossage had to pitch two innings, sometimes [Bruce] Sutter had to go three," he says. "I go one. Don't want to say my job is easy. But it can't get much better than this."

The Athletics' great talent helps. "I can only stay sharp if I pitch a lot," he says. "I only pitch when we win. And we win a lot. So I stay sharp."

For gravy, LaRussa is one of the new-school managers who believes that bullpen aces should be protected: never get them warmed up unless you're going to use them. LaRussa also tries to bring his man in to start innings—with the bases clear. Stoppers need such psychic assistance so they won't burn out emotionally. "This job is pure stress," says Eckersley. "Just thinking about it is a tough day's work."

Finally, Eckersley has discovered that all those extroverted devilish qualities that made the Eck such a self-destructive party animal are perfect traits when channeled into relieving.

Go on, Dennis, yell at the hitters. Pump that fist after you strike them out. Even pretend you've pulled a six-gun out of your holster and blow smoke off the barrel after you end the game.

"This has been great for me because I can expose my emotions—and not too many people get offended. As a starter, the stuff I did looked showboat. People thought, 'What a jerk.' It's accepted if you show emotion in the ninth.

"You know," he says, "to be the one who comes in to finish the game, you have to be fairly bold."

That part of the old Eck never died.

Orel Hershiser
and Kirk Gibson

May 12, 1990—Orel Hershiser and Kirk Gibson were the heroes of the 1988 World Series. Now at ages thirty-one and thirty-two, respectively, their careers may well be finished. The same gung-ho attitude that brought them glory then has made them casualties now.

Hershiser's right shoulder and Gibson's right knee are wrecks. Doctors aren't sure either will ever play again. If they do, they may be shadows of the men who were the National League's Cy Young Award winner and Most Valuable Player just two years ago.

The Bulldog and the Caveman have paid a high price for their utterly unselfish styles. They repeatedly risked their careers for their team, the Los Angeles Dodgers. And, it now seems, they have lost their careers—five to ten years too soon. At least we can pay tribute to their sacrifice. They treated the baseball diamond as though it were a field of honor, not a business office. Maybe that's naive or unnecessary, but you've gotta give 'em points for style.

One looked like an angel, the other like a Hell's Angel. But underneath they were pretty much the same. Throwbacks. Dive-on-the-hand-grenade kind of guys.

Gibson didn't "play hurt." He played to *get* hurt. You can't be that hell-bent and not break. Then he usually kept playing after he got hurt. Gibby's one at bat in the '88 Series was merely the apotheosis of his whole career progression. He dragged himself out of an ice vat and could barely walk to the plate. But he hit one of the most famous home runs in history.

Hershiser always answered the bell, no matter what. Sometimes he even heard a bell when others heard nothing. When his arm finally blew up last month—ligaments, rotator cuff, the whole ball of wax— he had not missed a start in 195 turns. That's more than five years of "Doesn't hurt too bad, Skip. I can make it." Mike Flanagan, released by Toronto this week, once pulled the same Iron Man stunt. With similar results. He was never the same.

In the '88 playoffs, Hershiser started three games against the Mets and saved another when he volunteered for relief duty. Finally—and this is the part that's still hard to believe—Orel snuck into the bullpen to warm up in yet another game. Tommy Lasorda about fainted when he saw who was throwing. (And Tommy has burned out some good arms in his time.) Nobody does stuff like that. Not since Grover Cleveland Alexander anyway. Your agent's liable to have a coronary in front of his 50-inch projection TV beside his Olympic-size pool.

Now it seems that '88 was just a preamble for Hershiser, a way of preparing us to understand what he did this spring. Orel's surgery probably will become the Symbol of the 1990 Lockout. Hershiser is the most visible victim of the owners' greedy labor strategy and the union's pointless "don't workout without a contract" dictum.

As the Dodgers' player rep, Hershiser felt honor-bound to the union not to throw a pitch until an agreement was signed. But he also felt honor-bound by his contract to get ready in just three weeks so he could pitch on Opening Day to please the Dodgers.

Maybe Hershiser forgot an artist's responsibility to honor his own gift.

Just nineteen months ago, Orel and Kirk were the nation's twin symbols of hard-nosed hardball. Gibson challenged walls and ran the bases with a Death to Infielders sign over his head. Hershiser got three hits in one Series game and found a way to slide into every base.

With the help of a few stuntmen, they won a World Series that will never be forgotten. But they made a devil's bargain, too. Without a doubt, the very attitude that gave them an extra dimension of lasting greatness also made them doubly vulnerable.

Gibson never really recovered from his last crazy playoff slide into second base against the Mets. Of course, that final awkward twist was just the straw that broke his camel's back.

Naturally, Gibson tried to come back too quickly to start the '89 season. Everybody knew it and told him so. But Gibson was too macho not to try and the Dodgers were too weak to tell him no.

Gibson made it for Opening Day of '89, just as Hershiser did in '90. But before April was over, Gibson was on the disabled list for a month. Then, after just 253 at-bats (and a .213 average), he was back on the shelf in July for the rest of the year. To date, his knee still doesn't work properly, at least not when he tries to run full bore. And the former All–Big Ten end won't play any other way So, he may decide never to play again. Put it this way, he'll never resemble Kirk Gibson again.

How often and how badly did Gibson hurt himself? In eleven seasons, he played in only 1,114 games. He was on the disabled list seven times for a total of fifty-five weeks. No minor injuries for Capt. Kirk. Someday it's going to seem implausible that Gibson could have been so famous. He never hit 30 homers, had 100 RBI, or batted .300 for a full year. Career RBI: 603. Keith Moreland had more.

Hershiser's last win was his 100th. Not 300—just 100. Doctors say he may return next year, thanks to a new procedure that allowed repair of his stretched ligaments, torn rotator cuff, and damaged anterior labrum without any muscles being cut. Nonetheless, even Hershiser says he's doubtful he'll pitch again.

Someday, we're going to be asked to explain our powerful feelings and our exaggerated respect for these two fellows whose place in the hierarchy of baseball statistics is so tiny.

After all, next to Gibson's name in *Who's Who in Baseball* there is not a single asterisk—he never led any league in anything. Except heart.

Hershiser won 20 games only once and never led the National League in ERA or strikeouts. (Come on, how good could he really have been?) Thank goodness Hershiser has those 59 straight scoreless innings to frame his name.

For once in a baseball discussion, we'll be forced to say: "Forget stats. You don't measure these men that way."

But how do you measure them? How do you convince a skeptic that one October, done properly, can stand for as much as a twenty-year career full of records and awards? How do you make it sound convincing, not dumb, when you say: "They played to win, at all costs. They played for the glory of one heroic moment, not for the money."

How are we going to convince the next generation that, in the case of the baby-faced Bulldog and the stubble-bearded Caveman, you just had to be there to do them justice?

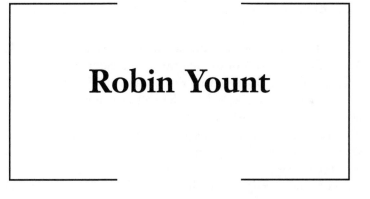

Robin Yount

September 12, 1992—Every year at family reunions, the Yount family shows the most famous, and secret, home movie in baseball.

Rick Dempsey, who's been Robin Yount's friend for twenty-eight years, narrates the film and holds the camera. Dempsey knows Yount's well-concealed background—that the 3,000-hit Milwaukee Brewer centerfielder is a daredevil, a speed freak, a risk taker. When they were kids in the Los Angeles suburbs, Robin was the neighborhood boy with a little mean/crazy streak in him when the playground fistfights broke out.

So director Dempsey hunkers down at the bottom of this California canyon in the mountains with his video camera and Yount gets on his motorcycle. This is years ago when Yount's supposed to be ultra-careful in the off-season because he's worth more than 180 pounds of platinum. Yount starts riding around the circular edge of this crater, going faster and faster, until, on the fifth loop, he swoops down and heads full bore at the camera like he's going to wipe Dempsey out.

That was the idea anyway. Yount would pop a wheelie and stop right in front of the lens. Robin and Rick forgot about the mud hole at the bottom of the canyon. "Robin's front wheel digs down into the mud," recalled Dempsey yesterday. "The bike flips and fires him over the front handlebars right at me. I don't know how far he flew. A long way, head first. He lands, helmet buried in the mud, at my feet.

"I said, 'I'm with Robin Yount here today, doing his famous motorcycle stunts. It's a good thing Bud Selig [Brewers president] isn't here with us.

" 'So, Robin, how many vertebrae did you just crush? Are you alive?'

"Robin looks up, covered with mud, and says, 'I think I'm okay.' "

Why haven't the rest of us seen this granddaddy of America's Funniest Home Video? Because Yount won't let you. ESPN called Dempsey and asked if they could show the cult classic when Yount got his 3,000th hit (on Wednesday).

"Robin said, 'Nope. Let's keep our private lives to ourselves.' "

That's the other side of Yount—the utterly quiet, semimysterious, leather-tough western male. He looks like a young Clint Eastwood except even more rugged and chiseled, like Mr. Nineteenth-Century American Frontier Hero.

Actually, Yount was very talkative last night. He gave three interviews, each about a half dozen sentences. Most sentences in each interview were identical. "It's sort of a catch-22," Yount starts each. Then he veers off, saying something that has nothing to do with any known catch-22.

"The excitement was great. You hate to see it turned off. You couldn't hide from this one." Not the record, mind you, or the fame. But the "excitement." The rush, the speed, so to speak, of a whole sports nation waiting for him to ring the bell.

To many in baseball, Yount is an odd character to find in the same company with so many of the game's greatest high-average hitters and batting stylists. He's hit .300 only six times in his nineteen seasons. He's had 200 hits only once. His stroke isn't pretty, his stance is extremely closed. He bends, a bit awkwardly, at the waist, as though looking for a quarter he's dropped in the other batter's box.

"I saw him for the first time in 1984 in Arizona, taking batting practice," said Orioles manager Johnny Oates. "In that thin air, it looked like he was hitting 3-woods off a tee. No effort. Hit the ball to both the deep power alleys, but it carried out of the park anyway."

Yount will be remembered more as a total team player than as a great hitter. His career average (.287) isn't too remarkable. His two MVP awards have come largely because of his leadership and his clutch hitting and fielding, first at shortstop where he was wonderful for eleven seasons and then in centerfield.

Despite appearances, Yount actually is extremely typical of the elite 3,000-hit group. The seventeen-member club is not a rough approximation of the greatest hitters ever. What these stars have in common, with a couple of exceptions, is durability and the talent or luck to reach the major leagues much younger than most players.

If you want to find out who's going to get 3,000 hits, don't count batting titles. Wade Boggs has five, Tony Gwynn four. Neither is likely to reach 3,000. Instead, look at a man's age when he first won a job. Yount played 107 games at eighteen! Boggs was locked in the minors so long by Red Sox misjudgments that he wasn't a regular until he was almost twenty-five.

Even players such as Will Clark and Ryne Sandberg, regulars at twenty-two, or Kirby Puckett and Frank Thomas, everyday guys at twenty-three, already are giving away hundreds of hits to 3,000-hit players such as Al Kaline, who was a batting champ in his third season at twenty.

With only two exceptions in this century, every 3,000-hit man has had at least 1,425 hits by his thirtieth birthday. (If you double a player's stats on his thirtieth birthday, you come so close to his final career stats it's eerie.) By that standard, Tim Raines may have as much chance at 3,000 hits—a long-shot chance—as such famous players as Boggs, Gwynn, Clark, and Don Mattingly. Even Cal Ripken Jr. had "only" 1,500 hits at thirty.

We should watch George Brett, Dave Winfield, and, perhaps, Eddie Murray, extremely carefully these days. They could be the last 3,000-hit men of the twentieth century. In fact, it's conceivable we won't see another until Ruben Sierra, Roberto Alomar, and Ken Griffey Jr. crack the barrier in 2005, 2006, and 2007.

Yes, those are the real Yount prototype players. None has yet won any of the Triple Crown titles, but they're way ahead of the immortality game. Griffey was a regular at nineteen, Alomar and Sierra at twenty.

When we look at Yount these days, we realize that, because he had 500 hits while his most gifted peers were still in the minors, the only way he was going to avoid 3,000 hits was to find a way to stop himself.

If we ever get to see Dempsey's home video, we'll find out he almost did.

Jack Morris

December 20, 1991—They jacked with the wrong Jack. And now they're going to pay. All of them.

If you thought Jack Morris was going to stay near his hometown of St. Paul and take a couple of dollars—or, to be more realistic, a couple of million dollars—less than he could get somewhere else, then you don't know Jack Morris.

He has a red mustache. And a memory.

For years, any time the word *collusion* was mentioned in Morris's company, that mustache seemed to twitch. To others, collusion was just an era in baseball history—a two-season attempt by owners to break the law and inhibit salaries with monopolistic practices. To Morris, collusion was a personal attack.

Morris went to New York City five winters ago in his nice fur coat to listen to a huge free-agent bid from a former Yankees owner. Instead, Morris got a cream pie in the face. Or a knife in the back.

George Steinbrenner offered Morris nothing, except excuses about why he wasn't interested in making an offer—even a deal cheaper than Morris's Detroit Tigers bosses. That's the day the world knew collusion was real.

Everywhere Morris went, trying to sell himself, he heard eloquent silence, even though he was one of baseball's top pitchers—thirty-one years old and coming off his best year (21–8).

"No one offered a penny," said Morris's agent, Dick Moss, yesterday. "In every city, we got excuses. We even publicly stated what we'd accept. Two-year, three-year, four-year deals—all the details, all below the top of the salary scale. Nobody offered anything."

How would Bobby Bonilla have felt this winter if he'd toured America and gotten no offers, then gone back to Pittsburgh hat in hand?

In 1987, Morris filed for free agency again, took the same humiliating trips, and heard the same orchestrated lines. And each year, back in Detroit—without the huge contract—he got older. His record fell to 18–11, 15–13, and then 6–14. He was a living object lesson in why a player has to take advantage of his market value while it exists.

For a long time, it looked as if the owners were going to have the last laugh on Morris—union man and client of Marvin Miller's friend Moss. It took a long time for the tables to turn. But they've turned with a vengeance.

Morris didn't just want money when he signed with Toronto this week for about $11 million for two years. He also wanted revenge. If you were him, you might too.

"Jack's decision wasn't vindictive," said Moss. "But a lot of players haven't forgotten, like Jack."

Morris will tell you he's an ornery guy with a mean streak. Black Jack is his nickname of choice. Under that gruff Man with No Name exterior lies a truly grouchy interior.

Perhaps no one has tilted the salary roulette wheel in the players' favor more than Morris, at age thirty-six, did on Wednesday. It's one thing for Roger Clemens in his prime to make $5 million. But Morris? What his deal says is, "If you have one big year, no matter how old or hurt you are or how recently you've been crummy, you hit the Big Jackpot."

Morris planned this bonanza last winter. Then he was granted "special free agency" by an arbitrator because he had been wronged. He signed a mere one-year deal, loaded with incentives, with the Twins, rather than a $9.3 million, three-year deal with Detroit.

"He was called foolish," said Moss.

You didn't think, after what he'd been through, that Morris was going to finish up his career with a multiyear contract based on 6–14 and 15–18?

No way. He was going to bet on himself, roll the dice, do something really special, and go back to that free-agent banquet for a really inflationary helping of the big boys' money.

So Morris won 18 games, added 2 wins in the AL playoffs, then was

Most Valuable Player in the Series, finishing the show with a ten-inning, 1–0 shutout. By the time the incentive calculator stopped adding, Morris was the highest-paid pitcher in baseball in 1991: $3.74 million.

Moss said he warned Morris this week that "you'll be called disloyal, a mercenary who'll pitch anybody to a title for the money. Jack said: 'I like that image.' "

This is the same Morris who as a Tiger loved pitching in the Metrodome against the Twins because boos inspired him and being booed in his own hometown in the loudest park on earth inspired him "in my weird little way."

When the owners pick somebody to pick on, they sure can pick 'em, can't they? Hadn't they read this guy's bio? He loves to make people mad.

Even Sparky Anderson, who likes the people Will Rogers hated, has been quoted as saying that Morris was the best pitcher, and one of the biggest egos, he ever managed.

"I've got to do the best I can for my future," said Morris on Wednesday. "I have some mixed emotions. Some good things happened in Minnesota, but good things could happen here" in Toronto.

"It was one of the greatest years of my career. I'm getting a ring out of it, and I don't want to say anything bad. I love Minnesota and I always will."

This has been a big week for Morris. He's made every baseball player richer, thanks to trickle down, while making the sport more of a nightmare for every owner.

In his own little unique way, that should all make Jack Morris very happy.

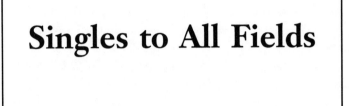

Singles to All Fields

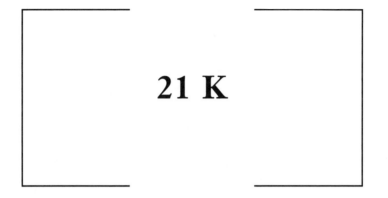

21 K

September 13, 1991—Twenty-nine years ago yesterday, old George Susce, the Washington Senators bullpen catcher, was warming up a pitcher in Memorial Stadium. Good Kid had seen some pitchers in his time. Susce called everybody "Good Kid," so that's what everybody called him back. But he'd never seen anybody with better stuff than the Nats right-hander had on that pleasant September night.

The rising fastball was on fire, jumping up above the belt. The overhand curveball had its bite. That goofy knuckleball was actually crossing the plate. And even the slider looked pretty decent too. Brooks Robinson, Jim Gentile, Boog Powell, and the rest of the Orioles were in for a long night.

"Good Kid, if you don't pitch a no-hitter tonight, it'll be your own fault," Susce told Tom Cheney.

He didn't pitch a no-hitter or a perfect game. He did something far rarer. Something absolutely unique. Something, actually, which may be the Baseball Record That Is Never Broken.

He struck out 21 Orioles on September 12, 1962.

You can win a lot of bar bets on that one. No, Roger Clemens does not hold the all-time record with his 20 K's. That is the nine-inning record. Cheney needed sixteen innings, which, in its way, is just as amazing. Especially for a pitcher who would blow up his elbow at twenty-nine and would end with a 19–29 career record.

Cheney is coming back to Memorial Stadium tonight to commemorate the record and wave to the crowd.

Cheney is the 6-foot-tall, fifty-six-year-old Georgian who looks like a fellow who might have spent some years farming and might now run a propane gas business in Cordele. That's 40 miles from Albany, which is 25 miles from Morgan, population 400, where Cheney was born. It's all a long way from 21 K's and fame. Cheney doesn't mind. He's a man who'd rather work long-hour days at a real job than go to a card show and ask a kid for five bucks to sign his name with a "21" after it.

"The money would be nice," he says, "but I don't think I could do it. I still sign a lot of autographs because of the record, but I don't charge anybody. If I see a gleam in a kid's eye, that makes me feel good. . . .

"I think it's real nice of the Orioles to have me back," he adds with a little chuckle that seems to say "since it was them I struck out."

Some athletes cling to their one moment. Others run from it. Cheney does not seem to need to do either. The Game is right back there, comfortable and mysterious, whenever he wants to rub it.

"I can't explain it and neither can anybody else," says Cheney, who was 7–9 that season with a 3.17 ERA and 147 strikeouts in 173 innings. "How'd I do it? That's a good question. Just something nobody knows. It was one of those times when everything works."

He came up with the talent-rich Cardinals, then was traded to the world-champion Pirates. He was just wild enough not to get much chance until he was twenty-seven and the desperate expansion Senators put him in their rotation.

"We called ourselves the Misfits. You knew if you gave up one run, you had a good chance of losing," says Cheney, who was 8–9 in 1963 despite a 2.71 ERA.

The cool night that he set the record, he did in fact give up a run. That's why he set the mark. If Charlie Lau's seventh-inning single hadn't tied the game, 1–1, Cheney would never have gotten those 12 strikeouts from the eighth inning on. In the end, he battled through a 10-hitter with 4 walks. Nobody kept a pitch count. Who knows how many? Certainly 200, probably 250.

Manager Mickey Vernon "told me it looked like I got stronger as the game went along," recalls Cheney. "I didn't feel tired at the time but, after I sat down in front of my locker, I could hardly get up."

Actually, Vernon tried to take Cheney out after twelve innings. But Cheney said: "Nope." When pressed, he elaborated: "I'm finishing. I'm gonna win or lose."

By the end, he'd struck out Gentile (46 homers in '61), Russ Snyder, Dave Nicholson, Marv Breeding, and reliever Dick Hall three times apiece. He also got starter Milt Pappas, Brooks Robinson, Jerry Adair, Lau, Hobie Landrith, and Dick Williams once. (Whitey Herzog never got a chance to hit. The only Oriole who didn't fan was Powell, who led the team in strikeouts.)

"I didn't know I was anywhere close to the record [of 18] by [Bob] Feller and [Sandy] Koufax until they announced that I'd tied it when I struck out Breeding in the fourteenth," recalls Cheney. "It must have shaken me up 'cause my next pitch to Hall was extremely wild."

The night of his 21, Cheney seemed on the brink of stardom. After the game, Vernon said: "When he is able to control his fastball, he's as good as any pitcher in the business. You gotta stick with a guy like him. Trade him off and he's liable to win thirty."

The next spring, Cheney remembers he picked up where he'd left off, starting the year 6–0. Then, one night with a 3–0 lead against the same Orioles, his career effectively came to an end on one pitch. "The pain shot through my arm."

Three trips to the Mayo Clinic got him a diagnosis—"epicondylitis, it's like tennis elbow but on the bottom of the elbow, not the top"— and a prognosis—no surgery possible and no cure known. Cheney tried pitching through pain. He tried taking a whole year off. He tried a comeback.

"I'd lost it," he says. "It was kind of a bitter defeat. Over a few years, I got it out of my system."

Could the sixteen-inning game have led to the elbow problem the next year? Who knows? Was he unlucky? "Oh, no," he says. "I was very fortunate. I even got to pitch in the World Series" in 1960.

What was his Series highlight? "I came in against the Yankees with the bases loaded," he says. What happened?

"I served up a grand slam to [Bobby] Richardson," says Cheney, laughing.

"I helped him set the Series RBI record. . . .

"At least we got the last laugh on the Yanks in that Series. They'd beat us, 15–3, then we'd win, 3–2. Gino Cimoli said, 'They set the record [for runs in a Series] but we got the money.' "

Ah, the money. These days, if a twenty-seven-year-old had a solid season, then topped it off by fanning 21, he'd probably get a multiyear deal for a few million dollars. He sure wouldn't have to sell propane for seventeen years before he could open his own business.

"Born too soon," says Cheney.

What he remembers about his magic game is that everybody close to him shared in it. His wife listened to the radio in Washington. A cousin came to the game. And, back home in Morgan, Georgia, the night was clear and the radio broadcast came in perfectly so his parents could listen to every pitch.

Cheney wanted to call somebody and say, "I struck out twenty-one men tonight."

"But I had nobody I could surprise," he says. Then, after a second, he adds, "Except myself."

The First
Shall Be First

THE FIRST COMMANDMENT of hitting was brought down from the mountaintop in 1969 by Ted Williams, chiseled by his own hand in the stone tablet of his autobiography, *My Turn at Bat:* Thou Shalt Not Swing at the First Pitch.

Williams *never* swung at the first pitch. Well, maybe once every two weeks. If the theory was good enough for Teddy Ballgame, perhaps the greatest hitter who ever lived, how could it be bad? Who'd have guessed that Williams was dead wrong? Who'd have imagined that, in fact, his idea was exactly backward? Who'd have believed that with this one perverse idea, Williams could damage a quarter century's worth of hitters and hurt the entire sport?

If Williams had consciously set out to sabotage every hitter who came after him—protecting his own legacy, as it were—he couldn't have done a better job. He propounded an illogical theory that worked only for him, and, incredibly, everybody believed it. If the pitchers union had conspired at a midnight meeting, it couldn't have dreamed up a better plot: Get the most respected hitter who ever lived to convince all the other hitters that they should spot us the first strike!

However, it's finally time to admit that the emperor has no clothes. For decades nobody could argue with Williams because nobody had enough data—who would keep a record of every pitch in every game, and do it year after year?—but this year the facts arrived, and it's official: Ted's pet theory is really Ted's big fallacy.

In the spring of 1993 STATS Inc. published a 501-page book called

Player Profiles. Yes, STATS has recorded every pitch thrown to every hitter for the past five years. The people at STATS didn't draw conclusions. They just gave us a bajillion numbers, and *Inside Sports* dug out the truth.

Somebody call a paramedic for Ted. We're sorry, big guy. You were a childhood hero, but you made the call, so you've got to take the fall.

Fact: An analysis of nearly 100 of the top hitters in baseball suggests that the best bat about 70 points higher and slug 130 points higher when they put the first pitch into play than they do in all other plate appearances. No, this isn't a misprint. Yes, this opens and closes the whole discussion in one sentence. Yes, these are astronomical differences. Yes, you're hearing it here first; we don't think anybody's figured this out before. Yes, Teddy Ballgame was a dumbo.

Fact: More than 95% of all big-league regulars hit better and slug better on those 0–0 at-bats (at-bats in which they put the first pitch into play) than in their other at-bats. Williams is virtually the only human being to whom his famous theory applies—that is, if it even applies to Williams himself. Maybe the man with the .344 lifetime average, the last man to bat .400 in a season, would have hit even better if he hadn't been so phobic about taking the first pitch.

Fact: Out of all the players in baseball, *Inside Sports* has found only six who don't hit better on the first pitch. And five of them hit worse by only a tiny margin; just one freak player in all of baseball hits measurably lower—16 points—on 0–0 pitches: Rickey Henderson. The conclusion? Everybody else should be swinging at a lot more first pitches.

Fact: Pitchers throw 55% strikes on 0–0 pitches.

Fact: Hitters put only 11% of first pitches in play.

Yes, we're all permitted to scream now. If virtually every hitter kills the 0–0 pitch, then why are 80% of first-pitch strikes not put into play? The answer, please: Because most hitters are idiots. They believe Old Ted tales. They come up to the plate 600 times a season and act like they've never seen a baseball before. "Let's see, the guy on the hill winds up, then throws the ball. And I'm supposed to hit it." Strike one. "OK, I'm ready now."

Wake up and smell the coffee, guys. The first pitch is often the best one you're going to get. Every pitching coach goes to bed mumbling, "Get ahead of the hitter." So what do you geniuses do? You let 'em get ahead of you! Wise up.

Pretend the first pitch is, say, a nice 2–0 pitch. If you like it, smack it off the wall. Don't swing wildly, of course, but go ahead and be a "zone" hitter—that is, divide the plate in half and look for a pitch that's up or down, inside or outside. Or be a "guess" hitter and look for a fastball or an off-speed pitch. But don't be ridiculously finicky. For heaven's sake, don't let 80% of those first-pitch strikes—the majority of them fastballs—go to waste. Be the aggressor. Give that pitcher something to think about next time. Attack his confidence. Make him mutter, "This guy thinks he owns me. He can't wait for me to throw the ball." Maybe then he'll start you off by trying for a perfect breaking pitch on the black. "Ball one." Then he'll really be in trouble. And you'll probably hit even better.

Hit the strikes, take the balls—what a radical approach. Use the same "now's my chance" tactics that are common among all hitters on 3–1 pitches. After all, the first pitch is the only pitch of every at-bat when you're guaranteed not to be behind in the count. And it's the only pitch on which the hurler hasn't had a chance to set you up, or mess with your mind, or expose one of your known weaknesses to get you worrying.

Statistically, hitters fare well in only two situations: when they're ahead in the count and on the first pitch. Surprisingly, the stats show that hitters fair almost equally well in these two situations. However, even the worst pitchers eat hitters alive when they're ahead in the count, and even 2–2 and 3–2 counts tend to favor the pitcher.

So why do the vast majority of big leaguers disdain one of the two situations in which the percentages of the game are dramatically on their side? Why don't hitters take advantage of the fact that if they swing at the first pitch and miss or foul it off, nobody makes them go back to the bench and sit down? It's obvious that you can't strike out on 0–0, of course, but, statistically, it's also a big deal.

For example, if hitters swung at two or even three times as many first pitches as they currently do, they'd raise their collective batting average by between 10 and 15 points, and they'd raise their slugging percentage twice as much. Many great sluggers, especially those who now take too many pitches, would pick up about five extra homers a season—for free. Just think how raising the major league slugging percentage by 20 to 25 points would jazz up the game. In fact, if you improved hitting by more than 10 or 12 points or 20-some slugging points, the game would have *too many* runs. The first team that ordered its entire lineup to be ultra-aggressive—the first team that praised players for attacking the first strike of an at-bat, rather than criticizing them—probably would lead the league in runs.

In addition, a crucial side benefit would accrue. The game's two biggest problems—low scoring and slow play—would be solved. Imagine a higher-scoring, faster-played sport that would keep fans on the edge of their seats, knowing that most hitters couldn't wait to start hacking. In particular, imagine the suspense with men on base, because that's when a hitter really ought to be aggressive. The only advantage to patience is that 8% of the time hitters draw walks. But with men on base, you need to maximize your team's batting average and slugging percentage. Strike while the iron is hot! Once a rally starts, every hitter's primary strategic goal should be to put one of the first two strikes in play.

Some may think that swinging at first pitches would lower on-base averages. Not true.

Fact: Big leaguers hit so spectacularly on first pitches that their collective OBA—without benefit of any walks—is higher on their 0–0 at-bats than in all their other plate appearances combined. Statistically, you give away nothing by being a first-pitch hitter. And there's more—so much more it's almost hard to believe.

Fact: Baseball's best hitter the last five years has been Kirby Puckett (.329). So who hits more first pitches than anybody else in baseball? You guessed it: Puckett. Twenty-five percent of his at-bats are over after one pitch!

Not only does Puckett hit the first pitch year after year, but he thrives on it. Puckett bats .383 and slugs .565 on 0–0 at bats; in his other at-bats he hits .311 and slugs .460. Gee, what a nonsurprise: He hits 70 points higher and slugs about 100 points higher—just like the league as a whole. Puckett proves that even if you hit almost half of all first-pitch strikes into play, your production does not have to fall.

How much does Puckett's style help him? Or, conversely, how much are other players hurting themselves by almost never swinging at first pitches? Compare Puckett and Ryne Sandberg—if you can stand the shock. Sandberg hit .400 last year on 0–0 pitches, Puckett .440. That mirrors their respective five-year trends: Both crush first pitches. On all their at-bats that did not end on the first pitch, Sandberg hit better, .301 to Puckett's .290. However, for the season Kirby hit .329 to Ryne's .304.

How is that possible? Because Puckett hit the first pitch 166 times, Sandberg only 20 times. Conclusion: Puckett improved his average by

36 points, relative to Sandberg, simply by swinging at eight times as many 0–0 pitches. (Note: Though Puckett's style caused him to have fewer walks—44 to Sandberg's 68—he still got so many hits that he had the higher on-base average. And though both the Twins and the Cubs got 100 runs from their stars, it's probably no accident that the always-attacking Puckett had 23 more RBI.)

Who knows? Maybe Puckett hasn't even pushed the envelope of what's possible on first pitches. Maybe he can get to 30%. Maybe 20 to 25% will someday be a normal first-pitch-in-play average for the whole league.

At this point, a logical question presents itself: Is it possible that first-pitch production is staggeringly good because hitters are extremely selective? If a hitter looks for exactly the pitch he wants on 0–0, he ought to be able to hit better when he gets it, right? However, if he starts being more aggressive, wouldn't he give away his advantage?

Intuitively, this idea seems appealing, but *Inside Sports* has studied this, too. We've looked at hitters who put 5% to 10% of first pitches in play, as well as those for whom the percentages are from 10 to 15 and from 20 to 25. What did we find? They all hit and slug equally well. The more "selective" hitters don't do better, as a group. There's certainly no pattern of decreased production with increased aggressiveness.

This, it should be noted, is not a scientific proof. It could all be a spectacular coincidence. Conceivably, hitters could be so intuitively wise that they know exactly how many first pitches they're capable of handling. Everybody could be operating in his own perfect comfort zone.

Yeah, right.

The more you look at the new numbers baseball has at its disposal, the more incontrovertible is the conclusion that, for a large majority of hitters, the quickest road to improvement is to be less "patient" and more aggressive. Why, for instance, would a team try to "tire out" the opposing starting pitcher by taking pitches? Folks, this is the age of five-deep bullpens. Nobody gets to hit against a tired pitcher anymore.

In fact, if you want to have a prayer against Jim Abbott, Steve Avery, Kevin Brown, Roger Clemens, David Cone, Doug Drabek, Dennis Eckersley, Dwight Gooden, and right on down the alphabet, the last thing you want to do is take pitches and let 'em work you over. Swing! It's your only hope.

Fact: Over the past five years, the league has hit better than .300 on the first pitch against all of the star pitchers in the previous paragraph. Less than 5% of pitchers can hold the league under .300 on 0–0 pitches. Look up any star pitcher in *Player Profiles.* Odds are the league hits about .310 on 0–0 pitches but .180 when he gets ahead in the count and .140 when he gets two strikes.

Seriously, folks, Kirby's got it right. Why wait?

In contrast to Puckett, let's take a typical example of a hitter who's been hurt by the omnipresence of the Williams Theory. For the last five years Jose Canseco has batted .363 and slugged .755 on 0–0 at-bats; the rest of the time he batted .268 and slugged .524. However, because Canseco is one of a generation of first-pitch "takers," he takes advantage of his fabulous 0–0 prowess only 9% of the time. Thus, Canseco gives away about 75 at-bats a year when he could be slugging .755, not .524. Over a whole career, Canseco probably will hit about 50 fewer homers than if he'd been an aggressive, 20% first-pitch hitter.

Canseco isn't alone, either. Dozens of the game's greatest stars could be a whole level better if they weren't so bloody "patient." In his career Frank Thomas has hit .435 on 0–0 at-bats, but he does so only 8% of the time. Come on, Frank, shoot for 20%. You might hit .350 with 140 RBIs.

Countless players seem oblivious to their monster numbers on 0–0 at-bats. Danny Tartabull's lifetime slugging percentage on 0–0 is .754, Fred McGriff's is .752, Joe Carter's is .687, and David Justice's is .645. In every case, that's 150 to 250 points higher than in their other at-bats. Yet they all swing at the first pitch less often than the league average.

Of all hitters, perhaps Juan Gonzalez makes you want to cry the most. Last year's major league home run leader hit .451 and slugged .941 on 0–0. Yet, like Thomas, he was an 8% man. If he could put the first pitch in play as often as Puckett—which is asking a lot—he'd have 100 extra at-bats every year on which he was Godzilla.

Gonzalez only has one large weakness: 143 strikeouts last year. However, he merely symbolizes a trend. Baseball is chock full of strikeout artists who fan from 100 to 150 times a year—yet take the first pitch. For instance, somebody should hit Dean Palmer in the head with a bat. Palmer struck out 154 times last year. Anyone who has this much trouble making contact should never take a strike, yet

Palmer hits the first pitch only 7% of the time. You say maybe he's not a good 0–0 hitter? For his career: .359 batting average, .750 slugging average. If he can hit 26 homers playing the game backward, what would he do if he kept it simple? With Gonzalez, Palmer, and Canseco—all colossal 0–0 sluggers who rarely swing at the pitch they hit best—on the same team, the Rangers have a unique opportunity to improve.

Many young phenoms paralyze themselves with analysis. For example, last year Phil Plantier hit .350 and slugged .650 on 0–0 at-bats, but he hit only 5% of the first pitches thrown to him. He "took" his way right back into the minor leagues.

Even the greatest hitters fall prey to the modern desire to see as many pitches as possible. Yes, Sandberg, this means you. For the last five years before this season, Ryno has batted .374 and slugged .691 on 0–0 at-bats, yet he put only 230 first pitches into play in 3,036 at-bats. Compared with Puckett in the same years, he wasted 561 at-bats.

Not every hitter has been dumb enough to believe Williams or the generation of forty-five-to-sixty-five-year-old batting coaches who parrot his doctrine—but it's close. In all of baseball, only four other regulars put the first pitch in play more than 21% of the time: Lance Johnson, Ozzie Guillen, Carney Lansford, and Kent Hrbek. Needless to say, all of them have helped themselves with the strategy—Hrbek in particular, who has slugged 101 points higher on 0–0 at-bats for the last five years.

If we look at the players who fall in the 15% to 20% range, we find some of the most accomplished hitters in the sport: Mark Grace, Mike Greenwell, Gary Sheffield, Larry Walker, Bobby Bonilla, Harold Baines, George Brett, Mark McGwire, Terry Pendleton, Albert Belle, Eddie Murray, Paul Molitor, Will Clark, Tim Raines, and Ken Griffey Jr. What a shabby group. Not more than about six of 'em will get into Cooperstown. The other riffraff are batting champions and All-Stars and such.

The hard reality is that most major league hitters are sacrificing 50 to 75 at-bats a season when they should be annihilating first pitches. Here are some more facts that should make your head spin:

- The better the pitcher, the more you should attack his first pitch. If the pitcher is great, you probably should always swing at the first offering.
- No pitcher in baseball is effective on the first pitch. Not one. They

are all vulnerable. In the last five years only two pitchers in the whole game have held opponents under a .266 average on 0–0 pitches. Digest that, please.

- Conversely, every pitcher in baseball—all of them—is tough when he gets ahead in the count. Dozens upon dozens of pitchers hold hitters under .200 when they get ahead in the count.

Look at Nolan Ryan, Roger Clemens, Rob Dibble, and Dennis Eckersley. Their stats are absolutely typical of all prominent pitchers. Over the last five years the league has hit .202, .225, .195, and .214 against them, respectively. When they get ahead in the count, the league is helpless: .143, .173, .138, and .151. And with two strikes, you might as well give the umpire the bat and take a seat: .125, .158, .114, and .124. Why on earth would you spot these guys a strike?

So is there any time when you have a prayer against these monsters? Well, of course: the first pitch. Over the last five years the 0–0 batting average off Ryan is .331 (131 for 396). Off Clemens, .307. Off Dibble, .408. Off Eckersley, .314. Why, batters slug an astounding .525 against Ryan on first pitches and an unbelievable .612 off Dibble.

Yet only 11% of all hitters put Ryan's first pitch in play, 12% for Clemens, 10% for Dibble, and 12% for the Eck. Good Lord, Eck's first pitch is a strike almost every time, and he walks less than one man a month. Why are 88% of the men who face him waiting? Swing away —it's your only hope.

How did the Blue Jays crush Eckersley in the AL playoffs last season? Watch the tape: Everybody went up swinging at the first pitch. As for Dibble, all three home runs he allowed in '92 came on first pitches, and all three of them lost the game.

For a quarter of a century, hitting theory has been completely dominated by Williams's approach. Batters have believed, to the bottoms of their souls, that great hitters take the first pitch—look it over, time the pitcher's delivery, make the pitcher work. The more you see a pitcher, the more you study him, the better you'll hit him. The benighted few who didn't obey the Williams dictum actually apologized for their idiosyncrasies. They'd shamefacedly admit they'd be better if they did it Ted's way.

Why did an entire sport fall in line with Williams's teachings? Because Williams may have been the hardest man in baseball history not to believe. He spent his adult life concocting theories on every craft he mastered, and he argued his points passionately. And as evidence of his unassailable judgment, he could cite the rather convincing fact that he was the best man on earth at almost everything he tried to master.

As a pilot he was an ace in World War II, then again in Korea. He once landed his plane in flames, rolled out of the cockpit, then started kicking the burning plane in a rage because it hadn't performed better. Was he the best fighter pilot alive? Maybe. One of the best, certainly.

Was he the best fisherman on the planet? Yes, he might have been that, too. From catching one of the biggest marlin in the ocean to bagging 1,000 elusive bonefish in a season, Williams either held the record or he was on its trail.

The man even married a former Miss America.

In the last decade, however, baseball statistics have gone from the Stone Age to the era of the computer chip. Gradually it's become commonplace to hear big-league players and coaches utter ideas they've learned, whether they know it or not, from nerds with pocket calculators.

For example, almost any manager can now tell you that baseball is a game of firsts. "The most important batter of an inning is the first batter," Skip will say, nodding sagely. "If he gets on base you have a fifty–fifty chance to score him; if he doesn't, you have little chance of a big inning. Also, the most important pitch to any hitter is the first pitch. The batter will hit .100 higher if the count starts 1–0 instead of 0–1."

All this came from the sabermetricians, and it's all true. But baseball may not yet have learned the most important of all its important firsts. Someday in the not so distant future, one of baseball's least-questioned clichés will be: Don't Get Behind in the Count. Thou Shalt Swing at the First Strike if You Think You Can Handle It. Especially with Men on Base.

How could we have overlooked something so obvious for so long?

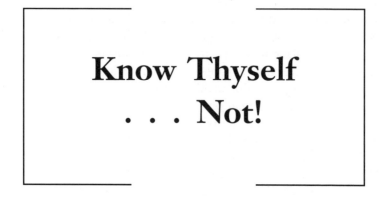

Know Thyself
. . . Not!

March 20, 1992—No spring training is complete without a visit to the New York Mets, heirs to the New York Yankees as baseball's most self-deluded franchise.

Everybody's talking about the Mets. Why? Because they're talking about themselves, of course. As usual.

This franchise has been to one World Series in eighteen years, but it thinks it's the center of the baseball universe. When the Mets are great ('86), they think they're the best ever. When they're good, they think they're great. When they're mediocre, they think they're very good but got stiffed. And when they're bad, as they were last season, finishing fifth, they think if they spend $30 million or $40 million, they'll be great again before the ink dries.

The Mets' reward for self-inflation is that they seldom learn the proper lessons from their annual disappointments and so almost never approach the next season with fitting expectations. For instance, at this very moment, the Mets think—and will actually tell you—that they should win the National League East despite their 77–84 record in '91, which was 20½ games out of first place.

Dream on. Once more, come October, the Mets—owners, fans, and press—will scratch their heads and find some Davey Johnson or Darryl Strawberry or Frank Cashen to pick as this year's scapegoat.

Let's make this so simple that even the Mets can get a reality check.

Two winters ago, the Mets lost free agent Strawberry. Last winter, they replaced him (for $29 million) with Bobby Bonilla, a fine All-Star who is getting chubbier every year. This is not progress. This is a net minus.

The Mets now have Bret Saberhagen (in trade), but they lost Frank Viola (to free agency). Talk about tit for tat. Both were once excellent. Both are on the slide. Both have arm trouble. But Viola's more durable. No progress here.

The Mets got Eddie Murray with his sour puss; but they had to trade Kevin McReynolds. Murray's a Hall of Famer. But so what? He's old. He's a statue at first base. And his stats are little better than those of McReynolds, who was a decent outfielder. A wash.

The Mets got ancient Willie Randolph and Bill Pecota to play second base. But they lost Gregg Jefferies. Why is this an improvement? Jefferies may still turn out to be a Royals star. "Mets fans are going to like Bill Pecota," said new manager Jeff Torborg this week.

Yeah? Why? He's thirty-two. He's never done anything anywhere. He's a .235 hitter. If the frequently disabled Randolph, soon to be thirty-eight, gets hurt, Mets fans may do a Pecota on Al Harazin's head.

Above all, the Mets fail to realize their greatest failings.

They have an absolutely horrible defense at almost every position. So what do they do? They move their worst defensive player, Howard Johnson (39 errors) to a really important position—centerfield. They move a first baseman to third base (Dave Magadan); he should be a nightmare. They get Murray, who hasn't hustled since 1979, to avoid smashes at first base. And they turn the catching job over to a rookie. At shortstop? The immortal stopgap Kevin Elster.

Torborg, asked about this, said—honest to God—"We're focusing on defense. We think it can be a plus."

You have to feel for Torborg, one of the game's nice, smart people. There aren't many honest questions you can ask him that won't cause him anguish.

How's HoJo look in center?

There's this wonderful pause while he reworks the company line: "He's looked better since Vada [Pinson, a coach] gave him a tip a couple of days ago."

What was the tip? Buy a motorcycle and wear a crash helmet?

Let's take pity and not ask him about Strawberry's autobiography just yet, okay?

Unfortunately, the Mets' biggest long-term problem may be the health of their two best pitchers, the young yet ancient duo of Dwight

Gooden, twenty-seven, and Saberhagen, twenty-eight. Both are in acute danger of the Fernando Valenzuela Meltdown Syndrome.

Studies of some twentieth-century pitchers have shown that those who are acutely overworked before they are twenty-five usually burn out by thirty. Gooden and Saberhagen, big-league starters at nineteen and workhorses by twenty-one, are the leading candidates of their generation for this sad end. Both already have had career-threatening arm problems.

The Mets can look at anything or anybody and, so long as it's in a Mets uniform, imagine greatness. Even Sid Fernandez. He'll be thirty this year and has probably already eaten away a fine career. Finally, last winter, after his extra weight forced him to have knee surgery ("Oh, no, he's going to land on us again!"), Fernandez lost about 35 of the 50 pounds he needed to drop. His conclusion after an off-season of diet study: "If you eat fats, you get fat."

Naturally, the Mets are counting on El Sid, who won one game last season. Right now, Fernandez has an itty-bitty injury and can't pitch, but the Mets aren't worried. At least he's not eating.

One new Met may get what he deserves. Pouty Eddie Murray has had his hand held by Earl Weaver and his feet kissed by Tommy Lasorda for most of the first fifteen pampered years of his career. Now he's going to meet reality: a two-year sentence in New York City.

Eddie's hands are tender and he hates to hit in cold weather. Shea is a wind tunnel. If Murray is hitting .160 on May 1, the tabloids will eviscerate him on Monday, Wednesday, and Friday, the home fans will boo him on Tuesday, Thursday, and Saturday, and on Sunday everybody will bring old vegetables to the park. By June, first base may look like a Caesar salad.

Mets fans always expect a lot. And the Mets always oblige by telling them what they want to hear: We're great.

When they aren't quite that good, no problem. Just find somebody to blame.

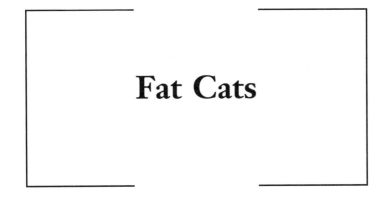

Fat Cats

July 31, 1991—In most sports, nobody loves a fat man. Not so in baseball, the last refuge of the hungry. Ever since 251-pound Babe Ruth gobbled hot dogs until he hospitalized himself, the game has had a perverse affection for the kind of player who might eat the infield grass.

Or, for that matter, the umpire. In 1928, Fat Fothergill, in the agonizing grip of a crash diet—complete with rubber suits and Turkish baths—became infuriated by a third-strike call by Bill Dinneen. The 5-foot-10, 230-pound Fothergill bit the ump in the arm.

Upon being ejected, Fothergill quipped: "Okay by me. That's the first bite of meat I've had in a month."

Ever since the Yankees billed 295-pound pitcher Jumbo Brown as "the man who swallowed a taxi cab," baseball has been selectively permissive toward the obese. That is, if they could play. Brown threatened to wear out his welcome in 1933 when, in a spring training game of leapfrog, he disabled two teammates, Sam Byrd and Cy Perkins.

These are the salad days of fat. The best slugger in the sport is Cecil Fielder, the Tiger whose waistline would make Ruth's look svelte. Fielder was enormous last season when he hit 51 homers, then celebrated by spending the winter locked in the kitchen. Sparky Anderson was appalled when he saw Fielder—tonnage unknown—in spring training. The trim manager has been temporarily assuaged by Fielder's 27 homers and 83 RBI, which make every other player in baseball this side of Jose Canseco seem, well, small.

If Fielder, twenty-seven, continues to make 50 homers and 135 RBI an annual habit, it may convince cleanup men to switch from Ultra Slim Fast to hot fudge. At the moment, Fielder doesn't hit the ball so much as he leans on it. His batting practice shots in the SkyDome at the All-Star Game were of legendary dimensions. Naturally, his deepest blasts landed in the Sightline Restaurant. Probably in the pasta.

It's been said that the only flaw in Fielder's game is a lack of discipline at the plate—not on balls and strikes, but with a knife and fork. At this, Fielder takes umbrage. With a side order of onion rings.

"I'm sorry if I don't look good for you in the lobby. But I'll go out there and play for you every day," said Fielder. "The criticism I take for my weight is not fair at all.

"They were ripping me in spring training. If you have any kind of heart, that gets you going."

Oakland's Dave Henderson, overhearing this, pointed to Circular Cecil's classic posterior. Fielder beamed. "That's the power joint," he said. "Where do you think the leverage comes from?"

Some speculate the Tigers traded for large Rob Deer and Pete Incaviglia just so Fielder, if he got the midnight munchies, wouldn't have to go to the International House of Pancakes alone.

Fielder is merely part of a broader trend. "Tony Gwynn is the best hitter in baseball and he has to take that all the time," said Fielder. Indeed, Gwynn does. "I hear the fat jokes about going to the snack bar between innings and 'Get the hamburgers out of your pants,'" said Gwynn. "I got hit with that all last year—not the right 'body type.' I don't know what my 'ideal weight' is. I tried all winter long to get to that weight. I worked out every day. I went from 218 to 215."

Since Gwynn is barely 5-foot-10, it may be fair to assume that, after some workouts, he cooled down at McDonald's.

"Everybody assumes if I lost twenty pounds, I'd be quicker. Well, I know I wouldn't be," said Gwynn, who is one of the few undeniably chubby players who also has been a superb Gold Glove fielder and a serious base stealer.

"This is not a game where you have to be cut out of stone like [André] Dawson, [Eric] Davis, or [Barry] Larkin. . . . I'd like to make a run at .400 just to hear what they'd say about my weight then," said Gwynn.

To his credit, Gwynn keeps his sense of humor about the Extra 20. "When I hit Chicago, they really go after me. I have to stick my face in my glove to keep from showing that I'm laughing."

Gwynn even tells the story on himself that, at the All-Star Game, he looked so rotund that a security guard would not admit him and demanded to see his press credentials. (Hmmmmm.)

The wisecracks and slights bother Gwynn only when he's in a slump. "If I slip to .340, they're really on me," he deadpans.

Everywhere you look, this is the year of the Big Man. The game's leader in saves is Lee Smith, who admits to 250 pounds but resembles a small nation. Asked about his off-season regimen, Smith said recently that he did sit-ups while playing with his son. "But my kid can only count to ten," said Smith. "And he misses a few numbers."

If Gwynn doesn't win the National League batting title, then Terry Pendleton may. Pendleton's shadow bears a strong resemblance to Gwynn's. In the American League, Kirby Puckett may again grab the silver bat. At 5-foot-8 and 213 pounds, Puckett would make a perfect bookend for Gwynn. He did, remember, in 1989.

"You can't please everybody," said Puckett, a fine centerfielder who is largely, but definitely not entirely, made of muscle. "So you do the best with the body you've got. You can't get another one."

Next to Fielder, perhaps the most out-of-shape star in baseball is Kent Hrbek, who has been accused by teammates of eating some of the vowels in his name. The 260-pound Hrbek is working on his ninth 20-homer season in the last ten years. He might even waddle into Cooperstown.

Everywhere you look, the heirs to Boog Powell and Aurelio Lopez are devouring the league. John Kruk, who looks like he invented the wheel, then had it for lunch, may drive in 100. Last but not least, the Mets' Sid Fernandez—the Human Luau—returned in time for the stretch-mark drive. Or maybe it was Free Bib Night.

Gwynn speaks for all his circular brethren when he begs the game's fans to show a bit more sympathy. "They tend to resent guys who look like me," he says. "It's hard for them to accept somebody with that body making that money."

Especially when they know where it will probably be spent.

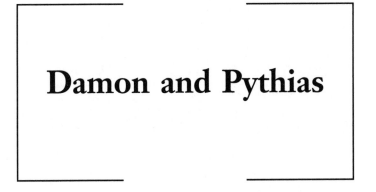

Damon and Pythias

Bart Giamatti

May 2, 1989—If ever a man was an advertisement for hard living—not wild living, but aggressive, committed, fill-the-days and fill-the-nights living—it was A. Bartlett Giamatti, the baseball commissioner who died of a heart attack yesterday at the age of fifty-one.

If that's the price a man pays for mastering the most serious works of the human mind, if that is the cost of presiding over a great university, and if that is the fee the world charges for defending a cherished institution when it's in a crisis, then perhaps Giamatti's death should be greeted with three cheers as well as many tears.

Giamatti was a student who never stopped burning the midnight oil, usually with a cigarette at his lips. The appetites of youth, which leave many of us too soon—for hard books, for new ideas, for ambiguous but worthy causes, for new friends—those, he never lost. It made the days too short and the hours rugged. But one look at Giamatti's bristling beard and barrel chest told you he wouldn't ask much quarter.

He loved to gnaw to the marrow of great issues, usually with a glass of something inspirational beside him. After he finished his long workdays in the tough world of academia and later baseball, he went home, cleaned his plate lustily, then wrote a few books in his spare time. His most recent work—*A Free and Ordered Space*—might have been a description of his view of what baseball, at its best, might be.

Day in and day out, all that Giamatti demanded of himself was everything. Although there are no true universal men left, Giamatti seemed tempted by the possibility of doing a tolerable impersonation. In the space of two minutes, he could make perfectly reasonable allusions to Marcel Proust, Robert Frost, *Rashomon* (the Japanese film), and the Heisenberg principle (physics' uncertainty principle).

To a more mediocre mind, Giamatti's passion for spreading his arms wide, pulling disparate ideas together, and then insisting that they belonged in the same embrace, could be annoying. With Giamatti, there was always a desire to say, "Keep it simple for the rest of us." Yet that was usually his ultimate destination. He studied complexity in the hope of reaching simplicity.

In the Pete Rose Case, for instance, Giamatti never let his eye wander from the ball. His goals were simple and they were the proper ones, too. Remove Rose from the game as quickly as possible. Leave open the possibility of eventual reinstatement—but only if Rose showed radical improvement of his basic character. And make sure that a capricious court system was not given the chance to damage the powers of the commissionership that had been left in his trust.

A week ago, in the single act for which his stewardship will always be remembered, and greatly valued, he achieved all of his goals.

Some said Giamatti's "indefinite suspension" of Rose was too harsh —that imposing what might become a lifetime banishment on a man simply because he bet on his own team to win its games was draconian. Some claimed that Giamatti buckled by allowing Rose to leave the game without a final "guilty" finding.

In the real world, a place where Giamatti dwelled very comfortably, the rookie commissioner actually got high marks for a solution that was long on realpolitik and short on aesthetic purity. He got the job done and even looked proud of the dirt left on his hands. He'd bobbled a couple, but he'd played hardball and won.

Some may speculate that the strain of the Rose Case, as well as baseball's other headaches, contributed to Giamatti's collapse yesterday on Martha's Vineyard, where he was staying with his wife and son. Yankees owner George Steinbrenner said: "He wrestled with all of baseball's problems. It may have all come in on him."

However, by a coincidence for which Rose should feel a little grateful, Giamatti himself addressed that issue at length last month. Giamatti insisted that the Rose controversy had taken less than twenty percent of his work time in recent months and had not consumed or troubled him inordinately. "While a serious matter," he said, "it doesn't take most of my time."

It is hard to imagine a man as accustomed to criticism as Giamatti—and as given to the sly cosmic laugh—letting the fairly straightforward issues of the Rose Case break his health. In private, Giamatti had little trouble laughing at himself and, in fact, liked to repeat the description of himself as, simultaneously, the most overqualified and underqualified man ever to become baseball commissioner.

When he took the job, Giamatti said, "Dante would have been delighted." By the day of his tragic death, almost everyone in baseball was delighted as well. Former commissioner Peter Ueberroth generously described him as the "finest commissioner in history" and a man who "encompassed everything that is good and enduring about America's national pastime."

Certainly no commissioner, not even Bowie Kuhn, loved baseball more deeply. As Yale president, Giamatti wore his Boston Red Sox cap around campus and, as National League president for two years, he wore it still, though only metaphorically. When the Red Sox were one strike from winning the 1986 World Series—which would have been their first since 1918—Giamatti later said: "Strange sounds started emanating from me. I did find myself shouting instructions from the wrong box. I'm not proud of it, but I admit I did it."

For those who love baseball, Giamatti's deep passion for the game —which was great all his life—was a lovely thing to watch. A year ago, in one of his stunning, picaresque monologues (which barely needed punctuation when transcribed), Giamatti said, "How people go about their pleasure is as important to me as how they go about their work.

"The largest thing I've learned [as a baseball executive] is the enormous grip that this game has on people, the extent to which it really is very important. It goes way down deep. It really does bind together. It's a cliché and sounds sentimental, but I have now seen it from the inside. . . . I think I underestimated the depth of this historical enterprise. . . . [Baseball] is an unalloyed good. Of course, there are passions [involved]. But passion is good if it is directed toward a noble end.

"There's nothing bad that accrues from baseball. [Realizing] that has been the most rewarding part of all this."

Nothing bad accrued to baseball from Bart Giamatti. He died decades before those who knew him would have wished. But he lived just long enough to complete an enormous service to the sport, the institution, the art form, that he loved.

Fay Vincent

CONSULT LA ROCHEFOUCAULD

August 1, 1990—If you want to understand George Steinbrenner to a depth you never imagined and if you want to grasp the source of his fall, Fay Vincent thinks he can tell you where to find the proper text.

"Consult La Rochefoucauld," said the commissioner yesterday, referring to the French author who died in 1680. "He's delicious on this. Look for the section on self-love in the *Maxims*. It's about pride and arrogance. . . . It's George."

What follows is a truncated version of the passage, a classic in world literature, which the commissioner of baseball believes illuminates the interior of the man he has just banned for life:

"Self-love is love of oneself and of all things in terms of oneself. It makes men worshippers of themselves and would make them tyrants over others if fortune gave them the means. . . . Nothing is so vehement as its desires, nothing so concealed as its aims, nothing so devious as its methods. . . .

"Nothing is so strong and binding as self-love's attachments, and even under the threat of the direst calamities it struggles in vain to loosen their hold. . . .

"Self-love is made of all the opposites: domineering and obedient, sincere and deceitful, merciful and cruel, timid and daring. Its inclinations vary with the varying temperaments that bend its energies now toward glory, now riches, now pleasures. . . .

"Self-love . . . even joins forces with its declared enemies . . . and, most remarkable of all, hates itself with them, plots for its own downfall and even works to bring about its own ruin; in fine, all it cares about is existing, and provided it can go on existing, it is quite prepared to be its own enemy. Hence, there is nothing to be surprised at if it sometimes throws in its lot with its own destruction—for the moment of its defeat on one side is that of its recovery on another.

"When you think it is giving up what it enjoys, it is only calling a temporary halt or ringing the changes, and at the very time when it is vanquished and you think you are rid of it, back it comes, triumphant in its own undoing."

Perhaps now it's easier to understand how Steinbrenner could hire the same problem drinker five times as a manager. How he could repeat the most amazingly self-destructive mistakes. How he could hurt so many people and then try to wash their wounds clean with money.

How could Steinbrenner be so mean and yet so generous, so smart and yet so dumb, so protean and yet so wasteful, so petty about the Yankees and yet so far-sighted about baseball in general? How could he get so locked in a cycle of destructive behavior? And how can he, right to this very moment, be so sure that nothing bad has happened to him and that he will rise again?

We still may not really know. But it's reassuring to know that the same guy was around—raising hell to glorify himself and damaging most of what he touched—back in the French court in the seventeenth century. At least now we know that we're right to knock him off every horse he rides and trip him every time he tries to get mounted again.

Why did Steinbrenner pay Howard Spira—a flat-broke penny-ante gambler—$40,000 for information to be used against Dave Winfield? Information that proved worthless. And why did Steinbrenner refuse to pay another $110,000 when he knew Spira would almost certainly go public with his story?

Maybe La Rochefoucauld knows the answer.

Perhaps the addicted self-lover cannot let go of the prideful fantasy that he can always start his cycle of gratification all over again. Just change the venue.

When Billy Martin—in whom Steinbrenner had irrational faith and to whom he was ludicrously loyal—died on Christmas, perhaps the Boss knew his Yankees run was over. Within days of Martin's death,

Steinbrenner paid off Spira and, thus, began his own inevitable base-ball suicide.

Vincent saw a man coming toward him who seemed to be conspiring in his own ruin. In his ruling, Vincent wrote, "I am able to evaluate a pattern of behavior that borders on the bizarre."

So the commissioner decided to turn that bizarre pattern of behavior to baseball's advantage. On Monday, Vincent offered Steinbrenner a two-year suspension as owner of the Yankees. That was exactly what everybody expected.

But Vincent also had a card up his sleeve—an offer he called "a functional alternative."

It was a deal so harsh no one grasped why Vincent bothered to bring it to the table. The author of *Maxims* would have.

If Steinbrenner was as self-obsessed, as addicted to fame, and as devoid of self-knowledge as Vincent supposed, then the worst fate Steinbrenner could imagine would be two years in limbo. What a living hell! "Such is the portrait of self-love, whose whole existence is one long and incessant activity," concluded La Rochefoucauld.

Bart Giamatti knew that Pete Rose was an addicted gambler who'd do anything, no matter how irrational, to deny in public he had ever bet on baseball. Giamatti used that card to turn Rose against himself. The public gasped as Rose agreed to a life ban in exchange for almost nothing: a formal no-finding decision on his baseball gambling.

Now Vincent has used the Giamatti Gambit to mousetrap Steinbrenner into banishing himself, just as Rose did. Giamatti let Rose keep the last threads of his delusions. Now Vincent has done the same for Steinbrenner.

With his shipbuilding company on the financial rocks, with his name a national joke, with the crowd at Yankee Stadium chanting, "George must go," Steinbrenner still thinks he can save face. After all, he just resigned. Steinbrenner can say he's still managing the money side, not the baseball side.

By yesterday afternoon, Steinbrenner was already claiming that the whole thing was pretty much what he'd wanted all along. Time to let the "young blood" take over the baseball operation. Time for the Boss to pursue other projects. Steinbrenner still imagines the U.S. Olympic movement wants him to help run the ship. Cue the spooky music.

Rose never realized, until it was too late, that he'd walked out of Giamatti's office stripped naked to face his enemies.

Now it is Steinbrenner—whose face might never again appear on the cover of *Newsweek* and whose public importance will dwindle toward zero—who may soon feel a draft around his hindquarters and wonder who stole his pants.

MUTINY

July 8, 1992—As usual, baseball Commissioner Fay Vincent followed his conscience on Monday, largely ignoring baseball's notorious backroom politics and acting in what he considered to be the best interests of his sport.

Vincent followed common sense and realigned the National League's two cockeyed divisions, putting Cincinnati and Atlanta, which are in the eastern time zone, in the East, and putting St. Louis and Chicago, which are in the central time zone, in the West.

The decision was obviously and incontestably correct—as it would have been five, ten, or fifteen years ago. The new arrangement makes for shorter, cheaper travel for almost all teams and promotes geographic rivalries.

For his pains, Vincent got the reaction that he has come to expect. The Chicago Cubs sued him yesterday.

The president of the National League, Bill White, did a little showboating himself, denouncing Vincent as a power-hungry law breaker because he overrode a veto by the Cubs, thus ignoring the sanctity of something called the National League Constitution. When did the National League become a nation? Who knew it even had a constitution?

Above all, Vincent's sworn enemies among owners—particularly Peter O'Malley of the Dodgers, Bud Selig of the Brewers, and Jerry Reinsdorf of the White Sox—could smile seditiously to themselves, delighted that their task of discrediting one of the game's most impartial commissioners could continue apace. That's to say, at any hour of the day when telephones are in service.

Vincent, one of the least celebrity-hungry men you'll ever meet in public life, has become Mr. Controversy this year. There are two reasons. He has the guts to make decisions—most of them the right ones. And the owners whom he necessarily angers by taking these stands are vindictive enough to respond with a vendetta against him.

"We have a handful of mutineers who will do anything to try to bring Vincent down," said one Vincent-backing owner yesterday. "To them, anyone but Fay would be a fine commissioner."

"What you're seeing isn't a firestorm that's been started by particular owners," said one anti-Vincent owner. "It's more like spontaneous combustion. I've never seen unrest like this. It's everywhere. And it's about how people perceive that issues are being handled—or not handled. I thought things had reached a point in the early '80s when they were as bad as they could get, but they're worse."

For the last twenty years, and perhaps the fifty before that, whenever a commissioner twiddles his thumbs and avoids issues, he makes friends and gets invited to stay on the job indefinitely. When he acts, as Bowie Kuhn finally began to do in his later years, he makes enemies. Finally, bizarre alliances are formed among owners whose only bond is that they all bear a one-issue grudge.

Selig and Reinsdorf are mad because they hired Dick Ravitch to head the Player Relations Committee, then made a push to get Vincent to give away his wide "best interests of the game" powers on labor matters. In effect, Ravitch would have become commissioner of labor relations. Of course, Vincent laughed in their faces as any commissioner would. The first law of the job is: don't give away any of the powers that previous commissioners fought hard to retain.

As a result, several hard-line owners who favor an all-out war with the union—similar to the one that resulted in the sixty-day midseason strike of 1981—have sided with Selig and Reinsdorf. Put Gene Autry of the Angels, Cal Pollard of the Twins, and Douglas Danforth of the Pirates in that group. "Antilabor feeling drives a lot of the anti-Fay feeling. They thought he was too conciliatory last time [in 1990]," said one owner.

Houston owner John McMullen once told Vincent that the owners' mistake in 1990 was allowing the commissioner to talk to them as a group and convince them to accept a compromise. "Next time," McMullen told Vincent, "we have to keep you quiet. You're too persuasive."

"We have a small group of extreme owners who fantasize that they're just one showdown [with the union] away from nirvana," said a member of baseball's Executive Council. "They don't seem to have much sense of baseball history."

Some AL owners are still miffed that Vincent did not give them a big enough slice of the $190 million expansion pie last year. Of course, some say they didn't deserve any of it. But they're mad anyway.

In baseball, it doesn't take much to make an enemy. It's a small, incestuous fraternity in which everybody not only competes against everyone else on the field but also cooperates with everyone else to get anything accomplished off the field. Getting and keeping behind-the-scenes power can become an obsession.

O'Malley, Selig, and Reinsdorf, for instance, have all been extremely influential with one or more past commissioners. None had much say in Vincent's arrival into power and none holds any particular sway with him. So they've gone from being ultra-insiders to being mere members of the lodge.

"Perhaps O'Malley simply has a very low view of me on the merits," said Vincent yesterday. "He certainly doesn't think I've been a good leader."

It's also possible that Vincent has inherited some of the chilliness that existed between O'Malley and Vincent's two immediate predecessors, Peter Ueberroth and Bart Giamatti. Once, O'Malley could pull all Kuhn's strings and was known as the de facto commissioner. Now, his gift for ventriloquism doesn't extend much beyond the ineffectual White.

Every time Vincent makes a tough call, he takes heat—usually with a passel of lawyers yapping at his door. He continues to keep Pete Rose out of baseball. He kicked George Steinbrenner out of the game indefinitely two years ago. Soon, he'll set conditions to allow the Yankees owner back, not that George III will be totally placated by this. In his cheerful buffoonish way, Steinbumbler has been suing, crying foul, and insulting Vincent since the day he got the boot. Ironically, those close to Vincent think that Steinbrenner wants to return to the sport so desperately that he's been a good, quiet boy in recent months, keeping his distance from the rebels.

"It's been a tough go," said Vincent yesterday. "You can't do this job counting noses. Maybe commissioners in the future should be appointed for x years with no chance of reelection.

"I'm concerned that we are becoming a selfish and litigious society. We tend to think that only in litigation can we find truth. I sometimes think of a president of Williams College who said he was retiring because he just couldn't stand dealing with one more lawyer."

A normal day for the commissioner begins with somebody screaming at him and ends, twelve or fourteen hours later, with somebody else screaming at him. If he isn't sorting out the implications of a Japanese minority interest buying into the Seattle Mariners, then he is, believe it or not, taking grief for kicking Steve Howe out of baseball after his sixth drug-related offense.

Sooner or later, the mare's nest of complications seems to take a toll. This week, Vincent gave himself a black eye when he didn't follow every conceivable nicety in grilling three Yankees employees after they testified at a Howe grievance hearing, saying they thought Vincent had been wrong to banish Howe for life. Vincent may have been wrong on the legal technicalities and timing of his chew-out of the Yankees flunkies, but he was right on the big issue. Who cares if the Yankees want to keep their left-handed reliever? The best interests of baseball clearly dictate that you cannot permit a man an infinite number of relapses into illegal drug use.

Perhaps the juncture has been reached when some of baseball's more sensible and civil owners—the ones who usually remain quiet—come forward on Vincent's behalf, if only out of decency. Vincent would never ask it himself.

"We have some owners who are very troubled that there's been so much opposition," he said yesterday.

For now, baseball will continue having the luxury of a commissioner who, basically, acts the way a commissioner should behave—in the best interests of the game, as he sees it. That makes three such bosses in a row, cut from the same cloth. When Vincent's term is over, it's likely that baseball's rancorous, shortsighted owners will reclaim their heritage of weak puppet commissioners. They've had enough of strong men with sharp tongues, such as Ueberroth, Giamatti, and Vincent. They'll probably come up with a warm body and nothing more.

Enjoy the carping, special-interest criticism of Vincent—arriving from all points on the compass almost daily—while it lasts. It's the surest possible proof that he's doing his job.

BLOW THE MAN DOWN

September 4, 1992—In case you wondered, the Chicago fire yesterday —with eighteen baseball owners issuing a vote of no confidence in Fay Vincent to try to pressure him into resigning as commissioner—was just a smoke screen.

The core desire of most of these insurrectionists is to turn the 1993 or 1994 season into 1981 revisited, if they wish. They want a free hand to reopen labor negotiations, lock the players out, shut down their industry, and force concessions—exactly as they tried to do unsuccessfully eleven years ago—even if it means wiping out an entire season.

And they want Vincent, a persuasive and independent man who's on the side of his sport and its fans, to be ousted from office and replaced by an empty suit as soon as possible so they can do the dirty deed more efficiently.

This fight isn't about whether Vincent is making lousy decisions on divisional realignment, allotment of expansion fees, or the proper way to spank George Steinbrenner. It's about money, of course. Some owners don't think they're making enough of it. They don't want to hear about the recession. They don't want to hear that it's their own fault, just because it is. They don't want to be told that the inflexible lesson of the free-agent era is that smart, frugal teams win (and make money) while dumb teams spend too much and lose.

The seditious owners who called for this roundtable Fay Bash want to do what they do best—blame somebody else, in this case Vincent, and talk tough about how they're going to smash the players union "next time."

These guys never learn. To them, history never happened. Even when it happened to them. They won't tell the truth when they negotiate. They always get caught in their lies and end up discredited. Sometimes, they even break the labor law and get fined hundreds of millions of dollars.

Earlier this year, White Sox owner Jerry Reinsdorf and Milwaukee President Bud Selig oversaw the hiring of Dick Ravitch as head of the Player Relations Committee, the same job held by Ray Grebey, who orchestrated the '81 lockout. They paid Ravitch $100,000 more than Vincent's $650,000 salary, then formally asked Vincent to relinquish his authority over labor issues.

Vincent flatly refused. That's when the owners hit the fan. Suddenly, they remembered who had opened the spring training camps in 1990, the last time they locked out the players. Yes, Vincent. They remembered the man who had spoken to them so eloquently during that labor battle about their long-view responsibilities as stewards of the national pastime.

Yesterday, eighteen owners voted to keep Vincent very quiet, demanding that he resign immediately. Next week, in St. Louis, at another owners meeting, the twenty-eight bosses will presumably take the next step of claiming they've fired Vincent.

Can they?

That question should be a beauty.

Fortunately for baseball, Vincent says he will fight 'em—all the way to the Supreme Court, if necessary. Not to keep his job, because he's so rich and in such difficult health that any job is the last thing on earth he needs. But rather to protect the powers of the office of commissioner. And to keep selfish shortsighted rotters like Jerry Reinsdorf, the coupmeister who owns the White Sox, from carrying the day and running the game from the wings.

To fully understand the open warfare between baseball owners and its commissioner, you have to go back to the aftermath of the sixty-day 1981 strike. That December, several bitter owners, looking for a scapegoat for their labor defeat, tried to fire Bowie Kuhn, claiming he'd been insufficiently hard-line in the last days of the strike.

Kuhn, who'd been the owners' loyal mouthpiece for a dozen years, was outraged to the bottom of his old boy's soul. He fought his foes in ownership for thirty months, stayed on the job until the last day of his term, handpicked Peter Ueberroth as his successor, and, as part of the price of forcing him out of office after fifteen years, got many of baseball's rules changed so that future commissioners could be more powerful and independent than he.

"I envy Peter," Kuhn said.

Kuhn's legacy, or perhaps his revenge, was an era of charismatic, controversial, increasingly independent, and autocratic commissioners. Ueberroth was *Time*'s Man of the Year for the way he ran the '84 Olympics. Now he's one of three leaders in charge of trying to rebuild Los Angeles after the riots. Bart Giamatti was a former Yale president and formidable scholar. Vincent operated at the highest levels of the Coca-Cola and Columbia Pictures empires.

To be blunt, Ueberroth, Giamatti, and Vincent all looked down on the majority of the people who paid their salaries. They had reason. But maybe it wasn't wise. Maybe they should have networked more and flattered. Maybe they should have consulted industry old hands more often instead of flattering themselves that they could concoct brilliant "lateral" strategies or rule by idealistic fiat.

Each year, baseball's lifers became more distant from the commissioner's office, more aligned with their league presidents, and more sensitive that they might be left out of the loop in an industry that they theoretically owned. They got sick of listening to high-minded talk about the good of the game and the interests of fans. Sometimes, they actually lost money. Their money! Meanwhile, the commissioners—without a dollar of their own at risk—took bows, made speeches, banned legends, and made Solomonic decisions.

Short-term, nobody can be sure whether Vincent can hold sway. Vincent told the owners ten days ago that he'd see them in hell before he'd resign.

Since 1920, the universal assumption in baseball has been that a commish can't be fired. How can you expect a person to act "in the best interests of the game" if the owners can turn around and fire him the day after he makes them mad? An easily impeachable commissioner is no commissioner.

Before September is over, we'll have some early answers. Nevertheless, the era of the charismatic, autocratic, independent, good-of-the-game commissioner is presumably headed toward the graveyard. He'll presumably be replaced by the equivalent of a head groundskeeper.

Baseball's best hope is a bizarre one. Some owners hope baseball salaries will soon go into free fall, depreciating spectacularly this off-season as a glut of famous free agents discovers that the law of supply and demand can work against them. Too many Ruben Sierras and Kirby Pucketts might actually drive the value of each star downward.

But what if it doesn't?

That's why eighteen owners think they can't risk having Vincent around—making noble moral pronouncements and, perhaps, making telling points against them during a lockout.

One thing is certain. Kuhn paved the way for a period of powerful commissioners who could act as he might have wished for himself. The powerful office that he helped to construct attracted the most accomplished men ever to preside over the game—with the exception of the first commissioner, Judge Kenesaw Mountain Landis.

After Vincent leaves, whether that is in two weeks or two years, it may be a long time before baseball has another commissioner worth remembering.

THE LAST COMMISSIONER

September 8, 1992—When you saw Fay Vincent, he was usually sitting in his golf cart beside a baseball field, smiling gently, peering through his thick glasses, holding his cane on his lap, and remembering everybody's name. He probably had a cigar in his pocket. If he wasn't chuckling already, he probably would be soon. His wit was sly and rumpled as befitted a huge, smart, gentle man with a suffering body that constantly kept him mindful of the pain in the lives of others. He wouldn't have shot a rabbit if it had been eating the lettuce off his plate.

What sort of men would force a man like Fay Vincent to resign from office?

What sort of people would disguise their selfish motives, so they could create a curtain of spurious slanders behind which to do their work?

Fay Vincent never sought the job of commissioner of baseball. He'd made a ton of money as a lawyer, as chief executive officer of Columbia Pictures, then as one of the corporate heads of Coca-Cola. He didn't need to start a fourth career, especially since his health had been suffering since he broke his back as a young man. He was wise beyond his years, but old beyond them too. He only got into baseball as a favor—to his best friend, Bart Giamatti, and to the sport itself. If Giamatti were alive at this moment, think how the ears of eighteen callow baseball owners would burn. If they could feel shame, they would.

To know Vincent, perhaps it helped to know his predecessor, Giamatti. The former Yale president was flashy, theatrical, ready to scrap, and full of himself—the Elvis of Ivy League academics. He could win the whole room to his side or rub people the wrong way, depending on the day. Vincent was, if not a true Yeatsian antiself, then at least radically different. Perhaps no one who ever wore a title as inflated as "commissioner" was so unpretentious, thoughtful, and quiet. His agenda was to study problems, find realistic solutions, then work with people in his calm, nonjudgmental way to implement them. His reputation, throughout his careers, was that he was just about the last man anybody would hate.

Vincent's handling of the 1989 World Series, after the earthquake, was typical of his judgment. He respected the sorrow of the Bay community and delayed the Series for a week. But he also recognized the needs of the business he represented. Too much "sensitivity" was both unnecessary and extremely unprofitable. So the Series was resumed and completed, surrounded by the vocabulary of uplift.

During more than three years in office, Vincent displayed one unexpected tendency that frightened the owners so much that, in recent weeks, they plotted against him. Vincent, perhaps more than any other commissioner, took his mandate seriously. He came to believe that he really should try to act independently in the "best interests of baseball." Like Giamatti, he viewed baseball as an American institution that was both indestructibly strong and constantly vulnerable. Nobody could kill it. But plenty of people, from Pete Rose to narrow-minded, dollar-obsessed owners, could tarnish it.

In the minds of many with no partisan ax to grind, Vincent became the first of baseball's supreme beings to act with almost shocking decisiveness. When the owners, after years of collusion, shut the spring training camps in 1990, Vincent was a force against the hard-line labor strategy of some owners. Perhaps he was actually embarrassed by the owners' reputation, established over generations, of having no ethics whatsoever in labor dealings. No regular-season games were missed at a time when many predicted a strike comparable to the sixty-day debacle of 1981.

The decisions, real decisions, and firm positions on issues kept coming. When many assumed that George Steinbrenner would get off with a light punishment for rubbing shoulders with unsavory types, Vincent treated the Boss with no more respect than if the owner had been a mere athlete who had gone astray and damaged the game's reputation for integrity. When he was asked to divide the expansion spoils, he divided them so fairly that no one was happy. When he thought it healthy for the game to put teams from the West in the NL's West division and teams from the East in the East division—a shocking notion that has been discussed for decades—Vincent actually did it, even though one team (out of twenty-eight) really didn't like it and threatened to cause lots of legal trouble.

What would he say or do next, merely at the bidding of his conscience?

So eighteen owners decided to douse the fuse on their lovable, rumpled loose cannon. For weeks, they bad-mouthed him, saying things so palpably foolish that anyone who knew the man had to laugh. Who but a baseball owner could call Fay Vincent "dictatorial" with a straight face? Or stubborn. Or not open to suggestion or discussion. The man lives to discuss and debate and reason.

At first, Vincent was righteously indignant and angry. He vowed to fight his back-stabbing, leak-planting, disinformation-spreading enemies all the way to the Supreme Court. But, in the end, Jerry "I'm

Michael Jordan's Boss" Reinsdorf of the White Sox, Bud "Me? Plot against Fay?" Selig of the Milwaukee Brewers, and Peter "I'm Just as Powerful as Dad" O'Malley of the Dodgers got their way. By an 18–9–1 vote, the owners asked Vincent to resign on Thursday.

Yesterday, Vincent resigned rather than drag baseball through the indignity and distraction of a long legal brawl that might have reached the Supreme Court. His final act "in the best interests of the game" was, he wrote, "resignation, not litigation."

Vincent was right when he said that "baseball can and will survive far more difficult times than these." He was right when he said that some owners want a commissioner who will "put aside the best interests of baseball" or one who will "represent only owners." And he may even be right that he should resign rather than drag the game through the courts.

Nonetheless, this is the saddest and most profoundly unjust day in baseball since Fay Vincent's best friend died.

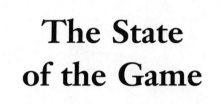

The State
of the Game

Damn Wild Cards

March 5, 1993—Abner Doubleday invents baseball in 1839 in Cooperstown. (Maybe.)

The Cincinnati Red Stockings declare themselves the first professional baseball team in 1869.

The American League is created in 1901.

The first World Series is played in 1903.

Babe Ruth inspires the creation of the lively ball in 1920.

Jackie Robinson breaks the color barrier in 1947.

Baseball expands for the first time in 1961 and 1962.

Baseball splits into four divisions and creates the League Championship Series in 1969.

Catfish Hunter becomes the first free agent in 1976.

And yesterday.

We don't know what to call yesterday yet.

But when the short history of baseball's most seminal events is written, March 4, 1993, will be on it. For better or for worse. Nobody knows which.

Because of yesterday's "straw vote" by owners in Phoenix: By 1995, baseball's playoffs will almost certainly be expanded from four teams to eight. At least two of the new teams will be wild cards. By 1995, American League teams will probably play National League teams in the regular season, just as in pro football, where the NFC and AFC play a limited interconference schedule. Each major league team will probably play ten to twenty games a season against the other league. By 1995, the American and National Leagues will probably each be realigned into three divisions—East, Central, and West.

Baseball owners tell us that nothing final was decided at their meeting yesterday. They say they just took a "straw poll" on expanded playoffs, interleague play, and realignment. Nonsense. If the twenty-eight people who own major league teams get in a room and by a "nearly unanimous vote" decide that they strongly favor these changes and expect to push them through, who's going to stop them?

There's no commissioner to act in the best interests of the game. (The players union likes all of these changes.) The owners control the basic structure of the sport utterly with nobody to stop them. They're hell-bent to rejuvenate the game financially by remodeling it along the lines of the NFL and NBA.

Of course, long term they could also end up damaging it irreparably by taking away its traditional uniqueness. Hold your breath.

The owners' primary goal is to make more money. Quickly. The owners want to hype interest with the novelty of interleague play. They want to generate more TV revenue with another round of play-offs—with four new series being played simultaneously. And they want to create more regional rivalries through realignment.

Such "popular" ideas may help some sports. But they can hurt others. Regular-season NBA and NHL games are now virtually meaningless. Losing teams get into the playoffs. Superstar power and the inherent virtuosity of the NBA are what sell that product, not the goofy, watered-down playoff format.

New ideas can be trendy, trashy quick fixes that hurt the game once their novelty becomes stale.

Baseball's two defining phenomena are the magnificent season-long pennant races and the abrupt, dramatic confrontation in the World Series between two teams that neither play each other, nor any common opponent, all year. Yesterday's straw vote revolution would knock all that into a cocked hat.

If there had been wild cards in 1951, nobody would ever have heard of Bobby Thomson's Shot Heard Round the World. Both the Giants and Dodgers would have had "playoff berths" locked up early. If there had been eight teams in the playoffs in 1978, nobody would ever have noticed Bucky Dent's home run off Mike Torrez. Because no one-game playoff between the Red Sox and Yankees would have been held. Both teams would have been cruising for weeks.

Isn't losing a great pennant race better than winning a wild-card spot?

The feeling here, for many years, has been that interleague play is a harmless idea. Some say it would take the "magic" away from the World Series. That seems a bit hysterical. The World Series can hold its own, even if the Braves and Blue Jays played a couple of games against each other in June.

However, the feeling, just as strongly held here, is that expanded eight-team playoffs are a horrible idea that strike at the very heart of baseball's summer-long appeal. When only one team from each division makes the playoffs, the purpose of the season is to find out who is the very best. With wild cards, the purpose of the season—especially the final weeks—is often to find out who the wild card—or fourth-best —team will be.

This is progress?

Baseball's current rush to judgment is particularly unseemly. Not long ago, the owners polled 11,000 season-ticket-holding fans on the issue of expanded playoffs, realignment, and interleague play. Questions were couched in ways that encouraged the responses the owners wanted to hear. All the owners' ideas were supported, but none by more than 65 percent. Hardly a landslide.

In fairness, it should be pointed out that some old-timers still hate the lively ball and will tell you the game was smarter, more strategic, in the dead-ball days. Some fans still long for the days of sixteen teams. Some purists still hate the League Championship Series. And some people have never been able to swallow free agency; they are determined to believe that athletes making millions of dollars must be lazy.

Yet baseball continues.

Francisco Cabrera, an unknown reserve, hits that miserable jacked-up ball through the infield in a game forced into the A.M. to please TV in the seventh game of an interminable NLCS between two teams of overpaid slackers. . . .

And the hair on the back of your neck stands up for an hour.

You talk about it for a week.

Six months later, you still don't believe it happened.

So, maybe, baseball will adapt itself to this new vessel and thrive.

Still, if you despise any of yesterday's developments, especially eight-team playoffs, which has the most backing, you better act fast. Only a major fan uprising can undo what was done yesterday.

If you like all the new-fangled stuff, just cheer. Because it's enactment is about a 99 percent certainty at the moment.

Shape Up
(or Ship Out)

July 12, 1993—For once, the state of baseball at the All-Star Game is crystal clear. Everybody knows what's right with the game. Everybody knows what's wrong. Everybody knows, at least in broad terms, what needs to be done. Everybody wants to do it. Or at least claims they do. Will it get done? Nobody knows. But if it doesn't, everybody's also going to know who messed up.

At the moment, more is wrong with baseball than is right. But since this is the eve of the 64th All-Star Game, let's look on the bright side first.

What's right with the game is fabulous attendance in the park, superb young talent on the field, improved regional marketing, and revolutionary old-is-new ballpark architecture, symbolized by Oriole Park at Camden Yards.

In other words, when baseball's brass gather for the All-Star Game, they should look at how the Baltimore Orioles are run, then go home and plagiarize.

Oriole Park is—and it's time to say this—the best stadium in baseball. Nobody in his right mind would trade Fenway Park or Wrigley Field for Oriole Park, even up. They're too old, too small by 10,000 seats, too destructive to the home team's pitching, and too poorly situated relative to the city's heart.

Long-term, the most important development in recent baseball history is Oriole Park. Long after Jerry Reinsdorf, Don Fehr, and Richard Ravitch are footnotes, the whole generation of parks built on the

Camden Yards model—starting with those in Cleveland and Texas—will be energizing the sport.

Slowly, baseball is learning that it's selling not just a game but, rather, an evening of family entertainment. The ballpark needs to become a quality restaurant, a mini-mall, a picnic ground, and even an urban plaza for milling and mixing. If you haven't walked Eutaw Street, Jacobs Plaza, and the bullpen picnic park, then you've seen only Oriole Park, not Camden Yards. Baseball can't just pitch itself to baseball fans. The Orioles want everybody.

By accident or out of necessity, the Orioles have also pointed the way toward other trends. In 1988, the Orioles lost 107 games. Then they were bought by a man who, as his fortunes slid into bankruptcy, pulled the team's purse strings tighter. Since starting over from the bottom—with a bad team, a lousy farm system, and no significant financial advantages—the Orioles have built a contending team that sells virtually every ticket to every game.

They did it with wise draft choices, emphasis on minor league development, and a commitment to re-signing key homegrown stars, like Cal Ripken, at fair market value. That approach works. Even when you trade Mickey Tettleton for Jeff Robinson. And Curt Schilling, Pete Harnisch, and Steve Finley for Glenn Davis. And make no serious offer to any major free agent in the past five years. And freeze at the trading switch when Fred McGriff is there for the taking.

You don't have to be brilliant. You don't have to spend for other people's stars. You just have to have a sensible big-picture plan and lots of patience. The Orioles farm system has drafted and developed Mike Mussina, Gregg Olson, Ben McDonald, Jeffrey Hammonds, David Segui, Arthur Rhodes, Brad Pennington, and, long ago, Ripken. General manager Roland Hemond has filled out the rest of the team with players who, when they arrived, had a market value of about $19.98 each: Rick Sutcliffe, Fernando Valenzuela, Jamie Moyer, Mike Devereaux, Brady Anderson, Harold Reynolds, Harold Baines, Chris Hoiles, Todd Frohwirth, Alan Mills, Mark McLemore. Such players are always available by the gross—if you have the baseball judgment to find them. Teams that pay millions for middle-echelon players are idiots. But about fifteen franchises do it exactly that way.

The Orioles have also shown how to market regionally, rather than locally. They were ahead of the curve in reaching out to fans who were 25 to 100 miles from home plate. If you court them, they will come. Sometimes for a whole weekend. The Orioles have co-opted the Washington market so successfully that few believe that D.C. will ever again have a major league team. Northern Virginia, yes, someday, because it's a gold mine. Washington? Ancient history.

Baseball attendance is up sharply, not counting the expansion teams in Denver and Miami that have doubled their own expectations. The sport has, in recent years, finally gotten in touch with its basic appeal —baseball is a regional game. No other group of fans cares so much about the affairs of the home team (and its foes) or cares so little about the rest of the sport if it has no bearing on the home team's fate. This, of course, is a double-edged sword. While the game tends to sell itself locally—by invading and enriching the lives of its fans at least 162 times a year—it also tends to be more difficult to market nationally. Baseball almost has too many stars. They dim each other. Check the record book: at any one time, baseball usually has about thirty-five future Hall of Famers who are active.

In recent years, baseball's wrongs have also come into focus. As have the solutions to most of those problems. Right now, baseball has:

An expiring labor agreement.

Fortunately, there's a solution for this. Study the NBA and NFL. Guys, the problem has been figured out. You have no excuses any more. Owners agree to share their revenues—especially local TV revenues—in a substantive, not merely symbolic way. In return, players agree to a salary cap system based on a percentage of the gross. See, that wasn't hard. One paragraph. (Call David Stern or Paul Tagliabue for details.)

Pathetic national TV ratings.

As a result of this trend, baseball's new network TV contract will probably bring the game a half billion dollars less in revenue than its previous one. That got everybody's attention. Luckily, the answers to the rating debacle are also obvious to almost everybody.

First, speed up the game by twenty minutes. The solution isn't rules changes. It's for the players to move a hell of a lot faster. Pace of play is 90 percent player (and union) responsibility. If the game could be played in two hours for generations, then it can be played in two and a half hours no matter how many TV ads and relief pitching changes delay it. Modern players dawdle. For a million-dollar average salary, it's not too much to demand hustle.

Second, owners must stop bashing their players and, instead, market their superstars far better. The players are the game. What sane businessperson attacks his own product? When Shaquille O'Neal signed a

$40 million contract, NBA owners welcomed him like a messiah. No-body said, "This rook hasn't scored a point yet." When Barry Bonds got almost $44 million—after winning two MVPs—baseball owners bellyached for months about the "bad precedent."

Baseball sits back and waits for shoe companies to anoint the next generation of mega-celebs with gazillion-dollar TV ad champaigns. So baseball has no Shaq Attack. The game's most publicized stars in recent years have been Bo Jackson and Deion Sanders because they played football too.

Why doesn't America know that Barry Bonds has skills comparable to Willie Mays's? Why isn't Ken Griffey Jr. seen as the next Hank Aaron? Why is Cecil Fielder's smile and on-camera charm and Ruthian tummy being wasted? Joe Carter's so cheerful he makes Magic Johnson look like the Grinch. When will young Latin stars even remotely begin to get their due? Juan Gonzalez, Carlos Baerga, and Roberto Alomar actually want to be role models—and live like it.

And, by the way, is baseball waiting for Cal Ripken to play in Con-secutive Game No. 2,131 before it gets excited? We may never live to see a bigger record broken. Yet all everybody wants to do is nag Ripken to death. Where is the TV ad, paid for by Major League Baseball, that says, "Sometimes Cal Ripken hits .323. (Ripken hits a home run.) Sometimes he hits .223. (Ripken strikes out.) But he al-ways gives his best. (Ripken bowls over a catcher.) Every day. (Ripken makes a routine play.) That's baseball. (Sweating, Ripken smiles.)"

Should Gregg Jefferies bat for the NL in Tuesday night's All-Star Game, millions of TV viewers will mutter, "Who's he?" Baseball won't bother to tell them that Jefferies, who may hit .350 with 100 RBI and 50 steals this year, already has 750 hits, even though he's only twenty-five years old—your basic 3,000-hit pace. But then, if baseball management advertised how great its players really are, it might not be able to complain so loudly about paying them great salaries.

Someday, when the All-Star Game returns to Baltimore—probably around the year 2020—we may look back on this Tuesday night with true disbelief.

Was this really the starting lineup for the American League home team?

At catcher, Ivan Rodriguez, a starter at nineteen and an All-Star at twenty, who ended up breaking Carlton Fisk's record for most games caught in a career.

At first base, John Olerud, who hit .400 in 1993.

At second base, Roberto Alomar, who had 1,000 hits by his twenty-fifth birthday and broke Eddie Collins's record for hits and steals by a second baseman.

At shortstop, Cal Ripken Jr., who played in 2,222 consecutive games.

At third base, Wade Boggs, who won five batting titles.

In leftfield, Joe Carter, who drove in 100 runs ten times.

In centerfield, Ken Griffey Jr., who, in a generation of unprecedented young bloomers, was the youngest of all. A standout at nineteen, he had 850 hits at the age of twenty-three. Though he retired at a younger age than his father, he still broke Pete Rose's record for hits. In fact, he broke it rather easily.

In rightfield, Kirby Puckett, who, although he made it to 3,000 hits, was better known for being the last man to start an All-Star Game ahead of Juan Gonzalez. Gonzalez, of course, had 120 dingers by age twenty-three—far ahead of Hank Aaron's pace—and finished with 801.

This entire AL lineup made the Hall of Fame, yet, ironically, the best player on the field may have been a National Leaguer. Barry Bonds, who won the Triple Crown in 1993, ended his career as the only man to win five MVP awards.

None of this is so terribly far-fetched. Actually, what may seem hard to believe with 20/20 hindsight is that an All-Star Game with such seminal performers, played in a ballpark of such historic significance, could have been viewed at the time as a symbol of a sport that was in trouble.

Long Goodbyes

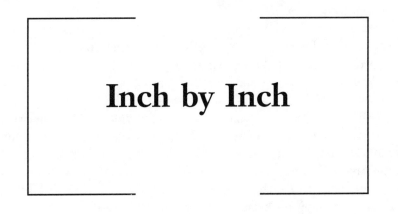

Inch by Inch

October 22, 1991—At first, Steve Palermo couldn't stand to watch the ballgames on television. He wanted to be behind the plate—the best ball-and-strike man of his generation—not lying in a hospital bed, partially paralyzed by a bullet in the spine.

But Cody and Mitchell wouldn't let him keep the TV off. They'd come up from the second floor, the children's ward, to Palermo's room on the third floor. They'd hit the remote, crawl in bed with him, one on either side, and ask him about the players, about the game.

"So what could I do?" Palermo said.

Cody, eight, had been dragged by a horse, his skull smashed. "At one point, they just said he was 'terminal.' They didn't think he'd live the night." Mitchell, eleven, was hit by a car. He wasn't supposed to walk again. But now he can.

"They'd come in and bogart my bed. The nurses would bring them ice cream and cookies," said Palermo. "They'd say, 'Turn on TBS. Let's watch the Braves.' Then after the game they'd leave and I'm sleepin' in ice cream and crumbs."

Steve and Cody and Mitchell measure themselves by each other. "Cody, he's something," says Palermo, who was shot in Dallas as he came to the rescue of two waitresses being robbed outside the restaurant where he was having dinner after calling a Texas Rangers game. "However far I walk on the crutches, he's going to walk one step further. 'I beat you, Steve.'

"Then I have to go a little further because I don't want an eight-year-old to beat me. . . .

"His speech is still a little slow, but he's from Texas, so it sounds good on him. He says, 'Gonna see Noooolan pitch tonight.' Mitchell wears this A's hat. I tell him, 'Mitch, bad move. This is Ranger country. You're going to get another head injury.'"

Palermo is home now, in the Kansas City suburbs. He sees Cody and Mitchell at rehab in Dallas. But in the middle of the night, when he needs some help and they aren't there, he turns on his bedroom light. The entire room is papered in letters and telegrams from all over America. Start with President Bush and work down. "I turn on the lamp and stare at the walls," he says. "If I don't make it back for myself, I'm going to make it back for all these people."

Palermo, sitting in the American League dugout at the World Series, stops to cry. "Majestically overwhelming" is how he describes the response to his tragedy. "It's very emotional," he says of being on a big-league field again, even with braces and crutches. "It's a reminder of what you're missing. I figure I'm out of hot water by now, but [the tears] just keep coming."

The highlight of the 88th World Series has been Palermo's slow walk to the pitcher's mound to throw out the first pitch. Palermo picked Al Newman, a tough, funny, much-loved, sawed-off utility man for the Twins, to catch the pitch.

"It was real touching. I was honored," said Newman, who bear-hugged Palermo at the mound, as did the whole umpiring crew.

We use the word *heroic* to describe Palermo, rather than a word like *wise*, because when you do the right thing, even though it's dangerous, sometimes you end up getting shot in the back.

If you could run out into the night to chase thugs who are robbing and beating a couple of women and know it would all turn out like a Kevin Costner movie, everybody would do it. Not just the heroes. But adults know better. Sometimes the bad guys don't run away. They double back in a car and mow you down in a gutless drive-by. Next thing you know, the prognosis is so bad the doctors can't face you; they get your brother to do it. Nobody knows if you'll walk without crutches again. No one can tell you if you'll be able to umpire again. And you're forty-two.

Perhaps Palermo wouldn't do it again if he had July 7 to live over and he knew the cost. But, if you've known Palermo a long time, you figure maybe he would. Being the good guy—wanting to do the tough job and be worthy of respect—runs to the core of the man.

Palermo was the best umpire in the American League. You couldn't even get an argument on it. Maybe he will be again, although he might be the only person alive who would not include the word *maybe*. He prided himself—and pride is the word you always heard first about Palermo—on being the best. He was cocky and had a temper if you crossed him, but he was so amazing at his work that people accepted the whole package and said, "In the seventh game of the Series, just give me Palermo behind the plate."

He and Doug Harvey in the National League were so far above the pack (the state of umpiring not being too hot these days) that many players viewed Palermo as one of the game's stars.

When you heard how Palermo got shot, all you could say was, "Well, of course." You think Steve Palermo's going to watch women get robbed at 1 A.M. and just finish his dinner?

Now is no time for reasonable medical doubts about Palermo's future. He doesn't need or want to hear them. He just wants to fight.

"As soon as I wake up in the morning, it hits me in the face," he said. "To get from the bed to the wheelchair to the shower, then shave and dress. It used to take me twenty minutes. Now, an hour and a half. I don't take any of that for granted now. And I never will again, after I come back. . . ."

He always says *when* or *after*, not *if*, which, the doctors say, is the attitude that gives you the best chance. "They just don't know enough about [nerve regeneration] to predict how I'll come out of it. I'm not going to wake up on a Tuesday at four o'clock after a nap and get up and walk. It's going to be slow. Inch by inch, life's a cinch. Yard by yard, it's very hard."

Whatever anger he feels, he seems to have sublimated into rehab motivation. He approaches therapy with a kind of fury. "I want my house back to normal as soon as possible. I want the railings, all those reminders removed. I'll have enough reminders. I'll have the mental scars."

Palermo even agreed to come to the Series, although he feared that he'd be a spectacle, because he thought it might help him. "I wanted to do this as a reminder why I'm working so hard, why I go to that gym every day . . . because I'm going to be back on the field."

Whatever Palermo's medical outcome, he is one of the few people who now know (and is shocked to find out) just how much they're liked and respected. No umpire has ever felt so appreciated.

He wishes he could answer every letter. "But I'd need a lot of hands." He was visited in the Dallas hospital by upward of one hundred players. "And a lot came after I asked them not to come because I didn't have enough time to visit properly. Robin Ventura, Bo [Jackson], Paul Molitor. I told Paul, 'I'm still going to beat you on that three and two pitch on the corner.' He understood. Sparky [Anderson] called more than once. Bobby Valentine came with his son. So many."

Now Palermo has one dream, one fixed idea to keep him focused. "It'll probably take 'em one pitch to start griping again. 'Same old horseshit Stevie,' " he says, laughing. "I'm looking forward to that first ejection. It'll be a nice one. I know them. It'll be their way of saying, 'Welcome back.' "

Leaving the Nest

BALTIMORE, October 7, 1991—Before the ninth inning of the last game in Memorial Stadium, the chant began: "We want Flanagan!"

"What do you say, Elrod, warm me up one more time, like you did those 350 straight starts," said Mike Flanagan to Elrod Hendricks, whose old knees haven't let him warm up pitchers in recent years.

"I'd be honored," said Hendricks.

With one out in the ninth Sunday, manager John Oates waved in Flanagan, the Baltimore left-hander who is the perfect emblem of what the Orioles were for twenty-five years, have not been of late, but desperately hope they can be again.

His black and orange jacket draped over his pitching arm, the thirty-nine-year-old war horse—assumed washed up and retired a year ago—walked to the mound, bringing back with him for a few minutes the very best of times.

He brought with him the night in a cold, steady rain when he started the '79 World Series by beating the Pirates when they were the Lumber Company. He brought with him the great failed pennant drive of 1982 when the Orioles swelled toward the wire for Earl Weaver on a 33–10 wave that crashed on the final day in a failure as glorious as any victory. And he brought with him the whole '83 postseason when he pitched against doctors' advice with a brace on his knee and helped the Orioles win their last World Series.

Flanagan knew, although the crowd did not, that eighty-five former Orioles—every star of any consequence and dozens of spear carriers like Dave Skaggs—were waiting in the dugout tunnel, preparing to fill the field after the game for a celebration of thirty-eight Orioles years in this park, most of them filled with dignity, craftsmanship, and almost too much fun.

"I told myself, 'They're chanting for you. Do this for yourself.' But I've never been able to do it that way. It's never been the stats. It was always the game. The Oriole concept—playing it the right way for the team. I saw all those guys in the tunnel. All of them had the Oriole concept."

So he pitched for them. Maybe this Orioles team lost 95 games. Maybe the three lousiest Orioles teams since '55 played here in '88, '90, and '91. Maybe the Orioles were in the process of being crushed, 7–1, by Detroit. But the old Orioles thought you finished the job right.

So Flanagan struck out Dave Bergman, swinging at a big full-count curve. Next, Tim Welke, an umpire with no soul, would not call a borderline 2–2 pitch a strike. "If I ever thought I'd get a call in my life, I thought I'd get that one," said Flanagan, laughing. "I'll never cry about another pitch."

Flanagan just came back with the best curveball you ever saw and struck out Travis Fryman by a foot.

The generations of Orioles in the tunnel, who couldn't see the field, asked Flanagan, "How'd it go?"

"Oh, I finished the ninth," he said.

The 50,700 begged for Flanagan, who hates any sort of curtain call. This time, he not only broke tradition, he relished the moment, waving his cap to all four corners of the emerald field where the Orioles will never play again.

"Of all the great Oriole pitchers—I don't even know if it was justified—I had the honor to be the last one," said Flanagan. Then he went and sat alone.

"Mike had a lot of tears," said Oates. "But then everybody did."

As the piano theme music from *Field of Dreams*—sounding a bit like a Bach fugue—played eerily, the field slowly filled after the regular game ended. First a Robinson at third, then one in right, then a Palmer, almost sobbing, running to the mound. The sun was already getting low—an autumn painter's light with only rightfield in an exploding orange glow.

"It was the most exciting moment of my career," Brooks Robinson said, echoing the comment of dozens of players. "It was really something wonderful. I cried anyway when I saw *Field of Dreams* and as soon as they played that song tears came to my eyes. It's the only movie I ever cried at."

Finally, there were almost fifty Orioles pitchers on the mound—from Bob Turley to Todd Frohwirth. Rick Dempsey, one of ten catchers, crouched and gave a sign. "It was incredible," said Flanagan. "All fifty of us shook him off."

Flanagan looked down. "I saw the marks I had just made on the mound. . . . I saw all the guys around me from our old teams. You have to say those were the best days of your life. There may be other big games in the future, but never like those games."

Finally, all 115 Orioles, old and new, formed a huge *O* around the infield. "I talked to a lot of the old players. Somebody said that we were the last team that had fun. That may be true," said Flanagan. "I told Dave Skaggs, 'I know you long for the old days, but it's not like it used to be.'

"I've been looking for those days elsewhere," said Flanagan, who pitched in pennant races for the Blue Jays, "and I've had to admit that they're gone. . . .

"Now, on this team, I'm the keeper of the stories. They all want to hear about Earl [Weaver]. That was the hard relationship for all of us. . . . Our common denominator may have been hating Earl. There's nobody like him left. Nobody who can get that much out of you. We gave. He'd never even say 'Hi' to you once in a season. Every night was a war.

"Only later in my career did I know he had compassion."

Sunday, Flanagan met Weaver before the game. Their history was long, tangled, and occasionally dark. "He always wanted everybody to throw sliders," said Flanagan. "Every time I gave up a home run on a fastball, I lied and told him it was a slider just to make him mad. He'd say, 'The guy got lucky.' So he said, 'Nice year,' when he saw me today. I told him, 'I started throwing sliders.' He said, 'Really?' I said, 'Nah, I'm still lying.' "

Then Flanagan took Weaver aside and, after all the years, thanked him—for the excellence he'd ruthlessly demanded, for the zaniness he'd patiently allowed, and, most of all, for the way he had built teams.

Long after Memorial Stadium saw its last pitch, those 115 Orioles stayed and talked. They almost could not leave.

Everyone has his favorite memory of the thirty-eight seasons of Memorial Stadium. But after the stunningly unexpected power of this day, many may feel the last moment was the best.